LEXICON OF BLACK ENGLISH

J. L. DILLARD, 1924-

A Continuum Book

THE SEABURY PRESS · NEW YORK

1977
The Seabury Press
815 Second Avenue
New York, New York 10017

Printed in the United States of America

Library of Congress Cataloging in Publication Data
Dillard, Joey Lee, 1924–
  Lexicon of Black English.
  (A Continuum book)
  Bibliography: p.
  1. Black English. 2. Vocabulary. I. Title.
PE3102.N46D5   427'.9'73   76-30389
ISBN 0-8164-9309-X

LEXICON OF BLACK ENGLISH

Contents

Acknowledgments

THE USUAL closely knit group of academic associates has provided invaluable aid in the production of this manuscript. William A. Stewart of the City University of New York has been a constant source of materials on Gullah, without which I could not have begun to treat the relationship between the general United States and the Sea Islands. Don Hatley and Joseph Johnson of Northwestern State University, Natchitoches, have provided valuable materials on Louisiana. Margie I. Dillard has read the entire manuscript and provided some check on my characteristic excesses.

The most gratitude, however, must go to the most energetic helper, Dr. Ian F. Hancock of the University of Texas. In addition to his productive studies in Creole and various Gypsy communities (from each of which I have taken useful material), Dr. Hancock now conducts a distinguished radio program dealing with the origins and development of Black music for Station KUT, Austin, Texas. My chapter on the blues has profited enormously from correspondence, conversation, and record playing with him.

Preface

THIS WORK is not a lexicon of Black English. An adequate dictionary would require more than the work of one man for a year or so. It is, rather, an attempt to demonstrate that the fields of linguistics, dialectology, language education, and early reading would be well served by a wordbook of the Black English vernacular. This book attempts to justify the production of such a dictionary on the grounds that there are enough differences between that language variety (spoken by younger, poorer Blacks as their only form of speech and retained as a special style even by some who have reached middle age and middle class) and ordinary or "Standard" English (including such familiar nonstandard dialects as "Appalachian").

At the current stage of work on this dialect, in my opinion, the most desirable kind of dictionary would be one produced according to historical principles. Early attestations of Black English (the Pidgin and Creole stages) are fragmentary, and some of them are suspect. Nevertheless, we have many mechanisms for evaluating the reliability of the documents; there are comparisons to be made with West Indian varieties that in some cases agree with the earlier attestations of the Black English vernacular, and the very mass of the documents virtually demands some kind of serious treatment.

The chief obstacle to a historical dictionary for Black English, as well as to the history of the Black English vernacular in general, is a deeply ingrained attitude in the American academic world that anything shared by the Black dialect and white dialects must have been transmitted *to* the Black *from* the white. But recent work makes this preconception seem eminently implausible (see articles by Wolfram and, especially, by Dalby in the Bibliography). Southern whites borrowed very much vocabulary—especially intimate vocabulary thought appropriate to less formal styles—from Black English during the period of slavery, just as white teenagers have borrowed a great deal of Black slang during the preceding two decades of this century. But without going through the requisite historical tracing, we are not able, at this point, to say a priori what the direction of borrowing was.

Although I am conscious that whites have borrowed much from Blacks, and although I am eager to reverse the earlier attitude described above, it does not follow that I consider every term discussed herein to have originated with the Blacks. In too many cases, the evidence is simply not yet in. I have felt free to discuss terms that are proved to be in widespread use in the Black community, especially those with specifically Black meanings, even though I cannot prove that they originated in that community—in some few cases, moreover, the evidence indicates that the terms originated with the whites.

I do not want to suggest that every term discussed herein is in some sense an "Africanism." It is true that there are many more Africanisms in American English than the older generation of language historians and dialectologists believed, but the influence of African language is by no means the entire story when it comes to differentiating Black American English vernacular from other varieties. As any reader of my *Black English* or of William A. Stewart's articles (see Bibliography) must know, our thesis is that a maritime Pidgin English became a Plantation Creole spoken primarily by West African slaves, and the latter "de-Creolized" (i.e., changed on the model of more "standard" dialects) in fairly recent times to form the Black English vernacular. Borrowings from the maritime tradition are always a distinct possibility, especially for the early stages of the Black English vernacular (including Plantation Creole). Furthermore, a certain amount of apparently spontaneous innovation took place in the maritime pidgins (see Hancock, Bibliography). The de-Creolized Black English vernacular certainly drew upon the results of that innovation, and of course, it is far from impossible that such creation continued into later periods.

Obviously, it is not impossible that the Black English vernacular should have retained British dialect forms now obsolete or archaic in other dialects of English or that it should have been somewhat more conservative than other (especially southern) dialects in terms of older language forms. There has been rare high comedy, however, in the way in which American dialectologists, who in their entire previous careers had not mentioned Irish dialect, began finding Irish sources for Black dialect forms—it having become transparently obvious that the old reliable sources like East Anglian dialect would not work. What I have objected to and continue to object to is the automatic assumption, which seems to be made by most dialectologists, that anything peculiar to the Black English vernacular *must* by the very fact of its existence represent some archaic British usage.

In the grammar, an excellent example of that type of faulty reasoning may be seen in the predictable attempt to find Black English vernacular durative or time-distributive *be* in Anglo-Irish. There is a basic grammatical difference: The Black English vernacular *be* can occur in a past-time context *(He be dancing last Friday);* the Anglo-Irish form cannot. There is also the more superficial difference that the preceding *do (do be* or *does be)* is much more nearly obligatory in Anglo-Irish than in Black English; in the latter, it is introduced primarily in negatives *(I don't be joking)*. While it is possible that the Black English vernacular has retained an English dialect form, it makes no sense whatsoever to assume that, because a certain form is present in the Black English vernacular, it *must* therefore be an English (or Irish) dialect form lost in the other dialects. If American dialectologists had traced many Irish forms to the United States *before* the Black English controversy arose, their case would now be more convincing. As it is, they seem merely to be clutching at anti-Creolist straws.

The opposite mistake—which almost no one makes these days—is to assume that anything peculiar to Black English is somehow an Africanism. It is true that in the emotionalism surrounding Black Pride movements extreme statements are sometimes made. There is no such emotionalism, however, in the work of careful scholars like David Dalby (see Bibliography).

The field in general, however, is burdened with emotion. In such a context, the man who turns in a fire alarm may be automatically labeled an arsonist. To point out, nevertheless, that Black children are not scoring so high on national reading tests as non-Black children and that they are generally not doing so well in our educational system as we could hope is to indulge in the merest truism. We might all wish that those problems were not there, but wishing will not make them go away. To point out that language differences may be partly responsible for that failure is also to risk misinterpretation. More than one of my professional colleagues has labeled me (as well as Stewart) a "deficit theorist"—one who believes that the language of Black children is somehow inexpressive or even inferior—because we have made statements about the possible effects of a different grammatical system, although all our works contain attacks on the deficit hypothesis. It seems necessary, however, to go on pointing out the possibilities, even though some of the misunderstanding seems willful.

To point out the function of language differences in educational performance is not to insist that language is the only factor. Labov, Cohen, and Robins, in the *Teachers College Record* (see Bibliography), have presented impressive evidence that peer-group attitudes have a great deal to do with it. But Stewart, the best-known advocate of dialect readers, was talking about cultural influences on reading failure as early as 1966, before the Labov group gave any sign of having heard of the problem. I feel that it is equally fallacious to assume that either language or nonlinguistic culture is a unique cause. For the Black student, the peer group that rejects him if he pays too much attention to books is the same one that transmits the dialect form to him. The sociologist who looks only at the social relationships and the linguist who assures him that his dialect has as much structure as any language are, from his point of view, equally "out of it."

Nevertheless, it seems that we can best cope with the problem by plugging along in our own areas of competence. A knowledge of the Black English vernacular lexicon will not solve ghetto educational problems, but those who do not know that lexicon will be severely handicapped in their attempts to solve the problems. Small advances in knowledge will make small contributions to progress. This work can hope for nothing better than to make such a small advance.

The method used herein is essentially a literary and comparative one. In terms of knowledge about Black English vocabulary, I cannot hope to compete with several works that have already been published. My hope of making this a significant addition to their work rests upon comparison to West African and West Indian varieties, hard work, and use of a large number of sources. In general, I have been leery of relying upon a sole source, especially when that source has been fictional—even if the author has been as good as James Baldwin or Richard Wright. In all cases, I have tried to corroborate the words and phrases taken from literary works from live informants, if not from a variety of literary works or recordings.

The works by Black authors who have a claim to special intuition about Black words deserve special attention in such a study. Although there are some major, and many minor, examples of such works, few have the linguistic or lexicographic sophistication to match that intuitive knowledge. The three most ambitious attempts, by writers either squarely in or fully sympathetic to Black militancy movements and Black Pride or "soul" groups, are Twiggs, *Pan-African Language in the Western Hemisphere;* Andrews and Owens, *Black Language;* and Major, *Dictionary of Afro-American Slang.* Haskins' *The Psychology of Black Language,* while slighter, has the same claims to attention.

Of these, Twiggs may be most shortly disposed of—but nothing about this cursory treatment should be taken as an opinion that the careful user of Twiggs' work cannot find a great deal of value. Twiggs overstates considerably; he is so eager to make Black (or "Pan-African") language use so completely different that he overstates minor differences. Some of his "words" are merely pronunciation variants of lexical forms shared by all, or almost all, varieties of American English. In many ways, he reminds one of the "dictionaries" of Texan English and the like, which make a great deal of quaint pronunciations like *war* "wire" and *tar* "the thing your car runs on." Also, Twiggs consciously reverses the traditional direction of study of American English and assumes that anything used by Blacks is a distinctive characteristic of his Pan-African language. This is, in principle, no worse than the prejudice of the Linguistic Atlas of the United States and Canada project, which has long considered anything used by both Blacks and Southern whites to have certainly come in from the white dialect. Nevertheless, correcting an earlier bias by a greater bias in the other direction is not the way to produce a reliable guide to the Black English vernacular usage.

Andrews and Owens have most of the values to be found in Twiggs and not quite so much of the overstatement. Although there is a lot of militancy in their book, their primary concern is with words and expressions. Seldom if ever does the militancy and political emphasis result in outright lexical distortion. They have no pretenses to historical accuracy; their treatment, although strictly non-technical, is also almost completely synchronic. Some of their terms (like *prick* "penis," *balls* or *nuts* "testicles") could not possibly be specific to any one American variety. In fact, it sometimes seems as though the authors indulge in sensationalism in discussing the "Escaped" (liberated, assimilated, or successful) Black's *fugg you* and the *fuck you* of the one still in the ghetto ("Hell," in the prevalent terminology). The expression could hardly be said to be "Black" or "white" or "ghetto" in any meaningful sense; perhaps it may be more "male" than "female." To equate *butt* with *ass* is to waste the time of any reader, Black or white, male or female. The only way to fill space with less-informative material would be to point out that the British spell it *arse*.

Elsewhere, though, Andrews and Owens can be very informative. Their feel for the language is considerably better than their methodology. On the face of it, one would be tempted to dismiss their entry

Gravy. Someone with GRAVY is into a lot of money.

as not Black in any meaningful sense. A look at some sources, however, suggests that they are probably right (see pp. 95–6). Their definition of *sididy* (spelled *siddity* in Major and other sources) is not formal, but it is informative: "Someone acting too big to be themselves." *Unass me* "get your hands off me," "Leave; get yourself away; cut yourself loose" may turn out to be relatively ephemeral, but it will no doubt be replaced by some related expression when it goes out of style. The discussion of compounds with *home* is an excellent example of the very strong points of their book. Like many other Black writers on Black English, they refer to someone (or something, like language) "from the 'community' " as *down home.* They point out how *home boy* refers either to someone from Harlem, Watts, or some other equally Black community or to one's best friend. The verb plus adverb *come home* "return to Blackness from a fantasy trip to Whiteland" may not occur so frequently as the other terms, but it has the smack of realism. *Back home* "Africa" may, on the other hand, be appropriate for the relatively few who still think in terms of Back-to-Africa movements.

Major's *Dictionary of Afro-American Slang* is probably the best of these. Its definitions agree, in general, with those of Andrews and Owens, and they come closer to lexicographic formality. Major is the only one to attest the fully historical common-noun use of the West African "day" names, like *Cuffee* "male born on Friday," to mean "Black person." Major even labels it "African word." His definitions of *fly* "to be fast and ecstatic, brusk" and other such terms are in accord with usages that have become even better known to the general public (especially through movies like *Superfly,* which some politically sensitive critics think of as being "exploiting"). His term *Georgiaed* "to be misused in any way" is familiar from the various books on pimps and pimping in the more specialized meaning "enjoyed sexually without receiving payment." Major's definition suggests that a term in the general Black lexicon may have been extended to pimping and then have taken on a specialized meaning. This seems likely because Blacks were using some of these terms long before they entered pimping.

To differentiate between a Black lexicon and usage of terms in domains like pimping is perhaps the most important objective not achieved by Major and the others. This aim requires great attention to the sociolinguistic domains in which a given term occurs. The overwhelming impression that has come out of my work on this book is that lexical materials cannot be explained out of context. My linguistic philosophy says that the discourse, not the sentence, is the real unit of linguistic generation. It may seem paradoxical to make such a statement in a work on the lexicon, but the feeling was fully developed in the course of such work. A term like, for example, *living sweet* may designate either living a Christian life (if the context is church) or having one's bills paid by a woman (if the context is pimping or the activity of streetcorner men who would be pimps). As must be the case with all other populations, the meaning of Black speakers' words cannot be fully understood apart from an understanding of what they are doing and why they are doing it. The sociologist of language calls this combination of language relationships and other behavioral patterns *domains.* They are, I believe, basic to an organization of the lexicon of Black English. The chapters in this book are organized according to my interpretation of some of the most basic domains of the Black English vernacular and are a basic part of my theory of that language variety.

LEXICON OF BLACK ENGLISH

1

On the Social Significance of a Lexicon for the Black English Vernacular

ALTHOUGH THE entire subject of Black dialect is a controversial one, all serious studies of the last few years have agreed that there are differences between the way words are pronounced in the Black vernacular variety of American English and in even closely related varieties of southern white English.[1] Admission of grammatical differences has been slower and more grudging, but it is now generally admitted that the contrast between, for example, *he working* and *he be working* (the former negated as *he ain't working* or *he not working,* the latter only as *he don't be working*) involves a category in the Black English vernacular that is not found in other American English dialects—and that is not identical to anything found in British (including Scottish and Irish) dialects.[2] Even more basically, perhaps, it is now acknowledged that speakers of other dialects usually do not even understand structures like

> You been know that.
> I been wanted that a long time.[3]

Once these relatively great grammatical differences have been shown, there is an opportunity to demonstrate more complex and subtler differences, such as the different realization of past tense. A great many linguists have exerted themselves mightily in order to provide an explanation whereby the teacher, who dimly perceives that his Black students "have trouble with past tense," can understand that there is no language malfunction and yet retain his perception of the difference between the language of his students and the language of the school (called, for want of a better term, "Standard English").

The battle about syntactic differences was a long and bitter one—it perhaps should not be described as being over—and it occupied most of the energies of those linguists involved. For them, it has been a convenient assumption that the vocabulary of the Black English vernacular is "exactly" shared with ordinary English. Actually, it has always been known that there are vocabulary differences as well. The most controversial workers on vocabulary[4] have been concerned almost exclusively with demonstrating that the influence has not been unidirectional—that more Africanisms than usually acknowledged have come into southern white and even into General American English. David Dalby provided perhaps the ultimate challenge to the extreme Anglicist position (the theory that almost everything in American English came from British English dialects) when he demonstrated how the most worldwide of "Americanisms," *O.K.,* was originally an Africanism. There may be few remaining demonstrations as inherently "catchy" as Dalby's, but there is much more about the quasi-autonomous state of the Black American English vocabulary that needs serious treatment. African origin is a serious, and always important, issue, but even those forms that have no such origin deserve full consideration.

As usual in such cases, *autonomy* is a relative term that has significance primarily with reference to the received viewpoint. It would be absurd, in the first place, to deny that many Black citizens of the United States use an essentially General American vocabulary, with a comparatively small (even if, in absolute numerical terms, appreciable) number of words and expressions not shared with Standard English and the nonstandard dialects. Measures of vocabulary size are so untrustworthy that it would be risky to guess whether it is Black English or Standard British English that differs more from General American. In the vocabulary that is outside the common core of all varieties of English, however, Black English does not agree with British as against American English. As I shall attempt to demonstrate in the following chapters, it has a striking number of similarities to the Creole varieties (including Creole versions of French, Portuguese, and even Spanish) of the Caribbean and elsewhere, especially in more abstract word-forming senses.

Twenty years ago, it would have seemed self-evident that any terms in New World Black dialects that did not trace back to the European "parent" must therefore be Africanisms. More recent research, however, has uncovered relationships to contact varieties (pidgins, largely) that were in effect more nautical in habitat than land-based. Historically, this approach is even more challenging to conventional theories than the derivation from African languages since it questions some of the bases of the theory of internal reconstruction.[5]

The theory of origin in maritime contact varieties (called herein the Creolist theory) provides an even greater challenge to deficit theory, wherein a number of psychologists (primarily behaviorists) have asserted that the language "problems" of Negro children in the schools of the eastern cities are the result of linguistic or even intellectual deprivation and have traced that "deficit" to something in the environment of the slum. If, however, the dialect of the ghettoes in the northeastern United States has a great deal in common with that of the Creoles of the Caribbean Islands, it is very hard to see just what environmental cause might be invoked. The problem would be the one that the Creolist has insisted upon seeing as the main issue all along—the tracing of a legitimate if admittedly complex language history.

In this respect, lexical findings lead one to the conclusion that the language, even though it is that of a severely "disadvantaged" group, derives from a complex set of cultural transmissions and is maintained primarily by an equally complex set of social relationships and communicative networks. (This is the "structuralist"—in the widest sense of that term—rather than the environmentalist approach to language.) The other notion has been very widely expressed; indeed, it is the orthodox point of view for a large number of educational psychologists.[6] If, however, both grammatical and lexical (as well as phonological) patterns existed in the southern plantations as well as in the northern cities, and were transmitted from one to the other, it is difficult to see how those patterns can result from one specific environment like that of the inner city.

Although it is tempting to see the movement of Black English into the northern cities as a transmission of southernisms, it is simply not accurate. The earliest records of the speech of plantation slaves reveal great differences from the speech of any white group, and on the basis of tape-recorded cues alone, listeners from the deepest South (Mississippi or Louisiana) can differentiate the race of the speaker. In fact, anyone, Black or white, from those areas proves surprisingly willing to volunteer information like, "I can always tell. On the telephone, around the corner—down a well, even—I can always tell." The color-blind liberalism hoped for by some prominent members of the Johnson administration will, seemingly, have to give way to an attempt to prove that people of other ethnic groups can have different behavior patterns and *still* deserve their human rights.

The discussion in this book returns repeatedly to the way in which those roughly color-correlated language differences arose, the Creolist theory. It cannot be presented in any more than sketchy detail here, but it has been dealt with in a large number of easily accessible books and articles.[7] Although it does not hold that everything in the Black American English vernacular—not even everything that is distinct from white dialects—comes directly from Africa, it does agree with the arguments of anthropologists like Herskovits (see Bibliography) that much more has survived from the homeland of the West African slaves than the older generations of historians, sociologists, and anthropologists wished to admit. In that respect, it finds inspiration and support in several new works on the history of slavery in the United States, especially Eugene Genovese's *Roll, Jordan, Roll.* The subtitle of that book is *The World the Slaves Made;* the subtitle of this one might be *The Words the Slaves Made.*

In line with the above considerations, it seems unavoidable that a Black American English lexicon should concern itself to some degree with the most debatable and most significant issue raised—the provenience of those forms that are uniquely or primarily Black. Because the etymologies are so hard to establish noncontroversially, it seems all the more necessary to take into account as much historical data as possible. There is no *Dictionary of Black American English on Historical Principles,* and the lack of one complicates the problem of the investigator immeasurably.

As interesting as such historical considerations are to the academic historian, however, there are deeper social problems involving language that make it unacceptable to build such a study around those words that happen to be more or less certainly of an African or Creole provenience. In the first flush of triumph over the Supreme Court ruling of 1954, ending or reducing segregation in the schools, liberals were inclined to believe that the Black child's literacy problems were solved. This has not proved to be true, and language has had a great deal to do with the persistence of the problem.[8] White schoolteachers in schoolrooms full of Black pupils simply were not prepared for what they heard and read. Black teachers were probably not so surprised, but many of them were not willing to classify the language as anything besides "bad" English. In Texas, "Black speech patterns, which differed from formal English," according to Alwyn Barr, "also led to problems for students because teachers viewed them as mispronunciations." Barr, however, had a more enlightened viewpoint:

> . . . many represented imaginative language creations which allowed more flexible expression. "Ageable," as a description of a person not yet old, or "journeyproud" as a verbal picture of someone excited about a forthcoming trip, suggested some of the possibilities.[9]

A student in a small Louisiana college, either groping unsuccessfully for *revenge* or finding her own alternative more expressive, wrote of a *payback.* Most of us will say, "I'll pay you back for that" (meaning "I'll take revenge"), so we understand what she is getting at. But it is a rare one of us who can suppress his pride in his book learning and admit that the word is as good as the bookish *vengeance.* A small girl in Washington, D.C., thought she had figured out her little brother's "dumbness" in school:

> [That's] why you so dumb in school because you always callin' fifty cent cash (Ha!) money.[10]

The term *cash money* is comprehensible enough, but it seems redundant to many speakers of ordinary English. It occurs, however, in many Black texts, notably Harry Middleton Hyatt's study of root-work conjure.[11] My Black students in a Louisiana college frequently ask to borrow my *ink pen,* referring to the ballpoint pen that I carry in my shirt pocket. Whites of the area know the term, but for them, it means a pen that has to be filled with ink—the type that all of us used twenty-five years ago.

    Individual teachers are troubled to varying degrees by these unfamiliar usages. (In the case of *ink pen,* it just seemed like a good idea to remember that the basic purpose of either pen was to write.) One teacher in a Louisiana "crossover" operation (wherein white teachers, willing or not, were required to teach in predominantly Black schools) reported that other teachers were disturbed but that she was prepared by experience for:

Some of their expressions, such as "He meddlin' me. . . ." I had heard "meddlin' "
all my life, but the Negroes on our cotton plantation said "meddlin' with me."
Anyway, I knew that meddlin' meant "bothering."[12]

It is just as well for this teacher that she had not become familiar with *meddle*
through Kyle Onstott's *Drum*, wherein it seems to have the meaning "have
intercourse with." Lurid fictional accounts like this have, of course, always been
suspect. Liberal white linguists have been so eager to show that they are on the
other side of the fence from a sensationalist like Onstott that they have adopted
the principle that the converse of what such writers say must be true. There have
been, nevertheless, many observers of Black language who, while not professional
linguists, have deserved better than to be classified with the fictional purveyors
of Black sex. Barr cites with approval Martha Emmons, whose *Deep Like the
River* (see Bibliography) cites not only *ageable* and *journeyproud* but also *car
house* "garage," *lip battlin'* "arguing," *misameaners* "misdemeanors, sins," *old
seeker* "nosy person," *pass* "die," and *funeralize* "bury, perform the funeral
ceremonies for." Some of these are widely attested, and all of them are at least
in principle believable Black forms. Emmons also attests *intown* (heavily stressed
on the first syllable) "expose to sophistication," *dislove* "hate, or at least have no
love for," and *onservice* "make unfit to do one's work."[13]

Works by professional linguists are depressingly rare, but some few indications
of the differences between the Black lexicon and that of ordinary English have
been published by academically qualified professionals. Almost all of them have
labeled the items under study "slang." The surprising exception is Norman
Eliason, better known as an exponent of regional distribution of dialects, who
published "Some Negro Terms" in *American Speech* in 1938, before the split
between social and regional dialectologists developed. He discussed words and
terms like *chip* "to steal," *boogy-woogy* "to enjoy oneself to the limit," *cow* "a
girl," *dog it* "to show off to advantage," *fay* "a white person," *funk* "body odor,"
gates "fellow" (perhaps related to alligator and its abbreviated form *gate;* see
Chapter 4), *Sam* "a Negro who demeans himself to secure favor from white
people," *sender* "anything that gives an emotional thrill," *shim-sham-shimming*
"a dance," *swab* "to whip thoroughly in a physical encounter," and the *swab train
will run tonight* "I'm going to whip somebody." Although the lack of historical
depth in Black vocabulary studies might make it difficult to put most of these into
chronological perspective, some of them are obviously quite old. Two other terms
listed by Eliason, *deal in coal* "associate with one of a darker hue" (never used
in the hearing of a white person, according to the author) and *coal-scuttle blonde*
"a dark Negro girl," are paralleled in the maritime trade in attestations from the
West Indian islands. Captain J. E. Alexander's *Trans-Atlantic Sketches* (1833)
quoted one Black worker in the harbor at Havana, who spoke a little English:
"She go for bring coal" (glossed by Alexander as "a Negro cargo").

Although not by any means scholars of the caliber of Eliason, many graduate students at small, out-of-the-way colleges have done creditable studies on Black English. Close to home for me, Ursula Genung Walker's 1968 thesis on the dialect of Natchitoches Parish, Louisiana, cites "distinctive idiomatic expressions," including *he pass* "he died," *my sister before* "my older sister," *contribute to a floral* "go in on funeral flowers," *I'll just face the grown days as they come,* and *One thing I don't like is when a teacher loud talks me.* She also includes *she is low* "she is short in stature," a phrase to remind the blues fan of Sam "Lightnin' " Hopkins'

> She little and she low
> She right down on de ground.[14]

One of the joys of writing on the Black lexicon is that it permits listening to blues recordings under the guise of "work."

Like others who have looked seriously at the language of the Black population in the United States (in her case, primarily Louisiana public school students), Walker found a use of "zero derivation" (e.g., making an adjective into a verb without changing its form—*to full* rather than *to fill*). This reduction of the derivation forms is fairly common in ordinary American English dialects (e.g., some nurses will use *to bath a patient* rather than *to bathe . . .*), but no other dialect equals Black English in that respect. Walker chose to express that perception in these terms:

> Some of these students create verbs with an insouciance that is sometimes thought to have disappeared from the face of this linguistic world: "I went site [sic] seening," "service my time with the Air Force," "If I don't success in that field," "Nobody could lap me" (i.e., hold me on his lap), "We always made it back up," "Maybe I would like to architect some of the world."

Examples come daily to those of us who teach composition to that population: "My father has worked on many construction jobs, but he is disable to work right now." The squeamish among us cringe when the almost inevitable comparison to "Elizabethan English" is made.

Zero or special derivations of this sort must have been used for a long time by Black speakers. One of the early narratives of ex-slaves recorded by the Federal Writers Project in the 1940s contains this sentence: "I's too wordless to sing 'em [songs, hymns, and Psalms] now."[15] The same informant says of the Yankees, "Dey made big promises, but dey was poor reliance . . . dey was mistol' 'bout a heap o' things."[16]

Semantic shifts and apparent innovations are also common, and workers on folklore have recorded, among other things, their astonishment at such occurrences. A writer on the "voodoo cult," writing down the words of his informant, heard:

"If you don't stop, I'll make you rabbit away from here." That was the first time I had ever heard "rabbit" used as a verb. But it is now more or less common.[17]

One particular usage, commented on by many teachers in the Louisiana area, is "May I speak?" The semantics of this Black phrase proved so striking to a crossover teacher named Manie Culbertson that she made it the title of her book recounting her experiences in a formerly all-Black school. She reported:

> This simple question has driven us transferees out of our minds. The pattern seems to have developed in the Negro schools so that this question is not a question at all but part of a ritual, repeated over and over in every classroom.[18]

In this context, *May I speak?* is a request to have a conversation with another person, as, for example, with a student coming from one classroom to talk to a student in another. One of the interesting implications of this phrase is that the students have apparently learned one of the shibboleths of English or Language Arts classrooms—*may* rather than *can* for permission. They are, therefore, more "correct" than the majority of white students—or teachers—by the artificial standards of the common school grammars. And they are still misunderstood.

In view of the educational conflict and its consequences to a Black child entering the mainstream educational system, it seems highly advisable for the teacher to learn the children's usage, in the case of words like *speak,* and to relieve them of that part of the burden of learning. Barr reports how students who could not understand "Bring down one and carry two" could immediately understand "Bring down de one an' tote de two." (A white teacher whose command of Black English phonology is not exceptionally good would do better, however, to use his normal pronunciation and change only the vocabulary. Such pronunciations are easily taken for ridicule.) The author of *May I Speak?* was struck by *stapling machine* "stapler"; surely, however, the linguistic adaptability of any teacher is great enough to keep him from "correcting" such a usage.

This common-sense attitude toward the language of schoolchildren has received a great boost from a writer like John M. Brewer, whose "Hidden Language: Ghetto Children Know What They're Talking About" is a highly sympathetic attempt to enlighten inner city teachers.[19] Bypassing grammatical considerations, and not really stressing ethnic slang, Brewer concentrates on the highly figurative language used by Black children. Thus, he reports that *trees without roots* is used for "broken homes," *toys on a fairy lake* for "outsiders looking for thrills," *flying backward* for "sad," *my special pinetop* for "my favorite teacher," *I am full of the joy of being upfront* for "I am disgusted with my circumstances." At first glance, this may seem impossibly high flown and figurative for schoolchildren, but the entire history of Black English is characterized by such metaphorical creations. From Blacks in general, the phrase *on you like white on rice* is frequently cited as an example of such expressiveness.[20] A freshman in my remedial English class wrote of violence in television programs: "Violence is really how an individual sees it. This could stem from a flower with man roots." Discussing several such examples, Martha Emmons asserts, "Many word coinages of unschooled Negroes are astonishing in force and character." Quoting a judgment in praise of the innovative diction of a modern poet, she goes on to say:

> In as full a measure this may be applied to the speech and song of such Negroes as may yet be considered of the folk group, without benefit of standardized education, standardized tests, standardized vocabulary, standardized thinking.[21]

Common sense tells us, however, that not every Black schoolchild is a poet. This praise of Black "inventiveness" runs the risk of lapsing into Crow Jim (Jim Crow disguised as a tolerant person). Emmons is undoubtedly not guilty of any such offense, but many a Black will shake his head knowingly when he reads the following passage from the Federal Writers Project in Alabama:

> The character and the apt imagery of the Negro are illustrated not only by his songs (see Music) but by his language. To him the V8 Ford is a "forked eight." A Negro woman goes through life known as "Flyaway" because, as her mother explains, "When she were a baby she were such a pretty little thing hit look like she might jest take wings and fly away." A husky man became "Clawhammer" because, "When dat boy 'ud get a whippin' he jest flop on de flo' and beller wid he laigs hooked back like a clawhammer."[22]

The rueful Black reader will remember only too well the difficulty that such users of "apt imagery" had in gaining admission to the University of Alabama.

It is probably this factor of skepticism, based on long and bitter experience, that makes even Black leaders like Kenneth Clark[23] negative about proposed attempts to incorporate Black English into the curriculum of the schools. A psychologist like Clark is all too well aware of the standardized nature of such intelligence tests as the Stanford-Binet, which are widely used as predictors of educational success and often have the effect of "self-fulfilling prophecies." (Teachers learn that a child has scored low on the test and may be expected to do poorly in school; they have low expectations of him and convey those expectations to the child; he does poorly in school.) Standardized vocabulary tests—often an important and even basic part of "intelligence tests"—make little provision for "forceful" coinages, and school assignments like those of the average composition class are only slightly more favorable to such innovations. The upshot is that Black children have passed for disadvantaged in the school system when there are none of the obvious physiological handicaps (cleft palate, brain damage), and the thesis of the nonverbal or "verbally destitute" Black child has played an important part in the literature of educational psychology in the last fifteen years or so.

Some of the more sympathetic teachers have come to suspect outright bias in the tests. Culbertson cites an example:

> Carlton has an I.Q. of 95. I know that this is not correct, and I question the accuracy of the test score. The test that has been in use in this parish is not valid for them, or there have been some serious errors in the administration of it. I suspect the former.[24]

No one who is around Black youngsters very much will fail to have the same kind of suspicions about the I.Q. tests and their supposed indications of "lack of intelligence." But the psychologists are often strongly committed to the I.Q. tests, which have now been administered for over half a century and therefore provide almost the only longitudinal data available to certain psychologists, and rationalizations have not been lacking. Jensen indulged in the famous ad hoc distinction between "analytical intelligence" and "associative intelligence," crediting Black children with a great deal of the latter.[25] And Shockley, a Nobel prize winner in another field, has not been dissuaded by criticism of the tests from some shockingly racist formulations.[26]

Against this, linguists have offered the suggestion that the language mismatch between the dialect of Black children and that of the I.Q. tests may be part of the explanation for the low scores. Elsa Roberts, of the Language Research Foundation in Boston, concluded after a long research project:

> High performance on this test [the Wechsler so-called Preschool Intelligence Test] entails nothing less than full socialization into the culture of speakers of the dominant dialect of English. . . .[27]

This bias was only part of a general pattern in American educational testing. Without exception, every kind of language test seems to discriminate against the lower-class Black child. Of the Wepman test of "impaired auditory discrimination," Robert Politzer of the Stanford University Research Center in Education and Teaching was able to say:

> [It] contains phonemic discriminations which are simply not found in Negro dialects or in other dialects usually associated with lower socioeconomic status. An examination of the Wepman test reveals at least seven such discriminations on each of the two forms of the test.[28]

Language testing of schoolchildren has become a big business in the United States. In some respects, especially where Black children are concerned, it is a highly questionable business.

Yet the really damaging kind of language-associated test is obviously the one that makes a statement about the child's basic intelligence. (Professional psychologists, especially when around their colleagues, are careful to distinguish between "I.Q." and "general intelligence." It is to be highly doubted, however, that the average school system does so.) An excellent example of the kind of bias involved is provided by Carson and Rabin.[29] In their test, based upon identification and description of ordinary objects in a picture elicitation, they rank "Categorization and Synonym," "Essential Description," and "Essential Function" highest; what they regard as "Vague Description and Function," "Vague Function," "Error," and "Don't Know" lowest. The examiners, predictably, found northern Blacks to be "superior" to southern Blacks but "inferior" to northern whites on such a test. The clear implication is that the Black children have poorer vocabularies and poorer communicative skills. But most of the "forceful" metaphorical usages described by Brewer and Culbertson would be labeled "Vague Description and Function" within the Carson and Rabin framework.

There has been at least one major rebuttal to the arguments about a linguistic bias on I.Q. tests. Quay's experiment[30] seemed to show that Black children scored no higher on a test translated into Black English than they did with the original wording. It is noteworthy, however, that on both versions this group of children scored in the "normal" range—I.Q. about 100. Apparently, these were not the "disadvantaged" children whose scores in the 70–80 range had touched off speculations like those of Jensen and Shockley. The I.Q. argument remained where it had been before. Admittedly, there is no conclusive experimental evidence for either side.

Children in school have not been the only Blacks who have scored low on standardized vocabulary tests. Levinson found that "non-domiciled" (i.e., homeless) Black men tested according to an interesting pattern:

> The homeless whites seemed to perform about equally well on all of the *Verbal* subtests, while the Negroes appeared to have scored relatively better on *Digit Span* and most poorly on *Vocabulary* and *Arithmetic.*[31]

The insistence that Standard English vocabulary is not the exact equivalent of vocabulary in the absolute has now been made frequently by linguists,[32] and the interpretation that the tests are biased against Black subjects is a familiar one among researchers. On a popular level, on the other hand, the damage had been done. Many people saw the results of the tests of the 1960s and found the notion that the Blacks were "verbally deprived" a comfortable one. If Blacks were making lower salaries (the differential having grown rather than diminished, according to some accounts, since the desegregation decision of 1954), it made mainstream America feel better to think that there was a "scientific" explanation other than simple prejudice. The same applied, of course, if Blacks were doing more poorly in the newly integrated schools, or if more of them were homeless.

The fact that Americans had traditionally been subservient to puristic ideals of language, especially as sponsored by the educational system, and that American English itself—not to mention *Black* American English—was still felt by many to be somehow inferior to British English paved the way for the general American willingness to believe that one of the "nonstandard" dialects of American English was in some way a limiting factor on intelligence.

A nation that believes in its ideals, however poorly it may actualize that belief, can be moved to do something for the disadvantaged. Unfortunately, such action is not always well informed. In spite of the potential for racism in connection with the notion of retarded Negro mental development, the people who took the activist approach in the 1960s—"enrichment" programs—were mostly liberals, and many of them were Black. Organizations like the NAACP, concerned with the practical needs of Black upward mobility and not so much with exactness of analysis, were often more willing to see "impoverishment"—which presumably could be compensated for—rather than a Black dialect that was "equal" but different. For one thing, the very phrase was an unfortunate echo of the "separate but equal" rule of the southern schools during the period of segregation.

"Enrichment" was the order of the day in Lyndon Johnson's abortive Great Society, and untold millions of government and foundation dollars were poured into such programs. Graduate assistants in the research projects, many of them Blacks, who were convinced—on no real evidence—that the mothers of ghetto children did not talk to their babies, undertook to provide "linguistic interaction" with the poor Black children who were in the process of language acquisition and putatively lacking in such interaction.

For anyone who even walked through a typically Black inner city community like the Adams-Morgan district of Washington, D.C., the notion that Black mothers did not talk to their children was ludicrous. Yet a ghetto mother, invited with her child into the fancy office of a psychologist, might be diffident about talking to the baby. "Scientific" evidence of such interaction was lacking, and there were always those low scores on the standardized tests.

A few field anthropologists, like Virginia Heyer Young, finally got around to going into Black communities to look at what communicative action went on. Looking for the assumed (and frequently reported) pattern of the stern, forbidding parents who never communicated with the children except in monosyllabic grunts of command, Young actually found the exact opposite. Parents, siblings, and even distantly related persons play with the babies constantly, even, Young suggests somewhat humorously, when the baby might prefer to sleep. Rather than being linguistically inhibited, the children are "urged to precocious speech development."[33] Young demonstrates that the very opposite of the "language deficit" assumptions is true for the very young Negro child: He is, if anything, more experienced in human interactions like talking than his non-Black counterpart. On the other hand, he may have been less exposed to material things of twentieth-century American culture and may have had no chance to become as proficient as middle-class children with blocks and building games. The poverty of the families seems an obvious explanation.

Young's explorations yielded an unexpected bonus in the terminology of child rearing. Georgia Negroes like those studied by Young—and there are confirmations from elsewhere—have terms like *knee baby* for "the ambulatory child who leaves the mother and returns to her, who stands at her knee whether there is a new baby in her lap or not."[34] The younger child is a *lap baby.*[35] Children of the same mother but different fathers characterize themselves in the terms, "We're halves."[36] There is even a terminological anticipation of an expression often noted in studies of inner city "slang": the "very common, admiring adjective *bad* is used, through 'knee-babyhood' of boys."[37] These boys are, as Young points out, not deviating from the behavior patterns of their group but are rather meeting the expectations of their elders. Thus, there is probably some cultural preparation, in child rearing, for song lyrics like:

> Stagolee was a bad man
> He was the baddest man I know.

As much as such studies do correct the misimpressions left by educational psychologists, they are vestigially culture bound. Surprised by the age-grading factor that places a child (especially a boy) of three or over primarily with his peers rather than with his elders, Young complains of the "abrupt ending of parental stimulation."[38] She adds:

> Often speech becomes an indistinct children's patois in contrast with the clear enunciation used by the knee-baby with his parents.[39]

"Indistinct," here, obviously takes its validity from the perceptions of the researcher, who possibly found the speech difficult to understand because it included so bewilderingly much more than the speech of the knee baby. (So the monolingual speaker of English finds it easier to follow *la plume de ma tante* than the conversations of Parisians on street corners.) The lessons that even sophisticated researchers have to learn involve the value of this "indistinct patois"; without it, the child is not functional, not an accepted member of his peer culture. He is a "square," a "lame," or even a "sissy"—depending upon the degree of deviation from his peers.

Like investigating anthropologists, teachers may find the language of these peer-stigmatized groups "clearer" than that of the peer-group-active children. Slightly after the age of three, the shattering experience of culture conflict comes with dramatic suddenness. Here, and at a cruelly early age (described with appropriate impact perhaps only in Richard Wright's *The Long Dream*), is the cultural crisis of which a linguistic crisis is one part. One suggested solution for this crisis is what has been scornfully styled "bidialectalism."[40] The recommendation has been made by sociolinguists like Stewart[41] because they recognize the need for a normal child to grow up with a successful orientation both to his peer group and to the school system. Without the appropriate dialect, the child cannot function well in either.

The "indistinct patois" of the Black child leaving babyhood behind assumes, then, an importance in the total picture that Young's casual designation misses completely. *Patois* is probably more accurate than *argot* because a complex grammatical structure is acquired with the peer-group language. The "hip" vocabulary of the inner city is obviously not what is involved. Some rural Blacks, possibly the families of those Young studied, never master anything like big city street talk. But any pejorative term for the language variety is unfortunate.

In spite of the fact that there is no historical record of large bodies of whites using grammatical features like durative *be* and preverbal remote perfective marker *been,* the assumption, found in most traditional works on dialectology, that Black children speak "archaic" southern dialect, identical to an earlier stage of the speech of whites, is such a deeply ingrained one that it can be found in much of the literature of education. Margaret Anderson asserts:

> The white children [in integrated Southern schools] notice the old-fashioned words and expressions, whereas the Negro children do not because they have never heard anything else.[42]

"Old-fashioned words," in this case, are only identified by such examples as "ast" for "ask" [sic!], "dunna" for "dinner," and so on.[43] Strangely for the notion that the words are old-fashioned, Anderson, a southern white adult, reports:

> Although I have always lived in the South, I often have difficulty understanding Negro children and have to ask them to repeat words or explain what they mean by certain expressions.[44]

The need to have certain expressions explained to white adults by Black children has been reported in many places. Bess Lomax Hawes and Bessie Jones detail their lack of understanding of Gullah Sea Islanders' use of the phrase *to clap with someone:*

> To Mrs. Jones and the Sea Islander [children], to be "with" somebody means to respond to them, to complement and support their silences, to fill in their statements (musical, physical, and verbal) with little showers of comment, to answer their remarks—to clap a different pattern.[45]

The first study to approach the problem from the viewpoint of relativism ("relativity" is his word) was virtually ignored. Ernest A. T. Barth's 1961 "The Language Behavior of Negroes and Whites" found different white/Black emotional reactions to some words *(father, minority, color, neighborhood, job, home, sex)* and no significant difference in the reaction to another set *(scholarship, slum, policeman).* Barth predicted difficulty for Negro children in integrated schools and even some of the (nonlinguistic) rationalizations that would be indulged in.

Such a relativistic approach as that adumbrated by Barth would stress the positives of the specifically Black lexical usages. It would not give way to the temptations that overcame even broad-minded writers like Culbertson when she concluded that a Black child writing about "My Family Tree" in terms of branches and leaves had a "limited experience [that] just didn't include any knowledge of genealogy."[46] It should be less ambiguous than the approach of Daniel Fader in *The Naked Children. Naked,* in this title, apparently means "without language," for Fader's flyleaf motto reads, "If language is the clothing of life, no child should be sent naked into the world." Fader, who taught an all-Black class in a northern ghetto school as part of an educational experiment, perceived some of the utility and richness of what he called "child's language" as the use of *vines* "clothing."[47] He was appreciative of "the rhetorical discrimination of children" after it had been explained to him how one boy, in a confrontation with a teacher, "used *mothah* as a way of stopping short of *mothah fuckah* without losing face and *shi-i* as not quite articulating *shit.* "[48] He speaks of Cleo, the girl leader of the otherwise all-boy gang with which he has a special association, as "lapsing into the black argot" in utterances like *We together. We goes with him,* but he also discourses at length on the practical advantages of "Cleo's several tongues."[49]

However ambivalent they might be about those "tongues," such observers could hardly avoid seeing that a great many Black lexical usages not only were different from the vocabulary of Standard English but were being picked up by non-Black users. Words now familiar to most Americans—*dig, funky, cool* (as terms of general approbation), *man* or *dude* (as terms of address), *fox* "pretty girl," *gone,* and *out of sight* (as terms of approval) and many others—obviously came to white America from the Black community, often through the medium of jazz, the blues, rock and roll, or some other musical type. For most of these, there is no evidence of prior white use in the same sense. The linguists, however, who attacked deficit theory generally mentioned this vocabulary only in passing. In his arguments in opposition to that part of the linguistic profession that did not want to see a distinctively Negro dialect (a large and still influential segment), William A. Stewart chose to posit, primarily for the sake of argument, "striking structural similarities in certain areas (such as vocabulary),"[50] in spite of the fact that he was fully aware of the body of ethnic slang. Actually, no one could have held so naive a view; the point was rather that those linguists were involved in their grammatical demonstrations almost to the exclusion of lexical considerations.

It was, of course, well known that certain white groups (first musicians attracted to jazz, then others like the hippies) were strongly influenced by the Black slang. On a journalistic level, it was often accepted that the hippies spoke exactly like the Blacks—although a simple listening test ought to have been adequate to dispel that belief. Somewhat paradoxically, even the very familiarity of a certain amount of the Black-associated vocabulary may have hindered the reassessment of the nature of the vocabulary.

The term "slang" itself no doubt contributed to this unfortunate effect. The general public has long associated slang with a transitory stage in the language development of teenagers, soon to be dropped by all except those few who never enter the adult, mainstream world. "Slang" was, for the average American, an exotic language phenomenon primarily for children—outside the domain of working language and not really to be considered seriously. Although many a reader of the Sunday supplements was convinced that he would score low on an "I.Q." test involving a lot of Black slang and questions on such ethnic behavioral patterns as the preparation of chitterlings, he was not convinced that the person who scored high (i.e., who was a master of that body of slang as well as the other cultural material) deserved any more linguistic respect because of his "nonstandard vocabulary." The famous demonstrations by Whorf—controversial as they still are—of the suitability of "unwritten" languages like Hopi for modern physics dealt with the verbal system and not with the lexicon. Professional linguists very seldom devote their attention to lexicography, and even when they do, they are not usually concerned with vocabulary size and function but with etymology or a similar matter.

Insofar as those concerns go, however, it would now seem impossible to continue to believe that the Blacks had learned (and perhaps distorted) a part of the lexicon of the English colonists who were in the New World when the Africans arrived. In the first place, there were not that many Englishmen here in 1619, when the African slaves began arriving. Slaves were brought to the New World before English colonists were buying any, and there is a slight chance that Africans had come over before the period of slavery.[51]

The influences that these many Africans and their descendants have had on the languages of the Americas, as well as the relatively autonomous language varieties of Black groups, cannot be appreciated apart from a consideration of compounds and expressions of two or more words. Dalby has pointed out how *big eye* "greed" is probably a loan translation from words meaning *big* and *eye,* which combine in the significance "greed" in several West African languages.[52] It is irrelevant that *big* and *eye* have been in English since long before the period of possible African influence. It is even less relevant that southern whites, who borrowed the expression from Blacks, have been able to rationalize the phrase as a kind of play on letters of the alphabet ("big *I,* little *u*").

The same, *mutatis mutandis,* can be said for *bad mouth* "curse" and for many other well-known "ghetto talk" expressions. Conventional dictionaries deal with such compounds and expressions haphazardly, if at all, and vocabulary tests are even further from a sensible approach. But the direction now seems to be obvious: If any real understanding, historical or otherwise, of the Black vocabulary (or of the vocabulary borrowed from Blacks by whites) is ever to be achieved, it will have to be done in terms other than the dictionaries' usual one-word-at-a-time method.

Although linguists and lexicographers have been remiss in dealing with such expressions, folklorists have excelled at such work for decades. The folklorists who have specialized in the Black community, most of them trained anthropologists, have never been deficit theorists. They have seen, much earlier than the other members of the academic community, the richness of the concepts embodied in whatever specifically Black terminology there is, and they have seen its essential independence of other groups. It is with the work of the folklorists, then, that I believe we could most profitably begin to seek an in-depth academic background for an investigation of the Black lexicon.

Among the unsung heroes of Black folklore research, there is probably no one more worthy than J. Mason Brewer (see Bibliography). A writer on Black culture long before it became fashionable to deal with that theme, Brewer provided, over the course of his lifetime, a vast—albeit somewhat informal—body of investigation of specifically Black beliefs and customs. He knew that the Negro who would be called "disadvantaged" in the 1960s told a different kind of ghost story or animal trickster tale, preached a different kind of sermon, and told a different kind of joke. He knew, furthermore, that he did so in a different kind of language. No formal linguist, Brewer expressed himself best in an area most easily accessible to the folklorist: the proverb. No Africanist, and certainly not dedicated to any African origins theory, he tended to feel that "the pithiest and most savory proverbs seem to come directly out of the Negro's own wisdom."[53] He documented that "pithiness" and "savor" by examples like *Don't say no mo' wid yo' mouf den yo' back kin stand,* and *Don't take no mo' tuh yo' heaht dan yo' kin kick offen yo' heels* "Don't worry so much about jilts in love that you can't go to a dance and dance your troubles away." In collecting a proverb like *De one dat drap de crutch de bes' gits de mos' biscuits,* he freely acknowledged that he (although a Black himself) had to ask the "folk" Black for an explanation of some of the terms: *drappin' de crutch bes',* according to his informant, signified "de one dat curtsy de bes'."[54]

In the works of J. Mason Brewer, Arthur Huff Fauset, Zora Neale Hurston, and others (see Bibliography), we have a priceless body of insights into the Black-white cultural differences and the language that expresses them. Their works span a period of fifty years or more, and the results are surprisingly homogeneous in the most important particulars. It seems foolhardy to undertake an examination of the Black lexicon without leaning heavily on those people and their body of materials. It seems equally absurd not to look at the domains in which they found the Blacks to be most significantly different from whites.

Anyone even halfway familiar with the study of folklore must be aware that the domains studied with so much profit by these and other outstanding scholars embraced conjure and the supernatural, religion and the storefront church, animal and trickster tales, sexual and courtship practices, and musical performance and lyrics. To proceed with an investigation of the Black lexicon without giving primacy to such domains would seem to be arrogant or stupid—or both.

Political expediency might well dictate another course. Especially where conjure and the supernatural are concerned, there are most unfortunate precedents to such an investigation. Racist entertainments like the blackface minstrels drew upon the notion of the "superstitious" Negro to a sickening degree, and any serious reconsideration of the same material is likely to be subject to the accusation of having resurrected the "coon song" attitude. On the other hand, any real accomplishment will probably have to be made in the face of those admitted risks. For purposes of honesty, as well as of efficiency, it is well to point out at the beginning an operational belief that holds that the conjure-related terminology constitutes the "deepest" (i.e., most different) and the least-known levels of Black English vernacular terminology.

To deal with these matters means to break with certain traditions, especially that of the "word geography" approach of the Linguistic Atlas of the United States and Canada. It means asserting the premise that an inventory of words associated with agriculture and the farm; home, kitchen, and cooking; and insect, plant, and animal names cannot possibly give an accurate representation of the differences that exist. It also means acknowledging that the traditional studies that have shown only trivial differences in those areas are probably correct—but *only where those domains are concerned.* Since both slaves and Black sharecroppers had to use the white man's farm machinery, it is to be expected that they would, by and large, borrow his terminology for such machines. Word autonomy would have to exist in other domains, but there is considerable evidence that it did so exist.

The Black populace itself, misled by the apparent advantages of other dialects, has often been the chief agent of the kind of concealment we refer to as folk etymology. The Gullah Sea Islanders, for example, seem to *want* to believe that their word *pojo* "heron" is a dialect pronunciation of Poor Joe, or that the day name Cudjo (given to a male born on Monday) is "really" based on Cousin Joe. Black English vernacular speakers who have learned some traditional grammar in the schools often rationalize their durative *be (he all the time be going there)* as "subjunctive" *(if that be true),* although of course the distribution is quite different (legal language utilizing the "subjunctive" would never have the negation *If that don't be true*). "Standard" English, the superposed[55] variety in the United States, has established itself in the linguistic folklore as "good" English, and each group would like to believe that its language is as close to the "good" variety as possible.

This defensive attitude is not abnormal, although it is more characteristic of "disadvantaged" groups that have suffered social and economic deprivation. One can find it among Puerto Ricans who want so badly to believe that their *zafacon* "garbage can" comes from English that they invent an English source, *safety can.* In the West Indies, *Mamadjo,* the name of a mermaid creature widely believed in, is taken to be derived from French *mama d'eau* "Mother of Water," although both the name and the associated ceremonies resemble the Yoruba water deity *Yemoja* "Mother of Fishes."[56] Virtually all of the Black-associated terms discussed in the following chapters have been subjected to the same rationalizing practices, wherein all possible efforts have been expended to find a European source.

On the other hand, there is comparatively little reason to believe that certain expressions, popularly believed to be Black, are in any historical sense products of the American Black community. It is even less likely that they are "Africanisms." First among these would undoubtedly be the terms associated with vice, especially narcotics and prostitution. A census would probably corroborate the visual impression that a majority of the prostitutes in Times Square are Black, but it is doubtful that anything in "Afro-American" culture would explain that predominance nearly as well as plain economic facts. Before a phrase like *mother fucker* can be taken to be "Black" in any meaningful sense, there has to be some objective demonstration that it came from the Black community. The mere fact that certain whites hear it more frequently from Blacks is not in itself very significant.

Imaginative tracings to the Black community have played their role in the unfortunate process of stigmatizing the English used by many socioeconomically disadvantaged Negroes. Edwin Newman, for example, has decided that the phrase *ya know* came from inner city talk, although there is not a shred of evidence that such is the case.[57] Newman does not like the phrase—considering it, apparently, one of the Americanisms that is going to be the "death" of English —and his bestselling book has propagated the notion that the Blacks are somehow the purveyors of this kind of sloppy expression—if "you know" is indeed such a phrase. In the first place, it is wildly improbable that the combination of the second person pronoun with one of the most frequently used verbs will ever be traced to its "first" use. The research project itself suggests all kinds of burlesque possibilities, but George Marshall of the University of Georgia has undertaken it, apparently in all seriousness and his tongue firmly out of his cheek. In what may be the most trivial article on language history ever published,[58] Marshall has found some evidence of the usage in British texts in the 1830s. With or without such jejeune contributions, however, we could have been sure that the phrase did not originate with Blacks. Furthermore, we could have been sure that it poses no greater challenge to the life of the English language than did "Forsooth" or "Methinks" in earlier centuries.

The lexical study of the Black English vernacular removes from the list, then, some of the terms that Negroes have been credited with (or blamed for). It adds some others. The aim should not, of course, be to make the list as long or as short as possible. The value that comes from such a study lies rather in the understanding of the nature of vocabulary usage by a majority of American Blacks. If, as there seem to be many reasons to believe, the inventory is an appreciable one, certain matters that have frequently been explained in terms of pathologies can be seen instead in the light of normal developments. If Black English has a lexicon in addition to the phonology and grammar that linguists have demonstrated for it in recent years, then it deserves the recognition accorded to a language. Some of the problems of Black schoolchildren and of homeless Black men in the streets can be seen to be, at least partly, problems of the type that we have always associated with bilingualism. Recognition of the language differences alone will not solve the problems or right the historical and present injustices of the American caste system. It would be arrogant to claim that kind of power for language. Furthermore, the typically American language prejudice is so all-permeating that the Black dialect speaker himself will sometimes insist, "Ah don' talk plain."[59] Much remains to be done before these deep-seated attitudes can be changed. But an accurate appraisal of the linguistic differences should contribute something to those endeavors.

2

Terminology of Sex and Lovemaking

IT IS rather easy to see how groups that have wished to avoid controversy, such as the Linguistic Atlas of the United States and Canada project, have stayed away from sexual terminology and have dealt instead in innocuous domains like farming practices, farm machinery, and kitchen utensils. A guilt complex that many liberal Americans retain because of the sexual exploitation of Black women by southern slave-owners has had far-reaching consequences. One historical picture has it that southern slave-owners kept harems of West African women. The influence of that historical formulation has been great enough to render the topic of sex almost taboo in certain academic disciplines. There are, however, some recent developments in the historiography of slavery that may remove or lessen that taboo. While the existence of a large number of mulattoes in all areas where African slaves were brought (perhaps especially in the South) must prove that some sexual exploitation took place, there is now reason to believe that some of the more lurid accounts were overstated (as in Kyle Onstott's sensational novels *Mandingo* and *Drum*). Fogel and Engerman have recently asserted a radically different interpretation based on demographic statistics:

> A demographic model of the slave population shows that the census data on mulattoes alone cannot be used to sustain the contention that a large proportion of slave children must have been fathered by white men. And other available bodies of evidence, such as the W. P. A. survey of former slaves, throw such claims into doubt.[1]

The older tradition, it is true, had it differently. Cohn represents the more conventional notion.

> In the slave-markets there was a constant demand for especially attractive women. Spirited bidding ensued for them at the auctions where the prices rose as high as $2,500 [an amount probably equal to at least $15,000 in 1976] for a really desirable bed companion. . . . The Delta, in the deep South, was no exception to the general rule. Here, too, white men resorted more or less openly to Negro prostitutes and mistresses. Their progeny are everywhere.[2]

Without taking sides in the controversy, one can see enough truth in Fogel and Engerman's thesis to realize that sexual activity was largely a domain in which Black communicated with Black and in which a distinctive terminology developed—or was carried over from the African past or from some other source. There was, obviously, some fringe interaction; whites learned some of the more prominent Black sexual terms like *jelly roll,* although they seldom understood the full implications thereof.[3] Other terms, however, remained essentially unknown to the white population until the fashions of the hippies and the ubiquity of rock-and-roll lyrics made them commonplace to the younger generation. It is interesting, coincidentally, that the fashion in interracial relationships shifted from white men with Black women to Black men with white women. Cohn's statement, made in 1935 and coming from a writer who had stressed the size of the mulatto population, is impressive: "In his religion and in his sex the Negro is on his own."[4]

The liberal's reluctance to deal with sex terminology has restricted, historically, the investigation of lexical differences even past the influence of Victorianism. It was the latter that kept James A. Harrison, whose 1884 article "Negro English" is an interesting pioneering work in spite of the fact that it did not measure up to the linguistic standards of its own time, from listing whatever Black terms he might have known for sexual intercourse and the genitalia. Guy B. Johnson's "Double Meaning in the Popular Negro Blues," while the work of a genuine scholar, shows in almost every line the influence of a climate of opinion not nearly so frank as that of today. Johnson is almost apologetic about bringing into the open the process by which the Negro group "has carried its ordinary vulgarities over into respectable song life."[5] A more open approach to sex and sexual terminology may reveal many more lexical differences than had hitherto been suspected.

Many of the specifically Black terms for sexual activity appear to be quite old, and their absence from the texts of the eighteenth and nineteenth centuries tells us more about the nature of those texts than it does about the Black lexicon. Slavery and postslavery relationships between Black and white left those terms among the strongest of taboos, and the literary fashions of that period reinforced the likelihood that they would never appear in print. Modern texts, which contain a very large number of such expressions, obviously represent the lifting of the taboo and even a somewhat self-conscious parading of the newfound freedom.

An excellent example of the half-familiarity of the white population with Black sexual terms is provided by the name Jody, if Bruce Jackson's derivation from *Joe de Grinder* is accurate.[6] According to Jackson, Jody is a term widely used among Blacks and current in the armed services for a superior lover (or "cocksman") who was known to be so good in bed that all men feared losing their wives and sweethearts to him. The term *grinder* and the verb *grind* in the sense of "copulate, indulge in sexual activity" are, at all events, extremely familiar in blues and Black folksong contexts:

> Now I ain't no miller
> No miller's son.
> But I can do your grinding
> Till the miller man comes.[7]

The verb actually refers to coital movement. It may be roughly similar to [*bump and*] *grind* from (white) burlesque, but in the Black culture, it is notably characteristic of either a man or a woman, whereas the burlesque usage referred strictly to the activities of a female.

Examples of the use of the verb are easy to find in specifically Black contexts. Roger Abrahams has quoted this one from the dozens played in Philadelphia:

> I fucked your mother from day to day,
> Out came a baby and what did it say?
> He say, "Looka here, Pop, you grind so fine,
> Please give me some of that fucking wine."[8]

In one specimen of the toast "Pimping Sam," the braggart speaker identifies himself:

> Say, "Bitch, this is Pimping Sam, the world's wonder,
> Long-dick buck-bender, all-night grinder, womb-finder."[9]

Grind is, however, also descriptive of a woman's role in intercourse. The old jazz song "Bawdyhouse Blues" contains the lines:

> I got an all-night trick again.
> I'm busy grindin' so you can't come in.[10]

Or, like so many other Black sexual terms, it can describe the action of either male or female:

> Well, I woke up this mornin', grindin' on my mind.
> Goin' to grind, honey, if I go stone blind.[11]

Some white country and western musicians have borrowed the grinding metaphor, with clear sexual allusiveness:

> Two old maids in a folding bed
> One turned over and the other one said,
> "What's the matter with the mill
> Can't get no grinding, tell me what's
>   the matter with the mill."[12]

Since the term does not occur outside song lyrics, and since Black influence on country music even preceding the rock-and-roll fad is acknowledged, it is very likely that the whites borrowed from the Blacks rather than vice versa.[13]

The most artistic use of the metaphor is, however, one in which the grinding is, Black style, restricted to neither sex but shared by both. In Bessie Smith's "Empty Bed Blues," the singer confides that she:

> Bought me a coffee grinder,
> Got the best one I could find,
> So he could grind my coffee,
> 'Cause he had a brand new grind.[14]

The familiar (to Blacks) sexual implications of *grinder* are enough, if the song title itself were not, to suggest double entendre—nothing noteworthy in the blues, except that it is exceptionally well handled in this song. Particularly interesting is the sex-shifting, which will play an important part in the ensuing discussion: The woman has the "grinder . . . the best one [she] could find"—thus it is apparently symbolic of part of her anatomy—but the man has to "grind the coffee," and it is he who has the "brand new grind." This semantic ambivalence of *grind,* either masculine or feminine in role, gives that part of the lyrics a sophistication not found in more routine (and simpler) lines like:

> Bought him a mattress so he could lay just right

in the same song. If the difference is not between ordinary work and great art, it is at least between an inventive mind working on folk material and a rather routine version of that material untransformed.

The food-and-kitchen suggestions of *coffee grinder* are no surprise to one who knows of the form *grayna* "eat" in Krio, the English-based Creole of Sierra Leone. They are a convenient thematic link (although the transition is seldom so simple in the actual blues) to other food metaphors for sex, like Bessie Smith's in the same lyric:

> He boiled my first cabbage, and he made it awful hot.
> When he put in the bacon it overflowed the pot.

Several commentators, including Guy B. Johnson, have noted that "another [Negro] term for the female organs is cabbage."[15] Nothing makes that denotation quite so specific as two lyrics by Jelly Roll Morton. In the first, he sings:

> I got a sweet woman; she lives right back of the jail.
> She's got a sign on her window, "Good cabbage for sale."[16]

In a mood of greater frankness (or perhaps the lady was no longer present when he spoke in occasional asides to Alan Lomax, who was manning the recording machine in those Library of Congress sessions), he changed the last line to ". . .'Good pussy for sale.' "[17] To the listener who understands the symbolism, both couplets say the same thing. Lines like these are completely lacking in ambiguity: The male is always the cook, and the cabbage is always the female organ. Morton's version of "Mamie's Blues," however, has the line, "I like the way she cook my cabbage for me."[18] Taken together, the two lines epitomize the sexual creativeness of the blues: Both partners are "cooking," and each shares in the food.

More general terminology related to cooking is commonplace in the blues and in Black writings. In Richard Wright's *Lawd Today,* an especially attractive girl is described by working-class Black men in the terms, "This is home cooking."[19] In "Tishamingo Blues," Peg Leg Howell sings:

> I'm going to Tishamingo to have my hambone boiled,
> These Atlanta women done let my hambone spoil.[20]

Another blues proclaims that "No coal black woman can fry no meat for me."[21] And Zora Neale Hurston, quotes a rural Black informant, "I got to have my ground-rations. If one woman can't take care of it, I gits me another one."[22] Citations of this type seem to contradict the facile assumption that the food metaphors can be explained away as references to oral sex. Although I know of no direct rejection of that interpretation, there seems to be nothing to support such an inference in any conclusive manner.

Food metaphors, animal references (especially the mule, the snake, and the dog), and machine allusions (especially automobiles and trains, although jet planes and satellites are becoming more frequent in recent years) make up an amazing part of the sexual double entendre of the blues. Baked products, especially jelly roll,[23] pie,[24] cake, and bread,[25] are frequently used for the purpose.

> Well, now, I can tell by the way she roll her dough,
> She can bake them biscuits once mo'.[26]

The raw product from which the pastries come, the dough, can figure with or without the finished product:

> Roll me, mama, like you roll yo' dough,
> Oh I want you to roll me, roll me over slow.[27]

The verbal resemblance to *roll* in *rock and roll* is probably neither accidental nor unintentional; in fact, both of the above stanzas could probably be said to pun on that resemblance. So does the term for the finest kind of sex, based on the finest product of the baker's art:

> Jelly roll, jelly roll, rollin' in a can,
> Lookin' for a woman ain't got no man.
> Wild about jelly, crazy about sweet jelly roll,
> If you taste good jelly, it satisfy your weary soul.[28]

As a symbol, the biscuit is almost equally important. At least in the days immediately after slavery, it was more likely to be on the table of the Black than pastry, and it is a good metaphorical reference to sex of a fairly steady and good quality—if not up to that caliber, it is *cornbread.* The "roughness" implicit in the cornbread metaphor is, on the other hand, a desirable quality for some, and we find:

> A yaller gal eats de cake an' pie
> A brown skin do the same;
> A black gal eats de ashy cake;
> But she's eatin' jes' the same.[29]

There are, in blues lyrics, many compounds like *biscuit brown:*

> Don't your kitchen feel lonesome when your
> biscuit-brown is not around?[30]

Oster asserts that *biscuit brown* has "three meanings: cook, brownskin woman, and sexual partner"; most probably, all three are being evoked at the same time. Somewhat more frequently used is *biscuit roller,* again because of the centrality of the term *roll:*

> Don't your house feel lonesome when your biscuit
> roller gone?[31]

A more direct symbolism, combining *biscuit roller* with *jelly roll,* occurs in Bessie Jackson's:

> You sure won't miss your jelly till your jelly roller's gone.[32]

Food symbolism combines with animal symbolism in songs like "Milk Cow Blues":

> If you should see my milk cow, tell her to hurry home.
> 'Cause I ain't had no lovin'. . . .

Usually, however, the suggestion is less direct than that involved in the use of the word *lovin':*

I ain't had no milk and butter since my milk cow's been gone.[33]

These combinations may occur frequently and even be stereotyped, or they may be spontaneous, imaginative, and even artistic. Some of them are possibly nonce creations. In the absence of adequate documentation for earlier periods, it is often hard to tell which is the case. Jelly Roll Morton's metaphor, in "Don't You Leave Me Here," has the mark of spontaneous creation:

> As the rooster crowed, the hen ran around;
> She said, "If you want my fricassee,
> You got to run me down."[34]

It must be remembered, however, that Morton often used traditional and even folk material and was not above passing off either as his own "invention." (In the musical world of the 1920s, where familiar Negro folk themes were passing as the "compositions" of songwriters like Irving Berlin, one can wonder what *compose* or *invent* would have meant to one familiar with both worlds.) From the French Creole-speaking community in New Orleans, of which Morton was by birth a member, we have fricassee allusions in a "signifying song":

> Si vous thoué ain poule pour moi,
> Melé li dans ain fricassy.
> Pas blié pou meté la sauce tomate
> Avec ain gro gallon di vin.[35]
>
> If you kill a chicken for me,
> Mix her in a fricassee.
> Don't forget to put in the tomato sauce
> With a big gallon of wine.

The sexual allusions of the first line of the "Don't You Leave Me Here" stanza are extremely familiar. Mance Lipscomb sings an obviously related stanza, although without the food-for-sex metaphor:

> Well the rooster crowed
> And the hen flew down.
> Wanna be a man of mine,
> You got to run me down.[36]

The last two lines also have familiar paraphrases:

> If you want my cabbage patch,
> You gotta hoe the ground.[37]

Although rooster and hen allusions have an obvious place and a relatively great frequency, the animals with the most prominent suggestive power are the dog, the snake, and the mule. None of these is, as might be expected from the very nature of the Black lexicon, entirely unambiguous. The mule, on the simplest level, can refer simply to the male person—or to the male sex organ, perhaps because of the proverbial size of that organ in the mule. Iceberg Slim's *Mama Black Widow* contains a striking quotation: "Fuck her! Fuck her harder! Oh, you gorgeous mule dick sonuvabitch."[38] This usage can, of course, be found in the language of southern and probably of northern whites; it may not be originally Black at all. But in Black texts, we often find figures of speech like:

Another mule kicking in my doggone stall.[39]

which are more complex and seemingly more typically Black. In a line like Sam "Lightnin' " Hopkins':

Some other skinner must be kicking in my stall.[40]

we have a new level introduced: The skinner is obviously the possessor and manipulator of a "mule"; the stall, as elsewhere, is the vagina. Transsexual shifting is so easily accomplished in the blues that we find the almost identical:

I know there's another mule been kicking in my stall.[41]

sung by the really old-time blues singer Ma Rainey. Lines like this are, however, very frequent both on older and more recent recordings by male and female singers. The line is not merely an inappropriate use of a man's line by a female singer; the first line of the first stanza, in Ma Rainey's rendition, refers to the erring lover as "My daddy."

Even more frequently, however, we find the mule (rarely, an ox) functioning in a different metaphorical application:

She tried to hitch me to a wagon;
She tried to drive me like a mule.[42]

This metaphor apparently expresses the same attitude toward a sexual relationship as the familiar line in which the lover asserts that if he cannot be the beloved's "man, I sho' ain't gonna be yo' mule." Although lines like these do not completely exclude the use of *mule* to refer to the man's sexual performance, they do add an extra dimension to the notion of mule as a mere penis symbol. (In addition, they add to the picture of the male as the mere possessor of a penis, giving him a depth of emotional involvement that can be easily overlooked by those who examine the blues superficially.) If the term *be your mule* can mean "be your submissive lover," so can *be your ox:*

> Now looka here woman,
> Let me tell you what you can do,
> You can hook me to a log wagon,
> Now I'll pull just like an ox.[43]

The "patient ox" seems, impressionistically, more in accord with European metaphorical patterns than "patient mule," and this occasional substitution may have come about under rural white influence.

Associated with the mule, the ox, and any other animal large enough to be mounted is the metaphor of riding as a symbol of the sex act. The verb *ride,* so used, is one of the most frequent in all the Black terminology. There are lines like:

> I want you to ride me, baby, till I say that I got enough.
> I got a coal black mare, you know she sure can saddle along;
> She can ride me a while till I be right where I belong.[44]

In *Wake Up Dead Man,* his study of blues in the prisons of Texas, Bruce Jackson shows how the rider metaphor frequently occurs among the convicts because "in the free world a rider is one's sexual partner, one's man or woman."[45]

Although riding is a figurative expression for sexual intercourse in ordinary English, and has been for centuries, there is in non-Black usage a strong tendency for the "rider" to be masculine—the one above the supine woman. In Black usage, on the other hand, it refers with approximately equal frequency to either sex. Both uses occur in the same conversation in a scene in Richard Wright's *Lawd Today,* where ghetto men are looking at pornographic pictures:

> "He's riding her like a stallion."
> "He's riding her like a bicycle."

The masculine reference is commonplace enough:

> My father was no jockey, but he sure taught me how to ride;
> He said first in the middle, then you sway from side to side.[46]

"See, See, Rider" (or "C. C. Rider") is perhaps the best known of the blues songs that can be easily performed by a male or female with minimal change in wording:

> See, see, rider, see what you done done:
> You made me love you, now you' man/woman done come.

We have, however, quite specifically feminine references:

> . . . thinkin' 'bout my easy rider, she don't
>   live here no more.
> I wonder if I could find a woman to do just like
>   my last rider done;
> She kept it all for her daddy, she didn't give nobody none.[47]

> Lord I ain't got me no special rider now
> Lord I ain't got me no plumb good rider now
> It seems like my rider she tryin' to quit me now.[48]

Only when the rider is masculine, of course, is the use of rubber prophylactic tubes describable by the phrase *to ride with the saddle on.*

The prostitute and pimp's argot often describes the pimp—or someone being flattered by comparison to a pimp—as the rider. Outside those domains, however, the riding metaphor easily extends beyond animals to automobiles and other vehicles. *Ride the train* means "have intercourse with several males, one immediately after the other." This can also be described by the phrase *pull the train.* The males engaged in such activity usually must have some bond, such as membership in the same gang; the act is also styled a *gang bang* (also widely used by white males) or a *gang shag.* The unenviable lot of the last one to engage in such activity can be expressed, within this metaphor, by calling him the *caboose.* [49]

Although one would assume that the figuring of sexual activity in terms of automobiles has not been around so long as either animal or locomotive comparisons, it is by no means new. Zora Neale Hurston quotes as Black the stanza:

> Oh de white gal rides in a Cadillac
> De yaller gal rides de same,
> Black gal rides in a rusty Ford
> But she gits dere just de same.[50]

Blues singer Sam "Lightnin' " Hopkins, who uses a lot of traditional material, entitles one of his songs "Black Cadillac":

> Step on your cut out and let you' motor roll;
> This ain't the only place, we got other places to go.[51]

Georgia Bill, in "Scarey Day Blues," makes the sexual imagery even more explicit:

> When my baby go to bed, it shines like a morning star;
> When I crawl in the middle, it rides me like a Cadillac car.[52]

Other blues singers frequently communicate the quality of the sexual act by the relative expensiveness of the model:

> Once he was like a Cadillac;
> Now he's like an old worn out Ford.[53]

The fact that pimps, who must maintain a reputation as superperformers in sex, love Cadillacs is obvious from any of the studies of inner city prostitution. Like the typically Black sexual terminology, the Cadillac is an in-group thing for the pimp and his whores; the "tricks" do not figure in that part of the life where the Cadillac is used. Otherwise, the terminological parallels to pastry, where different grades of food betoken different grades of love, is obvious.

Probably the most extended automobile-for-sex metaphor is Sleepy John Estes' "Brownsville Blues":

> Now I can straighten your wires; you know poor Vasser
> can grind your valves
> Man when I turn your motor loose it sure will
> split the air.[54]

Other singers extend the vehicular domain. Roosevelt Sykes utilizes space exploration in "Satellite Baby":

> I got a satellite baby with a red hot style that's new;
> Well, she got mo' speed than Sputnik No. 2.[55]

The same girl is described in these terms:

> I got a rocket baby, faster than the Asiatic flu.

Furthermore:

> When she gets in gear, you think it's the end of time.

The virtually unisex approach to the terminology is striking to the outsider, perhaps because "exotic" or "bizarre" terms attract his attention first. To such an outsider, the culminating bit of sexual semantics is in the word *cock,* masculine for most speakers of American (or British) English but feminine for Blacks—and for southern whites, to whom it has probably been extended. (The Africanism *poontang,* for the female organ exclusively, has also extended to southern whites.[56] A pun on the word appeared in the name of a Broadway musical as early as 1927: *Roon Tang.*[57]) It is probable that *cock* became "vulva" rather than "penis" in Black usage at least partly because the Blacks picked up a "low" English usage in which *cock* was a verb meaning "to copulate with, but generally in the passive." Eric Partridge's *Dictionary of Slang and Unconventional Usage* reports that particular use, although not *cock* "vulva." Farmer and Henley's pioneering work on English slang records the verb *cock:*

To copulate. Usually employed by women and in the passive sense: e.g., "to want cocking," or "to get cocked."

Extending from this sense of generalized sexual activity (i.e., focusing on either male or female participation), the term *cock* was somehow specialized by Blacks to mean only the female organ. The same triple semantic distribution (male organ, general sexual activity, or female organ) is still in use for *jelly roll;* for some reason, it has not so specialized. At any rate, the Black (and southern white) meaning has obviously gone a long way from the Anglo-Saxon usage in which the male fowl betokened the phallus as does German *Hahn* or the *Hähnchen.*

Other Black terms for the penis include *arm* (compare armed services *short-arm inspection* "examination for veneral disease"), *joint* (associated with and often punning upon the term for marijuana cigarette), *swipe, private, Jones, pecker, stallion, Mister Tom,* and *Johnson.* The last achieved a very wide dispersion through the film *Putney Swope,* in which it may have served a disguise function in that not all viewers knew the meaning. There are, of course, many other such terms current in ghetto culture. *Hambone,* very frequent in the older blues, may easily be understood by a modern listener. An occasional term like *lemon* may serve the same referential function (Bessie Smith's "I'll squeeze your lemon until the juice runs down your leg.")[58] That term is, however, one of the many sex-shifting terms; applied to the female, it apparently refers to the breasts:

> Please let me squeeze your lemons,
> While I'm in your lonesome town.
> Now, let me squeeze your lemons, baby,
> Until my love come down.[59]

For the female sex organs, there are seemingly rather few terms, except for those discussed above, not shared with General American English. *Trim* has a widespread distribution and has spread to some southern white males. Like many of the other terms, it can refer to sexual intercourse as well as to the vagina. It is one of the strikingly prominent vocabulary items in the militant novel by Hari Rhodes, *A Chosen Few,* occurring once or twice in even brief passages of dialogue:

> "Shiiit . . . I don't need trim that bad [enough to patronize a whore] and I don't like having to go through all this jazz every time I get some. You can have it."
> "Not me. I jus' wanted you t'see what was happnin'. I got 'nuff trim in Wilmington t'last me from now on."[60]

A disguise form, like *poly-nussy* for *pussy,* is frequently attested,[61] so too is *pocketbook.* None of these seems to be ambiguous; that is, also usable for the male organ or for the process of sexual intercourse.

More interesting factors of general Black semantic relationships can be found, however, in association with the word *nut,* which does not necessarily apply to the male testes as it does—usually in the plural—in colloquial white sexual terminology. At times almost synonymous with the sex drive in Black English, it may also be used for the female organs, perhaps specifically the clitoris.

Returning briefly to animals used for sex symbolism, the snake is the least ambiguous. A phallus by its simplest associations, it usually has that meaning in blues lyrics:

> I'm a rattlesnakin' daddy,
> Honey rattle all night long.[62]

It may well be that West African (also Haitian voodoo) religious fertility symbolism has been retained in this relatively simple usage distribution.

A considerable amount of complexity can nevertheless be associated with the symbol. In Sam "Lightnin' " Hopkins' "Black Snake," the snake has a function vis-à-vis another male:

> That mean old black snake . . . crawl across my trail.[63]

Apparently, the reference betokens cuckoldry because:

> . . . Po' Lightnin' can't get no mail;
> One of them old black snakes have crawled across
>   my trail.

The consequences are dire:

> The world get in a tangle,
> When that black snake crawl 'cross you' trail.

Perhaps the most effective use was one of the first recorded—Blind Lemon Jefferson's "Black Snake Moan":

> Oo-oh, some black snake's been
> Suckin' my rider's tongue.[64]

It was apparently from Jefferson that the symbol was borrowed by the British group, the Rolling Stones.[65]

The dog fits into the more basically Black pattern in that it has more than one characteristic symbolic value. It is not the case, however, that the ambivalence is the obvious one, varying between male and female. One of the values is attested in the expression "A man got too much dog in him" (i.e., to be a good husband since he is always roaming around).[66] This proverb comes rather close to one quite general in American English: Why is a man like a bird dog? Because he's always looking for a place to bury his bone (i.e., phallus). *Dog* as sexually eager man occurs in texts like *Mama Black Widow:* "he takes her on the spot or the goddamn dog foams at the mouth until he can get her to a bed."[67] The context here is that of a "carnal" (or "fuckish") girl reprimanding a "sissy" for not being sexually aggressive. *Dog* here comes close to meaning "rake" or the like, which is far from exclusively Black. It is notable, however, that Southern Nigerian insult language uses *dog* for "an over-sexed person."

One of the other meanings may be more meaningfully Black. It is reflected in many blues stanzas:

> I can't be your reg'lar,
> I shore ain't gonna be your dog.[68]

This term implies something very close to humility on the part of the lover. Charters refers to it as "abject love, the man who loves a woman generally mean or unfaithful."[69] It may even imply humiliation by the mistress:

> How many mo' years I've gotta let you dog me around.[70]

In context, this *dog me around* means almost literally "reduce me to the status of a dog," but the domain of sexual relations is as clearly implied. In Jamaican English, a *dog* is a man who gets into trouble, especially with women. The second Black English vernacular meaning is probably related: The lover gets into the specific trouble of being faithful (or, at any rate, still loving), while his woman has outside relations.

In order to understand a lyric like "Doggin' Me Around Blues, ' it is necessary to know the Black English terminology. In other varieties of English, *dog me around* means "follow me around (closely)." The relationship of *me* to *dog* is a "patient" relationship in the terminology of some recent linguistics, where ordinary English is concerned. In Black English, on the other hand, *me* is in an "agent" relationship to *dog* "act humble."

> I been your dog every [sic] since I entered your door
> I'm gonna leave this town; I won't be dogged around no more.[71]

The last half-line obviously means "I won't be humbled," not "I won't be followed." The same, *mutatis mutandis,* is true of the last stanza:

> I been your dog, been your dog all of my days;
> The reason I'm leaving you, I don't like your dogging ways.

Dogging ways are "arrogant ways" or "humiliating [to me] ways."

Either interpretation may be involved in Nate Shaw's philosophical comment in *All God's Dangers:* "The thing for a boy to do when he gets old enough for his nature to begin to teach him, don't make a dog of himself."[72] Since *nature,* in such an attestation, means "normal sexual desire" (Shaw also uses *nature-course* for *intercourse*), the sexual implication is beyond doubt. The statement remains ambiguous, however, because either "being a gay blade" or "being made humble by a woman" may be what the young man is being cautioned against. Perhaps the ambiguity is intentional, and Shaw is warning a young man to beware both extremes.

A related meaning of the dog symbol turns up in "Lightnin' " Hopkins' "Hear My Black Dog Bark," in which the dog is the messenger as well as the symbol of the woman's infidelity. It seems quite significant that the concommitant behavior of "my little girl" (the unfaithful woman) involves failure to prepare meals acceptably:

> I go home in the mornin', my breakfast it ain't never done.[73]

because, as we have seen before, food and sexual activity are symbolically related. Hopkins makes the association quite explicit:

> I can ask her for a glass of sweet milk,
> And I swear she'll give me cream.

Furthermore:

> Why she don't have my breakfast done,
> She's out on a four-day run.

Such a woman may be merely *fast,* or she may be a *run-'round woman.* The man doing the cuckolding may be a *creeper,* a term which occurs frequently in many contexts; one of the congregation shouts the word when the sermon turns to adultery in "Satan Is a Dirty Fighter."

The Glossary in Milner and Milner's *Black Players* gives a fourth and seemingly unrelated meaning to *dog* as used by inner city pimps:

> (extreme insult) A man who is sadistic, brutal, treacherous, and totally untrustworthy. Such a man deserves whatever evil may befall him.[74]

Nothing else in Black usage, however, seems to parallel that definition; it may be that the particular sense applies more specifically to pimping and prostitution than to Black usage.

A rather mysterious use of *dog* occurs in the song title "Salty Dog." Although the song is obviously an old one, the phrase itself does not seem to occur elsewhere —at least not with any great frequency. *Salty* meaning "angry, annoyed, in a bad mood" occurs frequently in inner city slang; *jump salty* can mean "turn sour or hostile." Both are in Mezz Mezzrow's 1946 Glossary (see Bibliography), and they were probably not new when Mezzrow recorded them. However, "angry dog" or "hostile dog" does not seem to be appropriate in this context. Wentworth and Flexner cite the "late jive usages" of *salty* meaning "smart, neat, vivacious, alert, hep" and other meanings, apparently unrelated, of "lewd, obscene." The last is, on the slim evidence of the rather formulaic blues lyrics that are heard in performances of the song, the most probable. The fragmentary stanzas usually sung deal in some way with sexual escapades.

Wright's *English Dialect Dictionary* (see Bibliography) characterizes *salty* "of a bitch, *maris appetens* [desirous of a male]" as obsolete; nevertheless, it looks most like the meaning used in the lyric. Transmission of the "obsolete" English dialectal term would be more likely through the nautical trade than by any other medium.[75] Insofar as the phrase came through Louisiana and "New Orleans" jazz (and because of the primitive state of philological information, this is far from certain), it could have been reinforced by French Creole *salté* "dirty," *jouer ein salté* "to play a dirty trick."[76] The term *dirty* "sexy" is well established in blues tradition. Reinforcing the sexy associations is the familiar variation on a stanza quoted above:

> I can't be your salty dog,
> I ain't gonna be your dog at all.

In fact, it might be said that *salty* before *dog* disambiguates the two possible meanings of the latter word.

The more familiar type of ambiguity, applicability to either male or female or to the action of either in sexual union, comes with the now-ubiquitous *rock and roll*. Widely used in musical terminology, the phrase has perhaps its most basic application in the familiar line, "My baby rocks me with one steady roll." Hurston quotes:

> Oh, she's long and tall [twice]
> And she rocks her rider from wall to wall.[77]

The second lyric happens, because of the pronoun, to refer to the female action, but *she* could become *he* as easily as *baby* could become *daddy* in the previous citation. The really interesting thing here is that nothing would be lost from either stanza if the sex were changed.

In the mouth of a male singer like inmate Hogman Maxey of Angola Prison, the lyrics are equally natural:

> Rock me, mama, rock me all night long.
> Oh, I want you to rock me, like my back ain't got no bone.[78]

And the metaphorical level can be extended:

> You see me comin' run an' get a rockin' chair.
> Oh, Lord, ain't no stranger want to lay right here.

The pun on *rock* and *rocking chair* is no nonce form (i.e., the sole attested occurrence). Charlie McCoy sings

> Let me be your rocker until your straight chair come,
> And I rock you easier than your straight chair ever done.[79]

Rock certainly applies to the contribution of either sex, and equivalent attestations for *roll* can be found.

There does, however, seem to be a basic difference in the total distribution of the two verbs, despite a great deal of overlap. The significant co-occurrence in the last line cited above is *easier*. *Rock* definitely fits in with *easy*, whereas *roll* would do so with difficulty, if at all. Looking at the same two verbs in work-song contexts—where they occur with surprising frequency—it is impressive how completely *rock* correlates with less-strenuous activity and *roll* with a more strenuous counterpart. In sexual activity, it is possible to associate the former with the less active role (female, or in some cases supine male) and the latter with the more active role (male, or perhaps superior female). There are complications to this pattern, however, as will appear below.

The Glossary in Bruce Jackson's collection of work songs, *Wake Up Dead Man*, lists

Rock. Sing while working.

Rollin'. Working

The citations themselves, however, do not bear out any such simple interpretation. One convict informed Jackson:

> When you're working the convicts get tired and say, "Come on, you all, let's rock a little," and they get together, you know, and that's the way they fool the boss. They come down with their axe and then they work it like it's stuck . . . if they was working they'd be choppin' fast like this . . . but if they rocking they got their time and they going slower. . . . They ain't doing much. They rocking.[80]

Another prison informant testified in these terms:

> They call it "rockin'," "rockin' dead easy." That's what they call it when they start singin' the river songs. . . . We do it [work] by time. We have a steady

rock. Everybody raise their axe up and come down at the same time, just rock.[81]

Rock can even be applied to the performance of a preacher. A responding member of his congregation exhorts the Reverend Cleophus Robinson, "Well you rock tonight—take yo' time."[82] This exhortation comes early in the sermon; *rock* in this sense is a good description of the performance of a preacher secure and confident in his ability but not at the very climax of the sermon. When his raspy voice has brought the congregation almost to the state of possession, the preacher's performance is much more nearly analogous to the *rolling* of sexual and work-song terminology. *Rock* can apply also to other parts of the church service:

> ... members of the congregation dance around a center table African fashion going counter-clockwise, doing what they call a "rock"—a rhythmic, hopping, shuffling step, as they follow the deacon, who bears a standard.[83]

The dancing, a well-known feature in the Black church, may be the most basic meaning of *rock.* Koelle's *Polyglotta Africana* indicates an etymon *-rak* in Bidyogo, a West African language, that obviously means "dance": *yírak* or *írak* "I dance," *a írak* "I don't dance." Given the basic importance of the church and religion in Black English vernacular (see Chapters Three and Seven), the church usage may be the original one.

In the sexual domain, on the other hand, the common factor in all these uses of *rock* seems to be the absence of the most frenetic activity. The term stresses steadiness of effort and durability; it betokens an activity that is under control. The comparison to the female reaction may be a totally accurate one:

> The women love me 'cause I takes my time.[84]

Roll generally designates a more violent action. For that reason, its most obvious resemblance is to the male (or mannish female) activity. In coitus, it may refer more directly to the heightened activity of the male just before or during orgasm:

> That gypsy woman told my mother
> Just before I was born,
> I got a boy child's comin'
> Gonna be a rollin' stone.
> He gonna make pretty womens
> Jump and shout.[85]
>
> Let me be your little wheel, till you' big wheel come;
> I do more rollin' than you' big wheel ever done.[86]

Although *roll,* in work contexts, often refers to long-term activity, it is the arduousness of the activity that the term more basically stresses:

> I ain't tired a rollin'
> But I got so long.
>
> Mama I'm tired a rollin'
> But my time ain't long.
>
> When I roll my long time, mama,
> Back East I'm goin'.
>
> I say, I work so long, so they call me Rollin' Stone.[87]
>
> I been rollin' all night long;
> You may call it stayin', but I call it gone.[88]

The rolling metaphor, a prominent one for sexual activity, combines easily with metaphors of a different type for the same matter:

> I don't mind rollin', from sun to sun,
> But I want my supper, partner, when suppertime come.[89]

The predominating theme in the work songs, on the other hand, is labor and fatigue:

> Well my mama and my papa done told me a lie,
> Gonna get me a pardon on the Fourth of July,
> Oh, July and August done come and gone,
> And left me rollin', but I ain't got long.[90]

The archives of unpublished materials of the Louisiana WPA project contain the following, rather revealing work song:

> A darkey is the funniest thing I have ever seen,
> When he gets through rolling dem wheelbarrows he's looking
>   for beans.
> Roll on darkey, roll on,
> If you don't roll it'll make the foreman frown.
> Boy be careful or he'll knock you down.
> So roll on darkey roll on and get your beans,
> Cause if you don't roll you won't have no flips
>   for Madam Queen.

As always, the striking thing about these figurative uses is their adaptability. *Roll* can be extended into many other domains—enough to confuse even fairly astute observers. Hearing "Jack o' Diamonds is a hard card to roll" in a Negro folksong, W. H. Thomas repeated the judgment of early collector Dorothy Scarborough that it was "a naive confusion of figures."[91] Editor J. Frank Dobie, slightly more sophisticated but probably wrong, intervened to object that "the figure is really not confused to one familiar with poker dice." Maybe, but to one familiar with Black terminology, it does not seem necessary to invoke dice at all. One can "roll" cards, if he plays them industriously and persistently, just as easily as one can "blow" piano—or as easily as one "rolls" in the fields or in bed, if that is the rhythm and tempo at which he is pursuing the activity. Louis Armstrong has been quoted in an amusing extension to the domain of activity after taking a laxative, "I take my Swiss Kriss; man, they keep you rollin'."[92]

Before one rocks or rolls sexually, however, one must get the desire to engage in such activity—not to mention finding a partner, which is what most blues lyrics are about. It helps if she is a *phat chick* (the first word meaning "attractive" rather than "plump," being perhaps the only formal use of an orthographic distinction in the Black English vernacular) or a *fox*. She can make a man *hot*—a term shared with the white community, although Herskovits traced it to an Africanism. *Get the nut hot,* particularly when applied to feminine desire, is apparently still specific to the Black community. But the strikingly Black phrase is that one's *love come down.* The term is used in this sense in the Gullah-speaking Sea Islands; indeed, it is used almost everywhere poor or working-class Blacks are to be found.[93] Robert Beck ("Iceberg Slim") presents, in the discussion of what is purportedly an actual case, the approach of a southern farm laborer and preacher who unsuccessfully and unhappily moved North to his now disdainful wife:

"Ah ain't drunk, Sedalia. Mah luv jes come down fer yu, sugah. . . . Ah'm yu man. Now loose up."[94]

That this particular pass results in the wife's rejection ("Ah ain't gappin' mah legs fer yu.") has little relevance to the meaning of the term. Bessie Smith sings:

When I tried to kill him,
That's when my love for him come down.[95]

Mezz Mezzrow's Glossary documents the use of the term where an intentional provocation to sexual desire is involved:

Make your love come down: Arouse your passion, put you in a romantic mood[96]

Mezzrow gives further documentation of the borrowing of the term by a white musician (himself) influenced by Black jazzmen:

A [Negro] woman who really knows how to sing and means it can make your love come down even if she's buried in a block of cement up to her neck—all she needs are healthy vocal cords and a soul, not a chassis with the seven-year's-itch.[97]

A character in Richard Wright's "Long Black Song" says, in an explicitly sexual context, "I feels ma' love comin' down."

One whose love has come down must, to avoid frustration, get his ashes hauled. In the familiar pattern, this can apply to either sex. Jelly Roll Morton sang:

> Do you see that little fly crawlin' on that wall?
> She's going up there to get her ashes haul'.[98]

And Richard Wright's *Lawd Today* has a female character's song stanza:

> He hauls my ashes
> He strokes my fiddle
> Threads my needle
> Creams my wheat
> Lawd, he's a damn good man to have around.[99]

The term also applies to the male reaction, however, as Willie Lofton proves when he sings:

> Oh, ho, [I] spied a spider climbin' up the wall
> Cryin' I asked the spider did he want his ashes hauled.[100]

The term is transsexual in the Black community. In the white community, which probably borrowed the expression, *ashes* is identified with semen, and the application is limited to the male.

Mezzrow believed that *haul one's ashes* was a "simple and hygienic" reference to the process of sexual release. It is true that we find other phrases like *my garbage can is overflowing* and *empty my trash,* with clear sexual allusiveness,[101] in blues lyrics. Muddy Waters, in "Garbage Man," sings of his baby who "run off with the garbage man":

> I need this good-lookin' woman so she can empty my can
>   . . .
> I need you to come back to me, honey, because my garbage
>   can is overflowin'
>   . . .
> I don't need the money, honey, I just need you to empty
>   my trash.[102]

The phrase remains in-group enough to escape the television censor, having been used on "Police Story."

Given the importance of ashes in conjure, the term may after all be originally Black. W. C. Handy quotes his "original" blues:

> I put ashes in my sweet papa's bed
> So that he can't slip out.
> Hoodoo in his bread,
> Goofer dust all about
> I'll fix him!
> Conjuration is in his socks and shoes,
> Tomorrow he'll have those mean sundown blues.

Hauling one's ashes just could have meant, at one time, getting out from under a voodoo spell that had ruined one's sex life.

A striking characteristic of the Black sexual terminology is its easy accessibility. Unlike the "stag party" atmosphere in which until recently white pornography was transmitted, the Black terms could be heard by anyone who bought a record. Many whites did not understand, but that was the result of lack of curiosity and not of disguise. Other terms, like *mother fucker*, which have been around in General American "obscene" usage for a long time, are much more easily observed in and elicited from Blacks. Even if the word was not originally Black, the use of a large number of circumlocutions (m.f., Marshall Field, Mister Franklin) and the existence of many compounds *(bad mother fucker, tough mother fucker, rough mother fucker, fine mother fucker, jive mother fucker, stinking mother fucker, dirty mother fucker)* testify to the wider distribution in Black usage. Even the terminology of prostitution, although it is the least likely of all to be Black (or Afro-Creole) in origin, is more readily available to investigators like Susan Hall *(Gentleman of Leisure)* or Milner and Milner *(Black Players,* see Bibliography) from Black participants in "the life" than from whites. In the very attitude toward sexual terminology, there has been a basic difference.

There seems to be good reason for regarding this attitude toward sexual expression as traditional in Afro-American culture. In the *ijala* chants of the Yoruba, for example, there occur:

> ... vulgar jokes which many an ijala artist, in order to excite laughter, nonchalantly resorts to, especially when he is tipsy and is unashamed to chant lewd remarks and indecent narratives. Such broad humor is not usually found in the chants of elderly ijala-chanters, who employ euphemisms in their references to sexual organs and sexual life.[103]

In the case of the Black American vernacular culture, the constraints of the "old" *ijala* chanters obviously apply in the blues, but not in toasts like "Pimping Sam."

There has been an inevitable reaction against the possible sensationalism of specifically Black sexual terminology and the too-prominent part given to prostitution and the other rackets in many popular treatments of "Black" language. Hermese E. Roberts, a Black public school principal whose *The Third Ear: A Black Glossary* attempted to explain Black speech to the world of industry, specifically bowdlerized "Many of those [terms] of the more earthy or 'gut' variety," marking the omission of "some aspect of [the] connotation of a term by an asterisk.[104] This is only the other side of a coin, the flip of which is represented by an overemphasis on sexual and sensational terms and equally distorts the true picture of the Black vocabulary. It is felt, however, that a truly comprehensive Black lexicon would establish how sexual terminology is only a part of the whole by giving it equal treatment with all other Black terms.

3

Terminology of Religion and the Church

As COHN and others suggest, only in sexual terminology has the Negro been as independent as in religious vocabulary. A young Atlanta gospel singer puts it more personally: "Church has always been the one place where we could be ourselves, be really black."[1] If that is true, the language of the church should prove of special interest.

Religion, considered in its broadest sense, has many facets, of which the church is only one. The extreme character of Black-white religious difference does not, in fact, show up in a consideration of the church alone. (See chapter seven for other material associated with religion that is, at most, peripheral to the church.) As a relatively superficial manifestation of the religious differences associated with African survivals, the Black church is easily observed to be somewhat different from white churches. Middle-class Black communities have, as frequently noted, closed the gap by assimilation. In the rural and storefront churches, however, kinesics (the characteristic patterns of body movement) and paralinguistics (qualities of the voice such as harshness, raspiness, or softness) are unlike the nearest white equivalents in at least some particulars, and there are distinctive elements of terminology. As Mays and Nicholson put it, "The church was the first community or *public* organization that the Negro actually controlled."[2]

As early as the nineteenth century, observers saw the difference in language practices associated with the slaves' religion. Charles Colcock Jones, Sr., in *The Religious Instruction of the Negro* (1842), pointed out that the Blacks might understand better if preached to in their *"broken* English," but still advised preachers to eschew that language. At about the same time, but reporting from the Southwest rather than from the Carolinas, Joseph Holt Ingraham observed and theorized extensively on his trip through some of the slave states. His lack of empathy with the culture of the Blacks led him to make statements like "the religion of most of them is made up of shouting,"[3] and he concluded that the "shouting is not produced generally by the sermon, of which every sentence will contain words wholly incomprehensible to them."[4] It should be noted, however, that because of Ingraham's superficial understanding he does not use *shout* to mean "a holy dance" as it undoubtedly did in the Black church of the time (see below), but only "a loud cry."

Nevertheless, Ingraham dimly perceived why there were failures in comprehension: The preachers whom he observed were whites who spoke a very different dialect. He reported that:

> . . . negro preaching, among the removal of other privileges which they once enjoyed, is now interdicted.[5]

Frederick Law Olmstead was in most respects a sharper observer than Jones or Ingraham. He reported, it is true, that:

> The frequency with which the slaves use religious phrases of all kinds, the readiness with which they engage in what are deemed religious ecstasies, with the crazy jocular manner in which they often talk of them, are striking and general characteristics. It is not at all uncommon to hear them refer to conversations which they allege, and apparently believe themselves, to have had with Christ, the apostles, or the prophets of old, or to account for some of their actions by attributing them to the direct influence of the Holy Spirit, or of the devil.[6]

But Olmstead was also capable of immediately seeing significant implications in a basically autonomous Black religion:

> It seems to me that this state of mind is fraught with more danger to their masters than any to which they could possibly have been brought by general and systematic education, and by the unrestricted study of the Bible, even though this involved what is much dreaded, but which is, I suspect, the inevitable accompaniment of moral elevation, the birth of an ambition to look out for themselves. Grossly ignorant and degraded in mind, with a crude, undefined, and incomplete system of theology and ethics, credulous and excitable, intensely superstitious and fanatical, what better field could a cunning monomaniac or a sagacious zealot desire in which to set on foot an appalling crusade?[7]

Olmstead was certainly not free of the prejudices of his own day, expressed in terms like "excitable," "intensely superstitious," and "fanatical." And he was probably incapable of projecting himself into the viewpoint of the Negro, who would have seen a liberator rather than a "cunning monomaniac or sagacious zealot." But he did perceive the structure whereby Black leaders from Nat Turner to Martin Luther King would rise up through the Negro's religious organization. He would perhaps not have been surprised at the title of a document like James Baldwin's *The Fire Next Time,* possibly the most literate expression of Black militancy. Utilizing as it does the familiar spiritual quotation ("God gave Noah the rainbow sign; no more water, the fire next time"), the title can be heard echoed in many Black sermons.

The somewhat radical thesis of Miles Mark Fisher, that Black religious texts (especially the spirituals) were essentially a medium for conveying disguised messages for the African cult of which Nat Turner was at least ultimately the leader, is provocative but undoubtedly far-fetched. In particular, the magnitude of Turner's rebellion hardly matches such a grandiose context. Nevertheless, it seems that certain disguise messages were originally contained in the spirituals. More importantly, the religious messages, and the terminology in which they were framed, were often somewhat closer to conjure or to voodoo than to orthodox Christianity.

At the very minimum, there seems to be an agreement that the religion of the Black slaves, although in most externals a branch of Christianity, was greatly different from that of the whites, although there were obviously some similarities. Black church historian William H. Pipes expresses it thus:

> The original, full-fledged, unique type of Negro preaching in America, existed during slavery, approximately from 1732 (the period of the great influence of White-field's preaching upon Negro slaves) until 1832 (following Nat Turner's insurrection). . . . Some of the original characteristics and manifestations are to be found, in varying degrees, in Negro preaching today.[8]

Ira Berlin's judicious study *Slaves Without Masters* provides a kind of consensus in its statement that "Southern clergy admitted that the style of preaching demanded by white congregations did little to arouse Blacks."[9]

What were the differences, and what were the linguistic components of the sermons that aroused Blacks who were unassimilated to the American mainstream? These may turn out to be closely related questions. We do have provocative reports from intelligent observers like Sir Charles Lyell:

> He [a Black preacher on a southern plantation] concluded by addressing to them a sermon, almost without notes, in good style, and for the most part in good English; so much so, as to make me doubt whether a few ungrammatical phrases in the Negro idiom might not have been purposely introduced for the sake of bringing the subject home to their family thoughts.[10]

Lyell also recorded an "ungrammatical" Black prayer:

> Make he good, like he say
> Make he say, like he good
> Make he say, make he good, like he God.[11]

Even today, we find that the skillful Black preacher, who may be perfectly capable of doing all his speaking in "good" English, takes advantage of another ability —that of expressing himself, where it is appropriate, in "the Negro idiom," the Black English vernacular.

At the time of Lyell, and much later, the religion of the slaves contained other elements mixed with Christianity. No insider has put it as formally, perhaps, as LeRoi Jones:

> In Africa, ritual dances and songs were integral parts of African religious observances, and the emotional frenzies that were usually concomitant with any African religious practice have been pretty well documented. . . . This heritage of emotional religion was one of the strongest contributions that the African culture made to the Afro-American. . . . "Spirit possession," as it is called in the African religions, was also intrinsic to Afro-Christianity.[12]

But virtually no one expressed it with the authority of the great W. E. B. DuBois. His summary expresses it best of all:

> This [the Afro-American] church was not at first by any means Christian nor definitely organized; rather, it was an adaptation and mingling of heathen rites among the members of each plantation, and roughly designated as voodooism.[13]

As modern anthropologists have observed, the common African heritage has meant a certain amount of similarity to such other Afro-American religious cults as Haitian voodoo. Alan Lomax, for example, has pointed out that when a Black church member had a vision that "it just seemed that something came up my leg, just like when your foot goes to sleep," and that there was a definite resemblance to the "state of religious trance" in Haiti, wherein the numbness begins in the left heel and spreads up the leg through the body.[14] George Rawick suggests that the "little man," an emissary from God to the slaves in early accounts of the slaves' religion, parallels Legba (Elegba), a messenger of the gods for the Yoruba and a prominent figure in Haitian voodoo, too closely for it to be a coincidence.[15]

Charles S. Smith has commented, as have many others, on the importance of African cultural vestiges in the Black church, pointing out that "Sinners won't get converted unless there's a ring" and "Someone has even called it [a "band," which seems to have been approximately the same thing as a "ring"] a 'Voodoo dance.' "[16] Lomax further points out the similarities to a possession rite in the Black sermon, where:

> The phrases come like rifle shots. The voice rasps the nerves like a file. Gasping intake of breath after each line. People shouting, women screaming. Pandemonium.[17]

Less scholarly observers found the same things in the early nineteenth century, although they were not professional anthropologists and could not offer such precise descriptions. They may even have been as ethnocentric as the notorious Mrs. Frances Trollope, writing in 1832:

One of these, a youth of coal-black comeliness, was preaching with the most violent gesticulations, frequently springing high from the ground and clapping his hands over his head. Could our missionary societies have heard the trash he uttered by way of an address to the Deity, they might perhaps have doubted whether his conversion had enlightened his mind.[18]

From stigmatizing the utterances of a Black preacher as "trash" to recognizing residual African elements is a long step, but the abilities of Lomax and the narrowmindedness of Trollope should help us realize that a professional and a nonprofessional are dealing with the same material. For the linguist, the problem seems to be to put observers like Lyell and Jones, although admittedly they were both more objective than Mrs. Trollope, into the same kind of professional perspective.

Insofar as that perspective deals with terms shared by the Black church and the more transparent Afro-American cults, one of the more important terms is *seeking.* Zora Neale Hurston provided early documentation of the use of the term in conjure practices.[19] An 1891 article reported that Blacks on southern plantations, during the time for "seekin' 'legion," tied a cloth about the head and that those who "sought" were expected to drop all work and look very woebegone.[20] Very similar activities are characteristic of neophytes to Haitian voodoo. Today, whether on the Gullah-speaking Sea Islands or elsewhere, the prospective convert to the Black church is said to be "seeking." William H. Garrison, in the Introduction to his 1867 *Slave Songs of the United States,* reported: "Of technical religious expressions, 'seeker,' 'believer,' 'member,' &c the songs are full." One of Lorenzo Dow Turner's Gullah texts, from his important pioneering work on the dialect, is on that topic, the informant being quoted:

> If yu sik relijan, yU kmpel tU si dat beb*i*
> "If you seek religion, you [are] compel[led]
> to see that baby"[21]

In the novel *Black April,* by Gullah-speaking Julia Peterkin, a young man is angrily informed by a more worldly woman, "You ain't got no business seekin' "
—with the implication that a person who found "peace and religion" could not bat ball on Sunday with his playfellows. One of the slave letters reprinted in Eliason's *Tarheel Talk,* a collection that, according to the author, proved that there was nothing specifically Black about the English used by North Carolina slaves, records:

> George made one of the most opens [sic] professions I ever saw . . . and Gorge [sic] had bind [sic, probably for *been*] seekin a bought [i.e., *about*] 3 months. . . .[22]

The way in which an examination of the Black English lexicon brings together strange bedfellows can perhaps be no better demonstrated than by comparing the listing of *to be a seeking* "to seek religion" from James A. Harrison's 1884 article "Negro English," the phrase being among his "Specimen Negroisms." Harrison represented the plantation tradition, expressing his gratitude to Joel Chandler Harris, John A. Macon, Sherwood Bonner, and others. Eliason, a noted historical linguist, was that type of new Southerner who assumed that if a statement about the language of the Blacks was found in the writings of the likes of Joel Chandler Harris it was probably for that reason inaccurate. Yet, unwittingly, Eliason corroborated Harrison—and Joel Chandler Harris.

It is true that "Seek and ye shall find" is in the King James version of the Bible, which eighteenth- and nineteenth- century Blacks could have been exposed to, but the Black church has specialized that usage of the term in a way that does not wholly derive from biblical usage. It also seems significant that no white church in the United States has focused on that particular biblical terminology. The earliest attested use, according to the *Dictionary of Americanisms* at any rate, is Black, from 1824:

> With the field slaves [in Virginia] Sunday is usually a holiday; wherein they deck themselves for frolic, or for their unintelligible methodist meetings; where those, who are tender in spirit, are said to be "seeking."[23]

The person who has not yet begun to seek can be described in many ways: a *sinner man,* a *sinner boy,* or a *sinner girl.* In the nineteenth century, at any rate, terms like *still in de open fiel'* and *settin' on the sinner seat* were attested. The seeker was probably so designated before he was approached by a *worker for Christ,* or even, grandiosely, a *worker in Christ's vineyard.*

One who has been converted, on the other hand, has experienced the process of *coming through.* Although the term may be used in a general sense, it sometimes applies to a specific performance at baptism in which the person being baptized comes out of the water shouting phrases like "Thank you, Jesus!" and is often held by members of the congregation. The phrase "Thank you, Jesus" is, in fact, so familiar in religious contexts that "commercial gospel singers, completely secure in their roles . . . may cry 'Thank you, Jesus' under the most secular circumstances."[24] In some marginally Christian cults, at least, a good preacher will *bring* a listener *through.*[25] In James Baldwin's *Go Tell It on the Mountain,* in the context of a sermon in which it is asserted that rebirth of the soul must be perpetual, that only rebirth every hour could stay the hand of Satan, the hymn is sung:

> I want to go through, Lord,
> I want to go through.

> Take me through, Lord,
> Take me through.[26]

The same 1891 article that listed *seeking* includes *She's done jes come th'oo,* but it also has several other terms for the same state. Other terms from the list include *He done been shuck over hell, He's done spilt de cup of damnation, He's done broke de bonds, He's trying on the gole waistband, He's waggin' wid de cross, He's shuck out de shine line gyarment, and he's ready ter put it on, He's on prayin' groun' and pleadin' terms, He's done been led a far way, She's sippin' de cup of salvation, He's tuck a seat wid de member men, He's gathered in, She's done told her 'sperience,* and *She's done profess.*[27] Such a person is *on the Lord's side*—or, as Joe Louis put it in a perhaps staged movie commercial for the World War II war effort, *on God's side.* Perhaps even more than in the white evangelical churches, the members are addressed as *Brother* or *Sister:* Brudder Tember, Mudder Charlotte, Sister Lucy. Like *member,* these terms have extended to secular contexts, where they mean "a member of the in-group" or simply "a Black."

Attestations of most of these are hard to find in the twentieth century, and a few may be completely obsolete. But there are others on the 1891 list that are still active and productive. Besides *come through (come th'oo),* there are significant terms like *He's a shoutin' member* and *She's a rockin' Christian.* Shouting is a basically important term in the study of Afro-American religious syncretism (see pp. 55–6), and the term is in use in many parts of Afro-America outside the United States. The Shouters Church in Trinidad, subject of an excellent study by George Eaton Simpson,[28] features, besides the religious dance that gives the group its name, "mourning" and "building" ceremonies. A rather early description can be found in Allen, Ware, and Garrison, *Slave Songs of the United States:*

> [Men, women, and] boys with tattered shirts and men's trousers, young girls bare-footed, all stand up in the middle of the floor, and when the 'sperichil' is struck up, begin first walking and by-and-by shuffling round, one after the other, in a ring. The foot is hardly taken from the floor, and the progression is mainly due to a jerking, hitching motion, which agitates the entire shouter, and soon brings out streams of perspiration. Sometimes they dance silently, sometimes as they shuffle they sing the chorus of the spiritual, and sometimes the song itself is also sung by the dancers. . . . Song and dance are alike energetic, and often when the shout lasts into the middle of the night, the monotonous thud, thud of the feet prevents sleep within half a mile of the praise house.[29]

Allen, Ware, and Garrison thought that such shouting was limited to South Carolina and the states south of it, but they had heard the term *shouting* used in Virginia in a slightly different religious context.

The term is, today at any rate, widespread. On Folkways Records, Dock Reed of Alabama sings:

I'm shoutin' shoutin', shoutin',
Tryin' to make heaven my home.[30]

There are some variants, like the term *Holy Dance* among the Holiness sects.

Although *coming through* seems to be reserved for an initial experience, either at a meeting or at a baptism, a longtime member may *get happy*. (If it is the first experience, the term tends to be synonymous with *get religion*.) A Mississippi ex-slave recalls:

> Old Daddy Young was 'bout de best preacher us ever had. . . . Old Daddy could sho' make 'em shout an' roll. Us have to hol' some of 'em dey'd get so happy.[31]

Although the term *church member* is extremely familiar in all denominational contexts except for Episcopalian and Roman Catholic *parishioner* or *communicant*, the term *member* has a special function in the Black English vernacular. Special extensions and compounds occur so that an ordinary member, not a deacon or other such dignitary, is described as a *bench member*.[32] Like *soul,* which in a nonreligious context means "quintessentially Black," *member* acquires special connotations when extended into a secular context. It does not indicate someone who is merely carried on the church rolls but rather one who really "belongs"—one who is totally and enthusiastically a part of the church. That the white community may have thought of the term as something especially Black is indicated by this quotation from the *Century Magazine* of 1887:

> Of late years, colored farmers who are "members" frequently give corn-shuckings where no dancing is allowed.[33]

Some "members," even today, define their status by refraining from secular dancing or from the "sinful" blues, but will engage in "holy" dancing and gospel singing that uses many of the same rhythmic and harmonic devices. It is interesting that *member* was adopted by the Black militant groups, becoming virtually synonymous with in-group participation terms like *blood.* The term *saints,* reminiscent of voodoo terms (it has frequently been noted that "When the Saints Go Marching In" could easily refer to the entrances of the Haitian *loa* or the Surinam *winti*) is also used, but has not extended to secular contexts.

Although the newly converted member may practice some of the ceremonies that anthropologists have found linked to the African-derived cults (even *de baptizin' creek* may reflect a survival of African water deity worship[34]), everything in his conscious awareness calls for him to abjure those cults. Conjuring is linked to sin and the devil, although a preacher may be valued for his ability to *counteract conjure stuff*:

> Old Satan is a liar and a conjurer, too.
> An' if you don't mind he'll conjure you.[35]

Probably the whole bag (or bottle) of conjurer's terminology has been applied to Satan in the entire unrecorded history of spirituals and sermons. We get a few examples:

> Just let me tell you how this world is fixed,
> Satan has got it so full of tricks.[36]

In this case, note that Satan has made *the world* full of tricks; it is not that Satan himself is "full of tricks," in the familiar idiom of ordinary English. The sermon usage is probably related to the conjure usage. (For a discussion of *trick*, the commercial act of a prostitute, see p. 89.) *Tricks*, in a Black sermon, is a grim and pejorative term. It is quite possible, however, for the conjurer's term *fix* (see p. 117) to apply to the actions of the preacher; antiphonally to the Reverend Cleophus Robinson's sermon "Sweet and Stinky,"[37] a responding member repeatedly shouts "Fix it!"

Other terminology, applicable to blues and secular music, if not to conjure, is shared by the Black church. One of the most interesting words is *rock*, as in *de ol' church rockin' tonight* and a *rockin' Christian*. One of the most intriguing sections of the late Black folklorist J. Mason Brewer's *Dog Ghosts and Other Texas Negro Folk Tales* is the one entitled "Rock, Church, Rock!" A preacher, too, may rock; in context, this refers to a rhythmic, highly proficient style that is in control and definitely not labored. The same meaning characterizes the term in work-song and lovemaking contexts. Rich Amerson sings:

> Rock, chariot, I told you to rock.
> Won't you wait, chariot, in the middle of the air.[38]

A line from another folk-religious song, this time by Dock Reed, confirms the desirability of this characteristic in a chariot:

> Jes' low down the chariot right easy.[39]

On the Reverend Cleophus Robinson's record, a responding member shouts, at one point, "Well you rock tonight—take your time and fix it."[40] As in the other contexts, *taking your time* is a familiar and perhaps defining feature of *rocking*. If the assumed parallel to work songs is valid, *rollin'* should apply to the preacher's frenzied speech, characterized by a lot of vocal rasp, as the members begin to go into possession. Unfortunately, I have no attestation of that use.

Coming into a hypothetical Black church or *praise house* (although the term has been growing rare except in the Sea Islands)—like the Shiloh Primitive Baptist Church of Bogue Chitto, Alabama, or the First Church of God in Christ in Dallas—the new seeker would see something like a rather poorly furnished white church except for the *amen corner* with its *mourner's bench*. The latter term has been used by white sects, but the feature itself is much less important than in the Black church. According to Lee's *Beale Street,* it is, in the latter, usually the first *three* benches nearest the pulpit. There is no clear early attestation to show where *amen corner* comes from, but it is thoroughly nativized in Black English:

> God in the pulpit
> God way down at the door
> It's God in the amen corner
> God's all over the floor.[41]

The altar is sometimes called the *mountain.*

The service begins tamely enough, with announcements, often by one of the pastor's assistants. Songs may be led by a *singing deacon,* who "hysts" and lines out a familiar hymn. Allen, Ware, and Garrison reported the phrase *deaconing a hymn.* Either a deacon or the preacher will deliver prayers, accompanied by a *moaning* backdrop.[42] There may be other assistants if the *meetin'* is a *tractable* one (perhaps from protracted) and not merely a *tarry service,* where various seekers await the experience of coming through. If it is a revival, the preacher attracts large numbers of the merely curious, who come to see how the stranger can "go." The best kind of preacher will "tear up the pulpit" the first time, and even many of the scoffers will return to see "Can he hold up?" Faithful members will be especially careful about their Sunday dress:

> Sunday, when she wore white, and with her head tied up in a scarlet cloth. . . .[43]

That such colors may have more than random significance may be indicated by drawings of turbanlike red headdresses in baptizing scenes by Louisiana's folk artist Clementine Hunter. An important part of the service is, of course, the collection, sometimes described by terms like *raising the offering*[44] or the *consecrated dime.*[45]

The sermon starts, typically, with a Bible reading and a discourse on the meaning of the verses selected. The Old Testament is often preferred to the new, although *Revelation* ("John the Revelator") is extremely popular. As the preacher proceeds, the congregation becomes more and more involved. They *bear him up* by calling antiphonally, "Dass right!" "Sho' nuff!" "Sweet Jesus!" and "Preacher!" or simply echo part of his words, all neatly on his offbeats. Perhaps the most significant cry of encouragement is "Ride on!" (see p. 114). Stylistic variants like "Hold your horse, boy!" ("Go on as you are," not "Stop!" as the expression would mean in ordinary English) occur frequently.[46] A friend encouraging a preacher may exhort him to "make them holler tonight."

Here, any sympathetic listener simply has to familiarize himself with some of the interaction rules of the Black sermon. If not, he may misunderstand completely the role of the congregation. For example, on a recording made by some of my Louisiana graduate students, a woman actually says "Thank the Lord" at the very moment the preacher is discussing the existence of sin. She is not, of course, thanking the Lord for the existence of sin. Her comment applies to the sermon context as a whole—Thank the Lord that the sermon is being preached, that the people are gathered in church—and not to the most immediate sentence the preacher happens to have uttered. On several sermon records, to give a different type of example, members of the congregation actually laugh.[47] They are laughing, of course, not at the preacher but at the lies and pretenses of Satan and his minions, in recognition of or even in anticipation of the preacher's denunciation. Here, as in so many cases, the discourse and not the individual sentence is the unit to which primary attention must be given.

As the tension builds, the responses become screams, although they never lose the rhythm and timing so peculiar to Black services. The preacher motivates this increased involvement less by the message he preaches than by his *straining voice;* it was said of one "fanatic cult" preacher that he "could holler like somebody cryin'."[48] The extreme feature, a vocal rasp that makes an outsider wonder how such a man can survive one sermon much less preach again, is sometimes called *gravely voice.* It reminds one strongly of Louis Armstrong, one of whose many nicknames was Ol' Gravel Throat. The rasp may be introduced early in the sermon, but full use of it is delayed until the climax.

The "cries," however, may come relatively early in the service and show the importance of tonal phenomena in the Black sermon. There is even a term for one such practice: *zooning,* "crying [a word or phrase] over and over with variations."[49] Harrison gives the highly questionable *to come a zoonin'* "to come running" and then salvages some probability for himself by the explanation "imitation of a bee's buzzing,"[50] which does make possible an explanation in terms of tonal phenomena.

The successful use of such vocal qualifiers to build emotional involvement characterizes what is called a *gravy sermon.* A preacher who uses the devices well is also called a *gravy train preacher.*

The preacher proceeds, more or less in the language of the Bible and of spirituals, but adding his own individual touches. He easily slips into the words of a familiar song—or perhaps he is sometimes singing. There is, at this point, so much excitement that it is almost impossible to tell.

Particularly after the vocal rasp has given the appropriate signals, members may undergo possession and do dances. This part of the ceremony is what is called *shouting,* according to Turner from Wolof *saut* rather than English *shout.*[51] Collected narratives have long referred to this process, but few have understood what is meant by a statement like the following from a Louisiana ex-slave:

> We didn't lak [certain preachers] caise ya could not do lak ya wanted to do. Ya could
> not be free to shout. Gawd say dat ya must shout if ya want to be saved. Dat's in
> de Bible. Don't ya know it?[52]

It would be easy to assume that shouting here referred to the loud cries sometimes
uttered by the congregation, but that is not the case.

A more elaborate version of the shout, known to anthropologists as the *ring
shout,* is also called the *drama shout.* In either type, the member must maintain
the shuffling gait and not let his feet *cross over;* to do so would be to turn the holy
dance into a secular dance, and some of the churches would expel a member for
such behavior.

For the first religious experience at such a meeting, a novice may report, "I just
fell off the bench, just fell out."[53] Colloquial General American has probably
borrowed *fall out* from the Black English vernacular, but in a slightly different
meaning "be surprised" or "break out laughing." The technical religious term
remains specifically Black. In terminology slightly reminiscent of conjure and
voodoo, the person so affected feels the presence of *power.* After *falling out,* the
member is *saved,* the universal term of evangelical groups.

Specific details of the conversion may vary greatly, of course. One informant
reports wanting to get "baptize" from the time she was ten years old, but being
forbidden by her parents, who felt that she still did not understand enough. When
she was twelve, she got on the *mercy seat.* (The term is apparently not recorded
in the dictionaries.) She was baptized soon after. This young girl came from a
family with close church associations, and by her late teens, she had "moved on
up" to *welcome address* (greeting the congregation) and singing solos. Everett
Dick records another interesting term:

> At the conclusion of the service the Negroes could not separate without the breaking
> exercise, so called from breaking up the meeting. One who attended such an exercise
> said they sang the grandest, wildest, most beautiful African music he had ever heard.
> They began to sing and move in a procession by the pulpit shaking hands with the
> minister as they passed. As the long column filed by, faces shone with delight as the
> music rose wilder and more exciting. Finally the handshaking ended, the meeting
> "broke," and the service was over.[54]

Even the *blood-bought soldier of God* may be subject to the *temptationin'* of
worldly pleasures. If he resists these temptations in order to enjoy the Christian
life, he is *living sweet* (used, ironically, of a pimp). If he succumbs, it will be
necessary to *get right with God.* (The term is also current in white evangelical
churches, and impressionistically, it seems like the kind of term that would
originate with them.)

Even a preacher has *nature,* which may cause him to cast his eyes (if nothing
more) on the admiring women of his congregation. The theme of the preacher

who finds a sexual advantage in his calling is a familiar one in Black lore. Mance Lipscomb, the blues singer, puts it thus:

> Well the preacher preached
> All the sisters moaned
> You want this collection
> You got to follow me home.[55]

Robert Beck ("Iceberg Slim") in his presumably factual *Mama Black Widow* makes this interesting, if somewhat scatological, comment on such a preacher:

> And that goddam freakish Reverend Rexford was no inducement to serenity. He'd walk right up to Mama acrobating his tongue across his sensual lips, advertising right there in the house of the Lord that he ate cunt.[56]

A more scholarly source, like the unpublished field notes collected by Black interviewer Robert McKinney for the Louisiana Federal Writers Project study, provides examples wherein a preacher (like his Reverend Gundy) would be thrown out of a church because of his popularity with women: "It was very easy for Gundy to recall how important it is to be familiar with the women; it was also easy to recall how dangerous it is too." McKinney also provided an account of how one Reverend Jackson was almost fired by a Baptist Preachers' Conference because of the same kind of alleged familiarity. McKinney suggests that this conference contained, along with fifteen preachers, three *backsliders* (not glossed), two *backbiters* ("persons who try to either take the preacher's women or his job"), and one *hush man* (a person used by a preacher to "quell arguments or anything that will cause the preacher embarrassment"). An unpopular suggestion to retain the Reverend Jackson because he was already incumbent and any successor would most likely be equally bad was "jumped on with a barracade [sic] of preacher words." Unfortunately, McKinney did not give specific examples (except, of course, for those quoted above) of "preacher words." Nor did he go into much detail about the "preacher's reasons," which he somewhat scornfully attributed to members of the conference.

Even an erring preacher can still be a *God-sent man.* The term is used in the transcript of Nate Shaw's speech in *All God's Dangers* and in Lomax's *The Rainbow Sign.* In the latter, it is asserted of a sinning preacher that "He'll get up, he'll acknowledge his sin, and he'll quit it."[57] It is considered worse if he is not really a *God-called preacher* but is only *church-called* or *college-called.*

Even though it is possible for suspicions of wrongdoing to fall on him, the preacher is an important man in Black communities, and the evidence is that he has been, since perhaps the early days of slavery. Even those who were not militants or political leaders commanded a great deal of respect and devotion, and the preacher's coming to dinner was an important occasion for country folk, Black as well as white. Like rural whites, the Blacks were likely to kill a chicken or two when the preacher came. There is, however, no evidence that the whites used the prevalent Black name for the fowl: *gospel bird.* Andrews and Owens, in *Black Language,* use the term *holy bird* and suggest that some preachers kept the working Blacks down by the pie-in-the-sky suggestion that there would someday be fried chicken for everybody. The scornful "race" song of the 1940s expressed the skeptical attitude: "Chicken Ain't Nothin' But a Bird." Maybe so, but even the Black Muslim literature uses the term *gospel bird.*

One of the additional activities of the church, and probably the last, is *funeralizing.* The member who has *passed* (not *passed away,* as in ordinary English) is taken care of by his church and his burial society, or *buryin' society.* The WPA Writers Project on Alabama reports that "He [the Negro] does not mind dying nearly so much if he feels assured of being 'funeralized big.'" One may be suspicious of that statement—the Alabama Writers Project was not entirely untainted by racism—and still acknowledge that such a society was the most important organization that the Black in the rural South belonged to. Its function is largely taken over by the storefront church, however, in the inner cities of the North.[58] Before the actual burying, a wake *(settin' up* or *happy wake)* was, in the past, celebrated. Jelly Roll Morton's account of the "New Orleans funeral" claimed scriptural authority: "Cry at the birth and rejoice at the death."[59] The corpse lay on a *coolin' board* during the wake. The term figures rather prominently in such speeches as prayers; in Goodwin's *It's Good to Be Black,* God is thanked in the following words:

> "First, Lawd, we want to thank you that when we rose this mornin' our bed was not our coolin' board, nor our cover our windin' sheet. . . ."[60]

The dead man was never left alone in the house, and all the mirrors were turned to the wall. (Many Jamaicans still do the same thing.) A Mississippi ex-slave reports:

> At de wake we clapped our han's an' kep' time wid our feet—*walking Egypt,* dey calls hit—and we chant an' hum all night till de nigger was *funeralized.*[61]

The pallbearers are sometimes called *holders.*

The elaborateness and emotion of the funeral vary, of course, with the sect involved. The so-called New Orleans funeral, familiar from the descriptions by famous jazzmen, is still remembered by older Louisiana residents—including those who lived in northwestern parishes and not in New Orleans. It seems, however, to be largely a thing of the past. The following description of such a funeral, from Dillon's *Fanatic Cults,* involves a departed leader receiving a much fancier funeral than the average member could hope for.

> When the great Leafy's corpse was less than fifty feet away [on the train, which was taking it from New Orleans to Chicago, where her family would receive it], the band struck up a lively tune. The mourners went home in tears, but the good timers, who wept when it was time to weep, wiped their eyes and made merry, when it was time for that, turning the funeral into a parade. The coming back spree was as exciting as the procession from the church and full of gaiety. The band accompanied the marchers and almost every one pointed to home in some kind of dance. . . . Almost all of them went back to the church to discuss the low-down and high-lights of Mother Anderson's death. An old gentleman suggested, "She is gone and dat's dat."[62]

The term *spree* is one of the most frequently used for this type of postfuneral celebration. Interestingly, Dillon also records its use in *voodoo spree,*[63] where it is specified that there is a great deal of dancing.

The church, with activities like preaching and burying, does not provide so much specifically Black English vernacular terminology as does lovemaking. This is partly because the music of the church is not so widely disseminated as is the blues. Even when it is, the words are likely to be those of hymns known to many denominations and to churches that, historically, have been exclusively white as well as to those that have been Black. This lack of publicity does not mean, however, that the church has any less of its own distinctive terminology. And perhaps more than even sexual activity (where universal semantic processes may be suspected), the church services reveal cultural survivals in the Black English vernacular-speaking community.

Church terminology transfers easily into other Black domains. Hannerz, *Soulside,* relates a case in which a man addressed as "Brother Wilkins" gives a street-corner man a quarter and is told, "Thank you, Jesus." This is mockery because, as Hannerz stipulates, the speaker was inclined to the Muslims and the giver was a relative outsider. Still, the phrase can be used in less cynical contexts. Even though recording some of these satirical usages, Hannerz concludes:

> . . . religion is still part of the ghetto perspective, even for those whom the regular church goers consider most obviously lost to the flock. It is something ghetto dwellers can more or less count on having in common.[64]

Many times in the past few years, when talking to audiences about such matters, I have been told by a Black, "That's what we mean by *soul.*"

Religious expression is not, however, exclusively limited to the church. McKinney's transcript, cited above, represents one of the Baptist preachers as saying:

Dey can shout and pray as long as dey want but dem darkies want dat hoodoo stuff, dat's what dey want. No Baptist preacher will give it to dem so dey go to the Spiritualist Church.

The fringe organizations described in works like Arthur Huff Fauset's *Black Gods of the Metropolis,* Joseph R. Washington's *Black Sects and Cults,* and Francis Dillon's *Fanatic Cults*—and informally by the preacher quoted above—are much less orthodox in Christianity than anything that comes even rarely to public attention. Their terminology, it might be suspected, may possibly reveal depths not suggested so far. Most basically, however, they approximate even more closely the voodoo and conjure activities that are historically related to and still marginally associated with the Black organizations like the storefront churches of the inner city. There is, then, no sharp break between the church terminology and the vocabulary used in root-work conjure, described in more detail in Chapter Seven. Only when these two are taken together can it be appreciated how much different the religious lexicon of Black English really is.

4
Music, Especially the Blues

IF RELIGION and sex have been the areas in which Black English has retained most of its own vocabulary during the long process of assimilation, popular music has established a countertrend in which Black terminology has virtually taken over the domain for American English. To a very great extent, there remains a Black in-group where music is concerned, in spite of about fifty years of borrowing by the white population. When outsiders are absent, very simple terms can be used to describe what is really Black music, something as simple as *sounds*. For other contexts and other purposes, however, there is a very elaborate terminology, changing to some degree as out-group awareness of the terms develops. Many of the terms discussed below have by now been absorbed by General American English, becoming merely the music-listening public's terms rather than the Black musicians' terms for certain musical devices, procedures, and experiences. Some of them have been abandoned (or publicly disowned, which is not precisely the same thing) by the hipper Blacks, but a historical treatment cannot leave them out just because today some few of them may be used as much or more by whites as by Blacks.

Where blues and jazz lyrics, especially, are concerned, it is well to bear in mind that no one has tried to maintain purity of dialect. Writing of "songs of the Negro wanderer and songs dealing with women" (as good a designation of the blues as most), Odum and Johnson state:

> The language is neither that of the whites nor that of the Blacks, but a freely mingled and varied usage of dialect and common speech.[1]

Like Trinidadian Sparrow and other Calypsonians in a roughly improvisational vocal music, blues singers use dialect where it fits their rhyme and metrical schemes and Standard English where that will do as well or better. Those who have gained nationwide recognition, whose records sell as well to whites as to Blacks, have by and large standardized their dialect. For that reason, the songs of lesser-known performers—or the early work of those who later became famous —often represent the Black English vernacular better than the work of the most famous.

Grammatically, the Black English vernacular does not find its best representation in any musical genre. Musical performances tend to be public, and Standard English is the public dialect even for many of those who use other dialects in private. (The exceptions here, of course, are children, who have little part in recorded music performances.) The durative *be* of Black English turns up occasionally in musical texts; the preverbal *been* of a definite, restricted past action appears almost never. The grammatically nonstandard forms that do turn up are not often unambiguously Black; that is, third person singular, present tense forms like *he sing* are so superficially characteristic of the Black English vernacular that not much could be made even of very many such occurrences. The nontransformed version of a question serving as a subordinate clause ("I wonder how long will I suffer") is perhaps the most frequent nonstandard grammatical device of blues and jazz singers, probably because syntactic manipulations are less within awareness and therefore less subject to "correction" than word endings. An occasional basilect form (outside Gullah, the most different form from ordinary English) turns up, as in John Henry Jackson's "What make I love you so" in a blues lyric.[2] Nevertheless, the study of the grammatical distinctiveness of Black English is best pursued in domains other than music.

Certain nonstandard usages are, however, deeply ingrained in Black folk music, regardless of whether or not they happen to occur also in other dialects. A good example is *lay* for *lie*. To "correct" the usage would mean giving up a useful rhyme with *day:*

> Woke up this mornin' 'tween midnight and day,
> Grabbed the pillow where my good gal used to lay.

Formulaic stanzas like these, occurring frequently in the blues, are freely exchanged with other popular music varieties like country and western, the nonstandard dialects of which usually agree with Black English in this particular. Use of the less formal *-in'* present participial ending, along with other Black dialect pronunciations, makes possible rhymes like *mind* and *crying.* This one is very important to "Trouble[d] in Mind Blues," which may have been originally Black but has been borrowed by many white bands.

The phonological characteristics of the Black English vernacular are extremely important to blues lyrics. The prosodic devices are, otherwise, relatively conventional—rhyme and stress-oriented meter—and the Black English phonology makes possible rhymes that perhaps give the lyrics their sole distinctive characteristic in that area. There are those who snobbishly object to the rhymes and those who find understanding difficult because of the different pronunciation. The classical three-line blues stanza, with the second line a slight variation on or almost a repeat of the first, has a rhyme scheme that offers marvelous opportunities for the observation of phonological processes at work. Many a singer will give a word the "Black" pronunciation the first time and the "standard" articulation the second.

A list of "words [that] have the same value for sound in rhyme,"[3] while not absolutely complete, proves accurate enough for guidelines to the rhyming processes. They provide a few major categories, with some combinations of categories possible. Final nasals, as in *along, one,* and *foam,* tend to neutralize (often being actualized merely as nasalizations of the preceding vowel), and such words rhyme freely:

> I wish I had a heaven of my own,
> I'd give all you girls a real nice happy home.[4]
>
> Children standing screaming, "Mama we ain't got no home";
> Papa says to children, "Back water left us all alone."[5]

Final consonants in general tend to be weakly articulated, and differences can be ignored if the rhyme scheme so demands:

> I got a gal, she's got a baker's shop;
> Her jelly roll is the highest thing she's got.[6]

Stop, block, and *top* can thus rhyme, as can *late, shake,* and *gate.* Even in a two-syllable word, this kind of neutralization can apply to the first syllable if it is heavily stressed. An added unstressed syllable does not disturb the scheme:

> You've had your chance and proved unfaithful,
> So now I'm gonna be real mean and hateful.[7]

Consonant clusters in final position, especially where the next-to-last sound is *l* or *n,* also simplify quite easily, and the neutralization of nasals can work along with this process to make rhymes possible with words like *mind* and *sign* (or *time, nine, line,* etc.). As in many dialects of both British and American English, postvocalic *r* is not given the retroflex articulation, making *hollow* and *dollar, sport* and *coat,* or *load* and *Ford* rhymes. (The hypercorrection that makes *hollow* into *holler,* as in *a holler tree,* occurs in Black English, but not so frequently as in some white nonstandard dialects.)

Lowering of vowels before nasals can make a rhyme of, for example, *whang* and *thing;* the last pronunciation is, of course, by no means peculiar to the Black English vernacular, despite its favored use in the ethnic-marking phrase *doin' your own thang.* Like many southern white dialects, Black English tends to simplify the "long-*i*" diphthong, reducing the difference between *like* and *lack* and making it possible for the former to rhyme with *track* or *back.* Sometimes identity of vowels where there are apparently no neutralization rules for noniden-

tical final consonants makes it seem that assonance rather than rhyme is the
device being employed:

> Some of these mornings I'm gonna wake up crazy,
> Gonna grab my gun and kill my baby.[8]

The phonological differences between the original language of the lyrics of
Black folk music and standard English have often influenced changes in the lyrics
and made it difficult to conclude just what is the original form of a line. Even
beyond that confusing influence, it is often difficult to distinguish what is distinctively Black in a lyric or in musical terminology. Many glossaries of blues and
jazz exist, but often they simply list words and expressions much used by Black
musicians, whether or not they are widely used by ghetto nonmusicians and
whether or not they originated as musical terminology. In the strictest sense,
many of them are not musical terms at all.

Popular studies, sometimes written by people who have no contact with the
Black community except through rock-and-roll lyrics, have contained some exaggerated ideas about the slang of Black musicians. Obviously, it is not to belittle
the influence of musicians to point out that they have been by no means the only
users of words like *dig, chick, crazy,* and *cool.* No doubt the jazz musicians—or,
in many cases, their commercial imitators—have been the most direct means of
transmitting some of these terms into American English. On the other hand, it
would be a gross distortion to attribute all of the influence to musicians.

The worst offender in this case is the terminology of drug use. In a source like
Mezz Mezzrow's *Really the Blues,* there are almost as many entries related to
narcotics as to music (by my count, out of a total of 437, there are 39 musical
terms as against 30 terms for narcotics and their use). Although the use of drugs
by jazz musicians has undoubtedly been something of a factor in the problems
of many, and although it has been much discussed, Mezzrow's book like many
others makes it clear that marijuana and other drugs were underworld and ghetto,
not strictly musical, associations. Jazz, which was forced to depend upon illegal
businesses for its revenue from the days of New Orleans players working in the
brothels of Storyville to those of playing in speakeasies during Prohibition, just
happened, later on, to be exposed to a lot of drug and addict relationships. The
music no more depends upon drug use than it does upon prostitution. Nevertheless, the lingo of the drug trade plays an important part in some jazz lyrics. The
classic example is perhaps Louis Armstrong's "Sweet Sue" (1933), in which Budd
Johnson engages in "viper [i.e., pot-smoker] language" and Louis answers in
"muta [marijuana] mumblings."[9] In his various biographies, Armstrong is quoted
as having a lot to say about the use of marijuana—but, perhaps significantly, he
has more to say about his favorite laxative.

A high degree of selectivity biases early glossaries like Mezzrow's (who was not interested in linguistics) and gives us more about such terms as *the climb's on him* "he's providing the marijuana," *tin* "small amount of opium," *pill* "pellet of opium," *roach* "small butt from a cigarette of marijuana," *put somebody on* "let somebody smoke marijuana," *salt and pepper* "cheap brand of marijuana," *shying* "the technique of cooking opium pills," and other such expressions than we really need to know in order to understand the relationship of the Black English vernacular to musical terminology. Mezzrow has only four terms clearly linked to religion (*Father grab somebody* "may the Lord take him away," *Head Knock* "God," *prayerbones* "knees," *skypilot* "preacher"—and perhaps *righteous* "good, right, satisfying" should be included to make five). The reason for the shortness of the last list is obvious: Mezzrow was Jewish and a young adult before he began his long and intimate associations with Black musicians. He did not interact with them in religious contexts. He did sell narcotics in Harlem—spending as much time in that activity as in playing the blues, according to his autobiography—and he obviously had a much better opportunity to pick up ghetto narcotics terms than to acquire the vocabulary of the church.

On the other hand, an occasional term assumed to be an underworld ghetto term may have more musicianly associations than it has usually been accorded. An interesting possibility of this sort arises in connection with *pig* "policeman, exploiter." The term is of very widespread dispersion; Black moviegoers, seeing on the screen a white plantation owner taking what John Dollard called "the sexual advantage," will often shout "Oink!" and make the noises of hog-calling. Women's libbers, fond of the phrase *male chauvinist pig* (probably based on something like *racist pig* or *white chauvinist pig*), generally assume that they took it from the ghetto's term for racial chauvinists, and they are probably right in the most immediate sense. There may be something more to it, though, than the notion of a pig as "a dirty animal," or "a greedy animal." There is some evidence that a small statue of a pig was passed around the early jazz bands and placed in front of a musician who played a bad note.[10] The semantic progression from "clumsy performer" to "exploiter" is not without parallel in the ghetto's argot. *Pig* is also the inner city's derogatory term for last year's Cadillac (i.e., a "hog" that does not quite make it anymore), a believable semantic approximation to the above hypothesis.

Printed treatments of Black musical terminology, whether popular or scholarly, differ greatly—and sometimes amusingly—in the terms that they consider typical of the "jazz" influence. The two considered below are by Norman D. Hinton and Whitney Balliet.[11] Although both lists are meant to be representative rather than complete, and although Balliet's especially is consciously shortened, it is amusing that only three items are contained on both lists: *square* "not in accord with a jazzman's aesthetic standards," *way out* "departing from the norm" (usually in an ameliorative sense), and *corny.* (Mezzrow's Glossary has *square, square from Delaware,* and *corn* "anything hackneyed.") In addition, both mention semantic reversals, Hinton using as his example *bad* "good" and Balliet citing *a mess* "something marvelous" and *terrible* "extremely good."

It might be thought that the almost twenty years intervening between these two articles explains this difference. Such an interpretation fits in with the popular notion that slang, especially Black slang, is "ephemeral." This hardly proves, on examination, to be the major cause of the differences. Both *square* and the reversal pattern have been observed in Black usage since long before the time of Hinton's article.[12] I have no information immediately at hand on *way out,* but if it is relatively new, it must be a replacement for some such expression as Mezzrow's *gone* "out of this world." *Corny* goes back practically into musical prehistory: It appears in Corrothers' *The Black Cat Club,* where the author speculates that it has connections with slavery:

> "Co'n" in Negro dialect stands for "corn." Negroes did not like corn because they were compelled to eat corn bread in slavery until they were disgusted with it. So, now, when disgusted with a subject, or when they wish to say, "You are giving me taffy," they say instead "You're feedin' me 'co'n.' "[13]

Whether or not this quotation incorporates an accurate etymology, it does establish that the term has been around in the Black community for at least three-quarters of a century.

The difference between these two lists (and between these and all other short lists) lies not in the years that elapsed but in the complexity of the whole matter of Black slang and its relationship to jazz talk. As Corrothers' attestation seems to document, *corny* has never been applied exclusively to the domain of music —and it would not, even if Hinton and Balliet and a hundred others authoritatively said so a thousand times. As far as that goes, it is altogether likely that *square* has been used in the domain of prostitution, meaning "someone who seeks sex to satisfy a biological need and not for profit," or in the drug traffic, meaning "someone who does not take drugs," for at least as long as it has been around in musical terminology.

All kinds of people, perhaps originally Blacks but not necessarily musicians, call a girl, especially an attractive one, a *chick;* the term is reminiscent of Spanish *chica,* which is as good an etymology as any so far offered. (The association with *chicken* could come about as a typical Black metaphor linking food and sex, as detailed in Chapter Two. Spanish, however, complements a desirable girl with "*¡ Qué pollo!*" literally "What a chicken!" Either way, it drifted into the food-for-sex symbolism; Mezzrow's Glossary gives *chick* "young girl" and *chicken dinner* "pretty young girl.") Hinton has the word on his list, with the rather lame justification that jazzmen look at "chicks" just as do any other normal males.

Cat "a person" comes from Wolof *hipicat* "an aware person," as do obviously *hip* and its white distortion *hep.*[14] As Corrothers' 1902 pun (*Black cat* = both

"Black person" and "the dark little feline important to voodoo and other superstitions") indicates, the term had been around a long time before there were any
jazzmen. Both jazzmen and other Blacks have used it for a long time (probably
at least four hundred years for persons of non-Wolof descent and longer for
Wolofs), and whites who use it may have borrowed it from jazzmen or from
rock-and-roll musicians, but it is hardly likely that other Blacks (say, pimps, who
have been style setters in their own way) got it from the musicians. Hinton
believed that "a musician can now speak of a "square cat"—a contradiction in
terms in the 1930s; but again, there is no evidence for this assumption beyond the
original meaning of the term, which is best understood in terms of the Wolof
source and to which jazz usage is not overwhelmingly relevant.

Hinton specified that *dig* "understand and agree with" is "not limited to music
alone," and we can well believe him. Hinton's speculation, on the other hand, that
the term, apparently assumed to be ultimately from English *dig,* comes from "a
sense of getting to the bottom of things," does not stand up in light of Dalby's
research. Dalby also shows a Wolof source for this *dig.* The term got widespread
attention from popularized pseudo-jazz, particularly that type that appealed to
teenagers in the 1930s. A song entitled "Well, All Right" had the refrain "Dig,
dig, dig, well, all right," which caused titters from adolescents less liberated
sexually than they are today. The homophony with English *dig* "delve" motivated some phrasal patterns like *plant you now and dig you later,* familiar from
popularized jazz jargon of perhaps the 1940s.

Since it is obvious that Blacks were not always singing and playing music—
for the same reason that it is obvious that they were not always eating possum
and watermelon—it follows quite logically that jazzmen (most of the genuine
ones having been Black) used the vocabulary of their dialect from other domains
when talking about music or composing lyrics. There are, however, some expressions that are centrally musical; the next few pages will concentrate on those
expressions. Slang expressions used by jazz musicians but also by all members of
the Black community will be left to other chapters.

To begin, today *swing* is a term used for musical expression but also extended
to many nonmusical domains. It may mean "be a very devil with the women"
or even "engage in wife-swapping." These senses are, obviously, not the original
ones. The fact that they are obvious extensions of the jazz term makes it, in my
opinion, more appropriate to treat them in this context than expressions like *cool,*
which has been widely used for the last twenty years to describe a musical style
but which, the evidence tends to indicate, was not originally a musical term.[15]

Swing, when it first came to American linguistic consciousness, meant "that
undefinable something that makes a jazz performance a good one rather than a
routine or mediocre one." To define the term was virtually tantamount to delimit-
ing what made a performance good, and many jazzmen are on record as saying,
"If you gotta ask, you'll never know."[16] Whatever it was, "swinging" was not a

technical proficiency that could be tested on an exam, like conservatory learning, and even the adepts might fail to swing at some times. (Or at the very best, one solo by a jazz idol might be less swinging than his performance on another occasion, even when the musical number to be "swung" did not change.)

Despite the reluctance of many jazzmen to define *swing,* an occasional exception can be found, like Count Basie in an interview with Stanley Dance:

> "No, I don't [have a definition of swing]. I just think that swing is a matter of some good things put together that you can really pat your foot by."[17]

What can easily be missed here is that Basie, although not giving all the features for a tight formal definition, almost instinctively introduced a historical factor, linking the "swing" tradition to elements of Black musical and dance culture of the past. Neither the listeners, dancers, nor musicians at a swing performance could ever be seen actually patting their feet, but the practice and terms to describe it have a long history among Afro-Americans. The *Dictionary of Americanisms* records *pat* in such a significance from 1869, defining it "to beat time for dancing by clapping the hands, tapping the feet, etc." The citations refer specifically to *juba,* which, along with *patting juba,* goes very far back into slavery. The earliest listing of *juba* (marked " = *juba dance"*) in the *Dictionary of Americanisms* is from 1834, the citation referring to "a darky dancing Juba." James Hungerford's *The Old Plantation,* which has an elaborate description of a "Juber Dance," was published in 1859 but reports the author's experiences on a Maryland plantation around 1832. Another attestation, from 1838, is to "a darky . . . patting Juba." *Juba dance* itself is recorded as early as 1850, and *Juba minstrels* from 1852. In an 1854 novel by William Gilmore Simms, the situation in which patting Juba takes place involves slaves from "a dozen plantations," and a person with a broken arm is commiserated with in the terms, "You got only one arm for swing [in patting Juba]."[18] The associations of *swing* with patting Juba seem fairly clear.

The etymology of *Juba* itself is asserted to be obscure, although it is at least homophonous with *Juba,* the West African day name for a woman born on Monday.[19] Since the dances known as Jim Crow and Zip Coon, the latter very important in the nineteenth century although almost forgotten today, are based at least ostensibly on personal names,[20] it would not be completely unthinkable that Juba was, at one time, "the dancing done by a woman named Juba"—and that "swinging" the arms was part of it.

The day names and "patting Juba" are all but forgotten and would possibly be considered absurd if they were remembered by the musicians who are now setting the styles, but the historically minded can easily see that the "obsolete" forms of the past had a great deal to do with what is current today.

This necessarily brings up another matter of importance to the consideration of any in-group terminology, the alleged ephemeralness of lexical domains like musicians' slang. While it is true that changes great enough to exclude the outsider who has learned some of the terms in earlier currency may take place at relatively great rates of speed, it is still true that the "new" terms are in many cases simply replacements for the old. Something of the old semantic, and even the historical, pattern can still be seen if a thorough investigation is made. It can be argued, even, that the old terms that are kept around and subjected to pejoration are undergoing more radical changes than the completely replaced forms.

That kind of pejoration has obviously taken place with terms like *licorice stick* "clarinet" and *slush pump* "trombone." Hinton asserted that jazz musicians used those terms only to describe "a particularly 'corny' or 'commercial' passage, usually in imitation-dixieland style," at which time the colleagues may use the terms in order to let the offender know that he has lowered his standards.[21] That is, of course, a classical case of pejoration—"worsening" in meaning.

The opposite semantic process, amelioration, can be seen in a few terms like *alligator* and *'gate*. These are characteristic of the verbal tricks played by jazzmen on aspirants to the in-group. Louis Armstrong tells about white musicians following Blacks who were playing on the riverboats of the Mississippi:

> We'd call them alligators . . . because they were the guys who came to swallow everything we had to learn.[22]

The square world, in turn, swallowed the terminological joke whole. Entertainers like Bob Hope's handlebar-mustached stooge, Jerry "Professor" Colonna, got a few laughs and a lot of pretense at being hip with "Greetings, gate. . . ." *Gate,* however, belonged mainly to those who used *hep,* not *hip.* Cab Calloway's horribly commercial parody of a jazz band did something called "Jumping Jive" for the teenagers of the late 1930s, admonishing listeners:

> Don't be an ickaroo [pseudo-jive talk for "square"]
> Come on do like the 'gators do.
> Hep, hep!

It is probable that most Blacks who heard that lyric found it very funny, at least inwardly, but the white world failed to get the joke at least into the mid-1960s. "See ya later, alligator/After while, crocodile," was perhaps the earliest and crudest pseudo-Black lyric of rock and roll.[23]

Other terms, like *tailgate* for a trombone style, may be nearer to complete obsoleteness. According to all accounts,[24] the trombone was named the *tailgate* because the New Orleans bands (and probably those of other cities and towns as well), used to go around in trucks (originally wagons), and there was room for the trombone only if it were stuck out over the tailgate. In the "battles of music" referred to in all the jazz histories, the tailgates might be tied together by spectators in order to insure that the band about to be defeated (or "cut") did not beat an early, strategic retreat. This procedure gave another dimension to *tailgate* and to *tailgate style*. And the trombone, especially as wielded by someone like Kid Ory, had an importance in the early jazz bands that it has not fully retained.

Obviously, battles of music are not so simple anymore, but a band or a player may still *cut* another of less proficiency. The basic semantics are the same as Surinam *kotsingi* "strife by song."[25] According to a memoir by guitarist Danny Barker, the crowd at the Rhythm Club in New York City in 1930 yelled "Seminole! Cut them cats!" after a series of banjo players had presented choruses not quite up to the legendary Seminole's level.[26] Since the term was used by musicians of the 1930s and is still used by Surinam musicians as well as by modern jazz musicians, there is every possibility that it was used by fiddlers and banjo-playing slaves on the plantations. Striking continuities can turn up even in areas of reputedly great change. There has been a tendency to replace *cut* by *carve,* but again, the underlying semantic processes remain the same.

Throughout a great deal of the recent history of jazz—although it may not happen to be "in" just at this moment—musicians have referred to playing as *blowing* so that one can "blow" any instrument, even a piano. The instrument, or "tool," used to earn one's living as a jazz musician has been an *ax,* although it is quite probable that from time to time there is an imaginative replacement. The piano itself has been the *eighty-eight,* the *box,* and any number of other things. Only in the most figurative of conversations is it a *horn,* although any other instrument, like the oboe, may be a "horn" if a musician known to and approved by the jazzman speaking is using it. The analogy to *ax* is obvious. The jazz musician may also speak of his *piece;* there is overlap with standard usage when qualified by a numeral, as in *100-piece orchestra.*

A jazzman who blows may do a *head arrangement* or *wig,* or he may *fake* "improvise." *Fake it* may have some reference to the days when jazzmen looked for jobs in "square" bands and were in danger of not getting the job if they could not read—or play "legit." Or in another once widely used phrase, the best jazzmen could not necessarily *see* "discern what they were supposed to play by looking at a page of notes." On the other hand, what constitutes really good jazz is not "seen"—it is *out of sight.*

One of the favorite devices for improvising is a *riff,* a short phrase repeated over the length of a chorus, more or less like an *ostinato* in classical European musical notation. Jelly Roll Morton discussed, in very explicit terms unusual to jazz and blues musicians, the relationship between riffs and *breaks* in his Library of Congress conversations with Alan Lomax. According to Morton, a riff is "a figure, musically speaking," "something that gives any orchestra a great background," or "a background, what you would call a foundation," like "something you could walk on."[27] The break, not defined but rather illustrated by Morton, was an interpolated bit of improvisation, collectively, in most cases, by two or three instruments. In other cases, however, the break could be for a solo instrument like the piano or even for the shouting voice—"Oh, Mr. Jelly!" Since jazzmen no longer play the Morton-style jazz, which is now regarded by the more progressive as being hopelessly old-fashioned, the break has lost most of its importance or has been entirely replaced by the solo of several choruses in length. The term is, therefore, obsolete. It is interesting, however, that the term *riff* has remained in use. To Morton, the break was the essential thing for jazz: "Without breaks, without clean breaks, without beautiful ideas in breaks . . . you can't even play jazz."[28]

Terms for jazz compositions of Morton's era like *stomps* and *joys* are, by now, almost completely obsolete. Morton, whose "King Porter Stomp" was picked up by a lot of white bands of the swing era, professed not to know the origin of the term *stomp*, "only that people would stamp their feet and I decided that the name stomp would be fitted for it."[29] It is interesting to note that Morton used the pronunciation *stamp* for the verb and *stomp* for the noun, while overtly stating a relationship between the two, but the noun and the exhortation "Stomp off, let's go!" are now obsolete. Another obsolete term is *joys*, which apparently does not even have any on-the-spot description; it probably comes from French *jois*—or perhaps more likely, *jeux*. Either French word would have been strongly anglicized in American usage, a familiar process in the Louisiana in which Morton and a lot of other jazz greats did their early playing.

A longer-lasting, and perhaps more important, musical type of the older days has an even more problematic name: *ragtime* or *rags* (of the compositions themselves). The *Oxford English Dictionary* will not commit itself to an etymology for this one; the *Dictionary of Americanisms* offers no etymological explanation. The latter, in fact, offers us a "first" attestation that is patently derivative—George Ade's *Pink Marsh* of 1897. Jazz histories, however, tell us of a "Harlem Rag" reported as early as 1895. Traditions have associated the term with *ragged time;* that is, the rhythm is supposedly varied so much that it is "torn" or "made ragged," perhaps by analogy to cloth. Gunther Schuller's rather technical definition "syncopated melody over a regularly accented rhythmic accompaniment" tells us rather little about the semantic processes involved in the selection of the term.[30] Early observers like George Washington Cable, whose indefatigability in getting around to observe phenomena was not always accompanied by a professional expertise in describing them, gave reports like "The rhythm stretches out heathenish and *ragged.* "[31] Blesh and Janis, whose book is entirely devoted to that musical type, report that "rags, true to one meaning of the name, were patched together from the bits of melody and scraps of harmony that all created."[32]

Minor descriptive terms for early jazz, of no such musicological importance as other types under consideration here, included *gutbucket* and *barrelhouse.* Mezzrow defines the former only as an "earthy style of music." The former, especially, is frequently used to shock the middle classes, or for what Karl Reisman has called "dramatic low status assertion."[33] Andrews and Owens, drawing on LeRoi Jones's *Blues People,* refer to the practice of getting a bucket of chitterlings ("hog's guts") from the slaughterhouse; by association, then, the term would imply a "real low down" type of music. Other commentators and observers are equally convinced that it is an especially basic type of blues or jazz. Schuller regards it rather as a "manner of playing" than as a musical genre. Mezzrow's Glossary refers to barrelhouse as, first a "low, boisterous dive" and, then, in what he styles an adjectival use, "the original style of playing jazz, once associated with such low dives." W. C. Handy, an earlier if not necessarily more authentic exponent of the "real blues," quotes the lyric:

> Mr. Crump don't 'low no easy riders here.
> We don't care what Mr. Crump don't 'low,
> We goin' to barrelhouse anyhow.[34]

"Easy riders" has an obvious association with both sexual terminology and prostitution (see Chapters Two and Five). The latter association, especially, would reinforce the impression of a "low dive" style. Later versions of the same lyric, with Mr. Crump (a Memphis political boss of Handy's time) replaced by "Mama," substitute the apparently nonsensical *easy woodlin',* perhaps in an attempt to "clean up" the music and make it more respectable.

The existence of a nonsense vocabulary associated with jazz or jive talk is one of the thornier problems of the Black lexicon. There is, obviously, a great deal of in-group terminology that is designed to confuse or to shock the outsider. Nonsense vocabulary would undoubtedly help in producing both of those results. When a succession of obviously nonsense syllables is used as the lyric of a song, the term applied to it is *scat,* a term of very doubtful etymology. (A reduction of *scatological* to one syllable seems a little better than absurd only because there is no real competitor. Gold calls it "onomatopoetic," one of the more amusing uses of that far-fetched etymological term.) Some relatively early works on jazz attributed the term and the practice to Louis Armstrong, but Morton was vehement in his insistence that Joe Sims of Vicksburg originated the practice "long before Louis Armstrong's time." Morton's dismissal of Louis Armstrong ("one of my hometown boys") as the inventor is more impressive than the attribution to Joe Sims because the use of nonsense syllables is common, perhaps universal, in folk music. Nobody who has listened to as many as two "scatting" choruses by a Black bluesman, however, can fail to appreciate that something at least quantitatively different from "Hey, nonny nonny" is involved. In many parts of Afro-America, remnants of ritual texts, in what are probably somewhat garbled versions of African languages, are sung by people who attribute an emotional importance to the words but are not fully aware of their semantic or syntactic structure. If it is true that jazz, and especially the blues, has a great deal to do with Afro-American religious survivals (see below), then "scatting" is neither isolated from other aspects of Afro-American culture nor some casual outcropping of a folklore universal. On the other hand, the very strong possibility that the "grunts" of assent and negation are of African origin has little significance to their use by singers. Fats Waller was probably being more self-consciously Black when he interpolated "Yas, yas" (ordinary American English *ass* masquerading as *yes*) into a corny tin pan alley lyric than when he approved a solo with [m?h?m].[35]

The term *boogie woogie* might even be called more interesting than the music it describes. Mezzrow's Glossary calls it "a happier style of music which grew out of the blues"; Schuller called it a "primitive" manner of playing the blues on piano, characterized by a repetitive figure in the bass. White folklore, at least, associated "eight to the bar" with that repetitiveness; those young adults of the 1930s who prided themselves on being "hep" (NB: not *hip*), or who might describe each other as "alligators," were fond of using the terms *boogie woogie* and *boogie.* It was the kind of in-group jazz that could fit into a movie starring Gary Cooper and Barbara Stanwyck and featuring a bit by Gene Krupa.[36] The phrase, which follows a rather noteworthy Afro-Creole derivational pattern,[37] is often associated with *boogie* "a Negro," at least in the popular imagination. Joe Frazier, the former heavyweight boxing champion, has frequently been reported in the newspapers as using "boogie, boogie, boogie" as a way of describing a session of perhaps somewhat self-indulgent pleasure. Dalby cites Hausa and Mandingo forms and Sierra Leone Krio *bogi-bogi* "to dance."

The terminology becomes very different when we enter the domain of the blues, the acknowledged main trunk of the elaborate tree that leads to jazz and rock and roll. It is almost universally acknowledged that Black folk music, especially the blues, is basically African in origin, incorporating some surviving traits from West African music, and that it has influenced the popular music of American whites very greatly.[38] In fact, there is in histories of jazz a tendency to overlook the fact that jazzmen have assimilated to the European pattern at least insofar as the melodies upon which they base their improvisations and the instruments upon which they play are concerned. It is noteworthy that the African-derived banjo (Dalby cites Kimbundu *mbanza,* whence also Black Jamaican English *banja* and Brazilian Portuguese *banza*) has been replaced by some such instrument as the guitar or eliminated from the jazz band completely. But there is the obvious danger that these externals will mask the inner "feeling" of the music, which has remained Afro-American even though superficial factors like the instruments on which it is played have changed.

The same problem exists with the terminology, beginning with the term blues itself. That the word *blue,* even in the meaning "despondent," was familiar in English long before any Blacks used it is extremely commonplace philology, although American Blacks may have been responsible for such compounds as *blues dancing* and for the associations with the dance, without which "in general, African music is not conceivable." The standard reference dictionaries, however, consider *blues* as "short" for *blue devils,* a metaphor for "low-spiritedness" that originated, in American English and primarily among whites, in the early nineteenth century. The proposition, however, that despondency is really the musical (or lyrical) essence of the blues is not completely unarguable. Even insofar as the "mournful, haunting Negro folk song[s]" *(Dictionary of Americanisms,* definition of *blues)* deal with despondency—and "mournful" may be largely an outsider's reactions to blue notes (to be discussed below)—blues lyrics are primarily concerned with getting rid of that despondency.

There are, however, possibilities not yet given any consideration for the origin of the term *the blues,* insofar as it applies to Black music. *Blue* is still widely used among Negroes in the meaning "extremely dark." That is the characteristic of Blueboy in Robert Deane Pharr's novel *Book of Numbers.* Sergeant Russell Higgins, of Hari Rhodes's militant Black novel *A Chosen Few,* is known as Blue because a childhood acquaintance teased him, "Boy, you so black you blue."[40] Zora Neale Hurston's Glossary to *Mules and Men* explains the nickname "Blue Baby" in almost exactly the same words. A *blue-gummed Negro* is often associated with African origins and a special knowledge of conjure by rural Blacks, some of whom believe that his bite is poisonous. *Blue-skin* "a Negro," considered obsolete by the *Dictionary of Americanisms,* is attested in Cooper's *The Spy* (1821). It is, in fact, just as likely that the term *blues* commemorates the origin of the music by Negroes as that it denotes the melancholy or "despondent" nature of the genre. To trace the term to *blue devils* is to sweep under the rug almost every important fact about the term.

The adjective *blue,* "improper, as the Puritans would use the term," has its associations with sex. None of these associations, however, seem peculiar to the Black lexicon, even though there are extensive associations between the blues and sexual relationships. The homophony of the words must have had, at any rate, some influence in making the name for the musical type familiar to non-Black speakers of American English. In the Black lexicon, the fallacy of the unique etymology very frequently confuses the history of the term. Creolists, or workers on Afro-American language varieties, have long known that, rather than one accurate etymology and several faulty ones, there is likely to be a group of reinforcing etymologies.[41]

A second important matter concerns the communicative function of the blues. Alan Lomax reminds us that "the blues were, first of all, a form of dance music, a way of singing out your troubles, and courting the girls at country dances."[42] With all due respect to Lomax, there is a deeper level that underlies those functions, the conjure practices that facilitate all those aims. But understanding those surface functions is important in getting to the "roots" of the blues.

Something of importance about the blues may come from a consideration

of the communicative function of the song type. As is the case with West Indian calypsos, especially in their more nearly pure folk music function, and
with certain African songs like the Yoruba *ijala* chants, the blues in its most
basic function is a music of social commentary. That is what makes possible
a song like Sam "Lightnin' " Hopkins' "Happy Blues for John Glenn," com-
memorating the now almost forgotten exploit of the man who was for a brief
time America's leading astronaut. (Trinidadian Calypsonian king Sparrow's
"Explorer" treated space travel in a more sardonic vein: "I don't care where
the heck it fall, long as it don't fall on me.") A leading blues critic puts it
thus:

> If a particular person is the subject of enmity in a Negro folk community the
> offended man would "put his foot up"—in other words jam the door of his cabin
> with his foot and sing a blues and put him in the Dozens at the expense of his
> enemy.[43]

The most familiar example of the blues message—one that has almost
completely preempted the genre for some people—is that of the deserted lover
telling both his or her lost love and the one who has replaced him or her
about the singer's knowledge of what has gone on and scorn for both of them.
We can well imagine that "Yellow Dog Gal Blues," although depersonalized
and commercialized before it even reached phonograph records, represents
some such original message: "Some yellow dog gal done stole my man from
me."[44]

There is yet a third characteristic of the blues that is not so well known, and
the demonstration of which will probably not be so willingly received and accepted. It is the grounding of the blues in a deeper level of Black religion than
the church, even the foot-stomping, shouting "sanctified" church. This level is
nearer to conjure than to anything else. Its presence gives meaning to a blues lyric
like Robert Johnson's "Hellhound on My Trail":

> You sprinkled hot foot powder umm around my door,
>   all around my door,
> It keeps me with a rambling mind, rider, every old place I go,
>   every old place I go.
>   . . .
> I've got to keep moving, I've got to keep moving,
> Blues falling down like hail, blues falling down like hail.[45]

Although the statements were generally overlooked, Jelly Roll Morton made
it explicit in his interviews with Lomax:

> When I was a young man these hoodoo people with their underground stuff helpea
> me along.[46]

After Jelly Roll's death, the consort of his last years, Anita, explained to Lomax:

> The woman, Laura Hunter, who raised Jelly Roll, was a hoodoo witch. Yes, I'm talking about his godmother who used to be called Eulalie Echo. She made a lot of money at voodoo.[47]

How else does one explain the supreme confidence of the sensitive artist who at the same time outraged most of his colleagues by his boastfulness? If it was not confidence in hoodoo, what made him believe that he could beat almost anyone alive at pool, hustling, or piano playing? Anita said, "Jelly was a very devout Catholic. . . . But voodoo, which is an entirely different religion, had hold of him, too."[48] The man who grandly called himself the Inventor of Jazz may well have felt so confident because he felt himself to be singled out for special consideration by the spirits, or hoodoo "gods."

In many ways, the basic text of the blues lyric is, perhaps even historically, the wordbook of a "trick" (see discussion of this term in Chapter Seven) to insure magically the love of another, to keep that lover from wandering, or to win the wandering lover back again. Texas Alexander expresses quite overtly the "acquisition" function of the blues: "When I counts them blues, that many women is mine."[49]

Of course, a man may want to roam, and his greatest restriction may come from a woman who has insured his fidelity by a "trick." Tommy McClennan expresses one part of this complex set of attitudes:

> Now friend don't never let your good girl
> Fix you like this woman got me.[50]

While a man who has been "fixed" may be unable to find an outside love interest, his "woman" is free:

> Now when you get one of them funny women
> (take your time now)
> She won't do to trust.[51]

And of course, a "trick" may be used to repel the advances of an unwanted lover:

> Don't you mention 'bout rolling
> Cause she'll play her trick on you.[52]

Martin Williams has obviously come close, in his analysis of Ida Cox's "Fogyism," to the relationship of at least some blues lyrics to conjure.[53] In his analysis, the first stanza states a subject, the second continues in that realm, and the third makes a transition to introduce the subject of the trouble, or "blues." The last stanza specifies the trouble, the threatened loss of a lover:

> When your man comes home evil, tell you you are
>   getting old,
> That's a sure sign he's got someone else baking
>   his jelly roll.

The three most widely recognized elements of the blues are all there: the personal commentary, the sex (even expressed in the good Black sexual symbolism of *jelly roll*), and the sadness. Because of these elements, the blues almost crosses with the *torch song,* an (ostensibly) white song of love loss and sexual longing. Yet there are elements, beyond the merely formal, that separate the two.[54]

The most important of these elements is that rather inaccurately labeled "superstition." Before the singer's common-sense "sign" (the behavior of the lover) in "Fogyism," she discusses the supernatural signs that the "old folks" go by. It is possible, of course, to have a song full of superstition and still not have a blues. But LeRoi Jones was obviously coming close to pinpointing the kind of "superstition" most closely related to the blues when he wrote, in his significantly entitled *Blues People:*

> The African . . . had to find other methods of worshipping gods when his white captors declared that he could no longer worship in the old ways. . . . The immediate reaction, of course, was to try to worship in secret. The more impressive rites had to be discarded unless they could be performed clandestinely; the daily rituals, however, continued. . . . In fact, many of the "superstitions" of the Negroes that the whites thought "charming" were holdovers from African religions. . . . Among less educated, or less sophisticated, Negroes the particular significance of dreams, luck and lucky charms, roots and herbs is directly attributable to African religious beliefs.[55]

Since Jones' demonstration is impressive, it would seem to follow that the most African of beliefs (those connected with charms, roots, and so on) and the most African of musical traditions (the blues) would have much in common. The most striking element in blues lyrics is the constant reference to the use of roots, herbs, and magic charms to acquire love and to insure its permanence.

Many a jazz critic, like Whitney Balliet in *The Sound of Surprise,* has asserted that "Blues lyrics don't scan, have faulty, strained, rhymes, are repetitive and ungrammatical, and abound in nonsequiturs." Some of these arguments, like that of "faulty rhymes," can be answered by the phonological materials presented at the beginning of this chapter. The charge of non sequitur is a more serious one; almost any relativist would allow a folk poetry its own method of dealing with rhymes and meters. If, however, the basis in conjure and root magic ("superstition") can be recognized, the alleged lack of structure proves illusory. Another blues, like Big Bill Broonzy's "Big Bill Blues," proves to have almost the same organization as Ida Cox's "Fogyism." Broonzy's song begins:

> My hair is rising,
> My flesh begin to crawl.

a clear enough indication of the supernatural background, except that it is usually disregarded. Although the next lines proceed to talk about a dream (surely close enough to the supernatural to comply with the standards of most folklores!) of his "woman's" infidelity, most commentators would assume that the first two lines have no literal content and are simply there to fill space and provide rhymes. Actually, as the general context of the blues makes abundantly clear, the success of another man with Bill's girl must have been due to a conjure trick. This is the frightening aspect of what would otherwise be a matter for sadness, jealousy, or anger.

This song may be worth following through to the end for an illustration of just how the principles work. After establishing the conjure context, Big Bill proceeds in the next stanza to establish the blues modality of expression, deriding those who think "the Big Bill Blues ain't bad." This is a complete digression unless the blues have something to do with conjure, influence on someone's love, and dreams —but they are obviously connected with just those three subjects.

The next stanza is an elaborate sexual metaphor based on the comparison of sexual satisfaction to "getting mail"; the connection with mail and the postman may be arbitrary, but the failure to maintain sexual relations with the loved one is the direct consequence of the conjure, and it explains the introduction of the blues in the second section. The last stanza, instead of announcing (as might be expected in the central blues tradition) the intention of going to another hoodoo person and buying a countercharm, rather declares Bill's independence of the strayed woman, in terminology that will be familiar to readers of Chapter Two:

> I can't be your wagon,
> Dang sure ain't gonna be your mule;
> I ain't gonna fix up your black plantation,
> I ain't gonna be your doggone fool.[56]

The more basically expected reaction would be that of Robert Pete Williams, recorded in Scotlandville Prison, February 10, 1961:

> I'm going to the hoodoo, I'm gonna put you under my feet.
> I'm gonna have you, baby, do anything in the world I
>   want you to do.[57]

Rather than being loosely strung together, then, the stanzas of "Big Bill Blues" make one complete, integrated, almost narrative whole. Without the understanding of the folk religion background, however, it cannot be perceived how the first stanza fits into Broonzy's careful organization. Moreover, failures to understand produce such familiar, condescending statements about the nature of the blues as "picturesque, rhythmic, but intellectually unorganized." More importantly, from our point of view, such misunderstandings inhibit knowledge about the way in which the Black lexicon's use of *blues* differs from that of other varieties of English.

Because the scope of blues' conjure associations is not fully appreciated, blues lyrics frequently contain "hidden" meanings not perceived by the non-Black listener, even if he does know something about the sex symbolism discussed in Chapter 2. A good example is Jelly Roll Morton's "Michigan Water Blues." The first stanza seems, on the surface, to be a simple expression of preference for the northern states over the South:

> Michigan water taste like sherry wine;
> Mississippi water taste like turpentine.[58]

Taste like turpentine might be simply a slur against the racist state of Mississippi, except that in the relatively modern "Love Potion No. 9" the potion also "tastes like turpentine." There are also many potions that "taste like sherry [or cherry] wine."[59]

Morton's next stanza emphasizes the conjure relationship so clearly that only those who listen with preconceived notions could miss it:

> Believe to my soul that gal's got a black cat's bone;
> She'll go away, but she's sure to come back home.

Black cat's bones—the giving and receiving of them, and the inhibiting effect that either may have on a potentially straying mate—are perhaps the most prominent facts in the conjure literature.[60]

The next stanza is the least clear of them all, but it can probably be explained in terms of some esoteric conjure practices:

> She looks like a frog, hops like a kangaroo;
> If you ain't got no hopper,
> Let her [?] be your hopper too.

And the final stanza makes the supernatural associations altogether explicit:

> Gal in Alabama, one in Spain,
> Another in Mississippi, I'm scared to call her name.

If fear to call the girl's name cannot be explained in terms of her being a hoodoo woman, who perhaps prepares potions that "taste like turpentine," it would be interesting to find out what other explanation is workable.

Folklorists, not surprisingly, have come closest to recognizing the way in which folk beliefs contribute to an understanding of the blues lyrics. Hughes and Bontemps have a seminal kind of statement:

> The superstitions of the Negro folk are frequently found [in blues lyrics]. There are blues about "Black Cat's bones," about . . . mojo hand.[61]

Conjure-tinged associations are exceptionally easy to find in blues lyrics. Billie Pierce, who plays with her husband Dede on *Blues in the Classic Tradition,* a special seeking out of old-timers, sings:

> I'm going over to Algiers, baby, to get myself a hoodoo hand;
> Well the hoodoo told me he would give me back my man if he can.
>
> Well, the hoodoo look me, look me right in my eye;
> Well the hoodoo sell something for you but your man said
>   his last goodbye.[62]

Perhaps this particular man is not recoverable, even by conjure, but at least prevention against future occurrences can be gained:

> Well, I'm going back to Algiers to get myself a hoodoo hand;
> I'm going to stop these women from trying to take my man.

And it may well be a hoodoo threat that closes Billie Pierce's "Goodbye Daddy Blues":

> The day you quit me, that's the day you gonna die.[63]

This particular session was, according to the liner notes at least, not even oriented especially toward folk-style blues (it is only somewhat "old-fashioned" in its intentions), but the conjure materials pop out as if naturally.

The same kinds of lyrics can be found in endless sources. Muddy Waters sings on "Louisiana Blues":

> I'm goin' down in New Orleans, get me a mojo hand;
> I'm gonna show all you good-lookin' women just how to
>   treat your man.[64]

And on "Hoochie Coochie" he adds:

> I got a black cat bone, I got a mojo, too;
> I got John the Conqueror Root, I'm gonna mess with you.
> I'm gonna make you girls lead me by my hand,
> Then the world'll know the hoochie-coochie man.[65]

Few lyrics establish the relationship as explicitly, however, as J. D. (Jelly Jaw) Short's "Snake Doctor Blues":

> I'm a snake doctor man: everybody's trying to find out my name;
> . . .
> I know many of you men are wondering what the snake doctor
>   man got in his hand
> He's got roots and herbs, steals a woman, man, every where
>   he land.[66]

This occurrence of *snake doctor,* which clearly belongs in the conjure tradition, suggests much more than has hitherto been suspected about the influence of the Black lexicon on American English. *Snake doctor,* innocently looked upon as the insect with iridescent blue wings that hovers over streams in rural areas, is one of the primary diagnostic words for area dialects used by the Linguistic Atlas of the United States and Canada.[67]

The conclusion seems almost inescapable that there is a close relationship between the blues and conjure rituals, especially *love potions.* Bottles, for example, are extremely important conjure paraphernalia (see Chapter Seven). Sam "Lightnin' " Hopkins' "Blues in the Bottle" contains the familiar motif "stopper in my hand" that is shared with countless other lyrics.[68] Just for one example, we could quote from Memphis Slim's "Gee Ain't It Hard to Find Somebody":

> I've got the world in a jug, I'm holding the
>   stopper right here in my hand;
> I'm gonna hold tight, mama, until you come
>   under my command.[69]

Insofar as the blues are concerned with sexual relationships, they reveal a strong association with conjure matters. Love problems bring "trouble in mind," and consolation is most often sought from hoodoo doctors. In fact, the trouble is often assumed—more often than is realized—to have come from a hex. Bessie Smith, appealing significantly to a "Gypsy," says quite plainly, "That man put something on me; oh, take it off of me, please." And she knows her own set of charms to deal with a domineering lover:

> Dug a hole for his picture, faced it to the ground;
> Sprinkled salt around, to keep him from around.[70]

The association of the blues with "that other religion, hoodoo" helps explain the Black church's antipathy for the music, although, as has been stated over and over again, apart from the lyrics many of the church songs have more in common with the blues than with any other type of music.[71] Statements of the opposition between the blues and religious worship (limiting the latter to Christianity, superficially, not an arbitrary limitation since those involved would probably accept it) are rather commonplace:

> Sometimes I sing the blues when I know I should
> be praying.[72]

The same song asserts that the singer engages in the blues "to easy my worried mind"—an unrevealing enough sentiment until one remembers that the church claims the right to be the agent for such consolation.

Musicologically, the relationships of the blues to African music seems beyond doubt. The derivation has been professionally summarized by Gunther Schuller, among others:

> When the Negro made his first tentative attempts to combine his African melodic heritage with the European diatonic system, he found that he could readily do so by alternating, as equivalently as in his native land, the two seven-tone scales he already knew. . . . At first these attempts must have been somewhat cautious, but by the latter part of the nineteenth century definite patterns in which blue notes were used became established.[73]

Schuller tells how these *blue notes* were made familiar to the American listening public by the recordings of singers like Bessie Smith, Blind Lemon Jefferson, and Big Bill Broonzy. In my research for this book, without any intention of establishing a parallel, I drew on quotations from the first and last of these in order to establish the relationship between the blues lyric and root-work conjure. Merely by chance, I kept numerous quotations from Blind Lemon Jefferson's lyrics for back-up documentation. There is really no doubt at all that the singers who used the "blue notes" also sang of the conjure associations of the blues.

In spite of the musicological similarities between the blues and spirituals, then, it is not surprising that the terminology is very different. The discourse worlds of the two are far apart, and the domain of the discourse is the best determinant of the vocabulary. Folklore researchers have frequently been impressed with the insistence of, especially, rural Black informants on the incompatability of secular and religious music. The former are sometimes referred to as "jumped-up, sinful songs,"[74] and there are other references to *jumped-up songs* in places like Jamaica.[75] One of the reasons for the "sinfulness" of the blues is its association with the behavior pattern of conjure. The latter is beyond any doubt non-Christian; it may even represent a carry-over from West African religion.

There are, of course, some similarities between blues terminology and gospel song terminology. The degree of verbal skill of the practitioners is one comparable aspect. Commercial gospel singers, by Heilbut's account as wordly a group as any in the field of blues, have terms "bristling with verbal wit" referring to singing, the songs that are performed, and the reaction of the audience.[76] What a good singer can do is described in terms like *tear up, plumb demolish the place, and leave nothing standing, not even dust.* High spirits, presumably on the part of the singer, are described as *judgment,* or *time for church to be dismissed.* A hit number may be called a *house wrecker,* a *song for sister Flu,* or a *stick.*[77] There are, however, still some terms that unconsciously echo conjure practices: "Paul was making a lot of changes, what we called *trickeration.*"[78]

The earliest detailed reports we have of Black slaves in the United States make much of the importance of music for those Blacks. Allen's 1867 report, perhaps the beginning of serious study of Black music, stresses the variety of Black musical forms and the terms used to describe them. Unlike Port Royal, where Allen asserted he "never fairly hear a secular song":

> In other parts of the South, "fiddle-sings," "devil-songs," "corn-songs," "jig-tunes," and what not, are common; all the world knows the banjo, and the "Jim Crow" songs of thirty years ago.[79]

The relative autonomy of Black music, and of the vocabulary for that music, from that time to the present is obvious to anyone who takes the trouble to make an investigation.

5

The Street Hustle: Prostitution, Gambling, and Narcotics

It is one of the more shameful social facts about the United States that Blacks have not had equal protection under the law and that crimes have been more quickly imputed to them than to whites, even though the two groups may have been engaged in the same activities. Any treatment of the vice vocabulary of the Black population risks an accusation of prejudice because of these very unfortunate social facts. Nevertheless, the very discriminatory social makeup of the nation has meant that certain activities generally regarded as marginal to or outside the law have been relegated increasingly to Blacks. Such terminology is much less likely to have been innovated by Blacks than that of other activities. Nevertheless, the Black influence on general American English is likely to have been strong at just those points since prostitution, especially, entails a high degree of interracial contact. Studies of these activities in the inner city, at just the time when the control of them has passed to Blacks, have multiplied in recent years, and there is a great deal available on the terminology. It should always be borne in mind that the likelihood of white origin is greater in such fields and that virtually nothing in the terminology under discussion in this chapter is an "Africanism." It is especially noteworthy that prostitution terminology and sexual terminology (Chapter 2) are diametrically opposed in this respect. There are, however, some ways in which the terms in this domain dovetail with general Black vernacular lexicon, and no treatment could have any pretense of completeness without a consideration of those areas.

Although, for example, the term *rider* belongs to general Black sexual vocabulary, it applies, in the inner city, most easily to the pimp himself. It is a facile assumption that the pimp, because of his aggressive stylishness in clothing, his love of fancy automobiles, and so on, is so supermodern as to be beyond the Black English vernacular vocabulary and, especially, its rural antecedents. On the contrary, even the Black folk terminology is encountered from pimps, as in the name Mojo for a San Francisco procurer.[1] The "in" characteristic of disguise vocabulary overbalances any disadvantages that "country" associations might bring, and even Gullah shares some features with the terminology of the inner city pimp. In addition to those discussed elsewhere, there is *he say, she say* "a girl's talk to another about her personal business with her pimp," strikingly similar to *she-she talk* in Gonzales' "A Glossary of Gullah."² Although the expressions are different enough to leave open some possibility of coincidence, the context in which the pimping term occurs in *Gentleman of Leisure* is convincing. Silky, the pimp whose activities are detailed in the book, is giving his whores a big lecture: "I don't want you to talk to each other. I don't want this he say, she say shit."³ Gonzales defines his *she-she talk* as "woman's talk, gabble"; the different extra-linguistic environment is enough to explain the semantic difference.

The metaphorical inventiveness otherwise characteristic of the Black lexicon (see Chapter One) turns up in inner city prostitution talk, even among novice whores: *weekend warriors,* for seventh- and eighth-grade girls who are "turning tricks."⁴ The term *trick* for the sexual performance of a prostitute probably comes, ultimately, from the voodoo term for achieving control (often sexual control), possibly reinforced by the nautical term meaning "a task."⁵ The sexual meaning has gradually forced the others out of existence so that *out tricking* may be "looking for a customer" for a prostitute or "looking for a sex partner" for a "square" person. (The latter is, however, much rarer in occurrence.) It is pretty obvious that the latter developed from the former. Among prostitutes, the first trick of the evening is an important one because "He break my luck," or "I break luck with him." It is considered that the succeeding customers will be acquired more easily and quickly.

Like other activities, prostitution and pimping tend to have their own speech acts, comparable to rapping, copping a plea, and other ghetto speech acts described by Abrahams, Kochman, and others. *Murphying* is a term for a prostitution-related activity that at least turns up frequently in Black texts like Richard Wright's rawly realistic novel *Lawd Today.* Foster quotes just one Harlem schoolboy in a way that suggests that the term has a wider application:

Loud talk the teacher. Murphy and psych him out with double talk.⁶

Descriptions of the act make clear how the extension of meaning comes about: *Murphying* has a basic connotation of fooling the victim, making him believe that he will get what in fact he will not. A student who "Murphys" the teacher will probably make the instructor think that the pupil is unusually cooperative in order to "set up" the teacher for a ruse.

Sources like Iceberg Slim's *Pimp* and Claude Brown's *Manchild in the Promised Land* give elaborate descriptions of the act associated with providing a prostitute, or rather making a "John" think that a prostitute is being procured:

All I had to do was walk down the street and see somebody who was looking up at the buildings like he was fascinated with New York. I'd walk past him, not even stop, and say, "Soldier, you interested in some nice young girls?" . . . I'd keep walking, and he'd usually follow.[7]

Iceberg Slim offers the modification that there are many "Murphys" and that the most adept players:

> . . . prefer that a trick "hit on" them. It puts the "Murphy" player in a position to force the sucker to "qualify" himself and to trim the mark not only for all his scratch [money], but his jewelry as well.[8]

Iceberg Slim and Brown agree, however, on the most immediate means of extracting the money:

> . . . you got him to put some money in an envelope and wait for it, as you were supposed to check his money before he went into the house because the girls might take it from him.

Brown tells how the sucker is gotten rid of:

> You'd send him up to a hotel room after he'd given you the money. Sometimes you'd just give him a key and tell him he could go on up to the hotel. Then you'd just come on out. A lot of times, you'd steal a hotel key beforehand and send him up to that room. It didn't matter, because you wouldn't be down there when he came back.

Although "favored lover" may have been its meaning in square usage, *sweetman* soon came to be understood as "a pimp in the world of prostitution." The woman need not be technically a prostitute, however; Zeddy, in Claude McKay's *Home to Harlem,* is described as "living sweet" because he lives for a time with Susy, a grass widow otherwise known as "Ginhead Susy." Because she restricts his movements, however, he is scornfully described as a *skirtman;* pimps, of the Iceberg Slim persuasion at any rate, take no orders from the girls and could not be so described. It is interesting, also, that *living sweet* also functions in the domain of religion, indicating that the subject is living a "righteous" Christian life.

Sweet man itself easily shortens to *man,* which, with a certain emphasis and in the appropriate context, means "pimp." (Nowhere is the domain more important, for in other contexts *man* is simply the generalized term of address, now partially replaced by *dude* and a few other expressions.) There was, for example, my personal observation of a Black woman in a New York bar telling her little boy, who had come to ask her for money, "Can't nobody pimp me but my man." Unless one is on the lookout, the context can be missed. Jelly Roll Morton's "Mamie's Blues" undoubtedly refers to solicitation by a prostitute, although those caught up in the glamor of old jazz can miss the point:

Stood on the corner with her feets all soaking wet
[Aside: Her *feets* was wet]
Begging each and every man that she met:
"If you can't give a dollar, give me a lousy dime;
I want to feed that hungry man of mine."[9]

In the days of inflation, and when the pimps we read about are affluent, it is easy to mistake the above for the pathetic appeal of a "straight" wife trying to provide for a husband. It would be harder to mistake Louis Armstrong's report of how a woman in a bar made the accusation, "Some old bitch in this bar is going with my man."[10] In such a context, the term could apply only to the pimp.

Sweetman and *skirtman* seem to have retained some currency, although they are both slightly old-fashioned.[11] The term *Eastman* is found in diverse sources, almost all of them older and rural. Odum and Johnson report, "The 'Eastman' is kept fat by the women among whom he is a favorite."[12] Independently, H. C. Brearley has pointed out that the "bad" man was often such a favorite with the women, as is the "nachel bohn Eastman, who may brag that he need not work 'cause I got it writ on the tail of my shirt.' "[13] This same motif figures prominently in a Furry Lewis blues entitled "Kassie [sic] Jones," with the railroad story of the white ballad heavily overlain with railroad-sex symbolism (see p. 30) and reference to a "Chaney" who is probably the sexual athlete Spavin Chain of Jelly Roll Morton's "Winin' Boy":

I'm a natural born eas'man on the road again
I left Memphis just to spread the news
Memphis women don't wear no shoes
Had it written in the back of my shirt
Natural born eas'man don't have to work,
   Don't have to work,
I'm a natural born eas'man don't have to work.[14]

In more modern and urban usage, a pimp or someone with a pimp's life-style may be described as a *player,* or a really successful player as a *boss player.*[15] The modifier in the second expression comes from a Creole tradition that still extends as far as Surinam. A less-effective player, who barely subsists on procuring, is called a *simple pimp.* The pimp who does not exhibit the Iceberg Slim-type dominance (which is styled old-fashioned in Milner and Milner's *Black Players*) can be either a *sweet Mack* (a variation on Mack man that goes back to French *maquereau* and therefore is almost certainly not originally Black) or a *sugar pimp.* The other type may be a *gorilla pimp* or a *hard Mack.* Dandy, a pimp in *Gentleman of Leisure,* describes Iceberg Slim as "cold on his bitches' ass" and as "pimping alley style."[16]

For the prostitute, there is, as might be expected, a fairly elaborate terminology. *Ho,* which is of course merely a dialect pronunciation of *whore,* is used by some participants in "the life" who do not always speak an *r*-less dialect and who might say *whore* in different contexts.[17] She may also be a *working chick* or a *working broad.*[18] In the drugstore that used to be a stopping point for most of the street-walkers on Washington's Fourteenth Street Northwest, an interviewer who asked, "How many of the girls who come in here are working?" would get a ready estimate of the percentage who were prostitutes. A slangier usage produces *trick broads.*[19]

A pimp may have a *stable,* in which case the girls are *stable sisters* or *wives-in-law.* The most trusted one—often the oldest in his service and not necessarily the most beautiful or the favorite—is the *bottom whore, bottom woman, bottom bitch,* or *main lady* and is given a certain amount of authority over her "sisters." She is also sometimes called *Mother.*[20] The whores plus the pimp are a "family," and of course, the prostitutes may be called *wives* or *old ladies.* A pimp constantly strives to increase his stable by *copping* new girls. *To cop* (also *to catch,* or *to pull*) as a transitive verb is not, of course, peculiar to prostitution, but *cop* without expressed object meaning "induce a girl to ally herself with a particular pimp" is.[21] To lose a girl to another pimp is *to blow,* and the (usually) more or less friendly competition between pimps is described as *cop and blow.*

These are grammatically transitive verbs in "straight" usage that are used without expressed object in the argot of prostitution. The same may be said of *choose* "voluntarily decide to join a pimp." For a girl who is *qualified* "a professional whore" rather than a *turn-out,* choosing may involve going to a new pimp and leaving the one who has copped her earlier. A pimp trying to acquire either the experienced professional or the new recruit will *hit on* the girl "try repeatedly to win her." (The term is, of course, common in other domains.) If his initial approach (also, like many other ghetto approaches, called his *rap*) seems about to succeed, the pimp switches to talk of *taking her application.* One of Silky's girls describes the *copping fuck* of the newly accepted member of the stable—fifteen different positions.[22] All of the sources seem to agree, however, that the pimp's relationship to the whore is something other than that of lover.

To keep another pimp from copping his girls, or to refrain from "blowing" them himself, each player has a *game*—romance (in the case of Silky) or violence (in that of Iceberg Slim).[23] The expression *run the game* is also common in other domains. In Iceberg Slim's purportedly documentary *Mama Black Widow,* the phrase is used to describe the activities of one who picks up, beats, and robs homosexuals.[24]

The prostitute, or pross, is called the pimp's *stick*—the tool with which he solves his economic problems. (Compare the jazzman's use of *ax* to refer to his musical instrument, a saxophone or even a piano.) In early blues lyrics, perhaps to some degree prefiguring Black involvement in large-scale prostitution, the woman who provided support was a *meal ticket* woman. Her sexual equipment may be a *moneymaker* or a *money 'cumulator.*[25] A prostitute whose abilities do not include conning the John out of his scratch (i.e., money) is a *flatbacker.* [26] Her area of operations is *the street* or *the stroll* in the ghetto area, or *Hell.* She participates in a *trick* with her customer, who is also a trick. A man who is REALLY interested in the prostitute's services may be an *all-night trick,* or for special purposes, two girls may work on one customer in a *party.*

The concept of fooling the customer is the dominant one, reinforcing the possibility that the trick terminology has something to do with the same word as used in conjure. A woman with conjure powers can "play her trick on you." [27] To have a baby by a client is to produce a *trick baby,* a term of opprobrium for both the mother and the child. The biography of such a child is recounted in Iceberg Slim's supposedly authentic *Trick Baby.* The young man is called White Folks by those of the ghetto community who are favorably disposed toward him and *trick baby* by the others. (He stoutly maintains, incidentally, that his mother was never a prostitute.)

The prostitute's approach to commercial sex is generally regarded as acting. One of the pimp's best approaches to a "square" girl, who may be "turned out," is to offer to make her a *star.* Iceberg Slim tells one of his prospects, "I'm going to make a star out of you, angel." [28] He gives the report on another, "She was on her way to stardom." [29] And his "game" in seeming to welcome the departure of a girl who wants to leave him involves saying, "It gives some worthy bitch a chance to take her [in context, any whore who wants to leave] place and be a star." [30] The expression is used so often in the literature of Black prostitution and the practices of the streets that it should be considered part of the lexicon, although the relationship to and probable derivation from the vocabulary of the movies and stage is obvious.

Slight value is attached to the prostitute who is a *come freak* (multiorgasmic) or a *fuck freak.* Iceberg Slim definitely states that a pimp, to be successful, must control his sexual appetites. Milner and Milner quote "The Book," the mythical guide to pimping that Iceberg Slim presumably came closest to writing down, ". . . a pimp must never 'chippy' (make love to a woman for the pleasure of it)." [31] Iceberg Slim uses the term *be Georgiaed* for the same error. Except with the pimp, the prostitute herself is not *getting down*—having real sex. The term *get down* also applies, in prostitution, to starting work for the evening, which is *git-down time.* [32] There is an overlap with *get down* as used in church *(get down and preach)* and of course with that of "straight" sex.

In return for a major portion of the prostitute's earnings, the pimp provides her with a certain amount of protection. A "trick" who refuses to pay may be threatened with violence from the pimp, who is often described, in such a context, as a *bad mother fucker.* The term is also widely used by streetcorner men, for whom it is a term of near flattery—perhaps because toughness has a prestige function in that group. *Pimp* is also a term of praise or flattery to such men, being a high-status activity because of the pimp's income and his control of women.

A pimp also instructs (or at least pretends to instruct) the whore in the methods of plying her trade, and such information is probably necessary at least to the turn out or a prostitute from another town (a frequent situation since police tend to become familiar with the prostitute who works a certain area). The pimp who gives this kind of instruction is *running down the game* to his whores. The pimp's automobile, a Cadillac or a Lincoln with many added extras and gaudy decorations, is an important part of his "game," particularly since an occasional ride in it gives the girls the necessary delusion of luxury. The term *hog* "Cadillac" is probably general ghetto slang, but it occurs more often in the literature dealing with Black pimps than elsewhere. The pimp's elaborate dress (virtually a uniform) is proverbial; the slang terms *vines* and *threads* "clothing" appear constantly in the literature on pimps—although apparently never used of the clothing of prostitutes. There is rather scant chance, however, that either originated in prostitution; they seem to represent a kind of synechdoche that might have taken place, at some unknown time in the past, under almost any conditions of the use of argot.

In spite of the dangers of sensationalism and, more seriously, misrepresentation in dwelling on the character of the pimp—since in the very nature of things pimps must represent a very small portion of the population—the procurer is a heroic enough figure to the ghetto subculture to wield a disproportionate amount of influence. Pops Foster, who told how pimping was associated with good looks and fine clothes, reported, "All the musicians back in New Orleans wanted to be pimps."[33] *Rapping* is a ghetto verbal ideal, and a pimp must have a superb rap or perish. *Walking that walk and talking that talk* is almost the extreme standard of excellence for the ghetto male, and the pimp excels at both of these, or he does not survive at his trade. Insofar as skill in talking is concerned, there seems to be little terminology specifically referring to the pimp. Where walking and dressing are concerned, however, it is an entirely different story. The most spectacular performance insofar as walking is concerned is the *pimp strut*. Kenneth Johnson describes it thus:

> First of all, it's much slower [than the aggressive young white male's nearest equivalent walk]—it's more of a stroll. The head is sometimes slightly elevated and casually tipped to the side. Only one arm swings at the side with the hand slightly cupped. The other arm hangs limply to the side or it is tucked in the pocket. The gait is slow, casual and rhythmic. The gait is almost like a walking dance, with all parts of the body moving in rhythmic harmony.[34]

Johnson also describes a kind of "stationary pimp strut":

> This means that while the young Black males are talking, they stand with their hands halfway in their pockets, and they move in the rhythmic, fluid dance-type way (without actually walking) to punctuate their remarks. The arm that is free will swing, point, turn, and gesture as conversation proceeds.[35]

Pimping and prostitution may well be activities forced on the Black population by American social prejudice and the caste system, but the kinesics typical of the pimp must go back to other sources. (The admiration and imitation directed toward the pimp by young ghetto males may well be, if this is true, rather the identification with traditional Black folkways than with any special attraction to "immorality.") Johnson's work makes elaborate comparisons to West African kinesic patterns, and even Negroes of the Ecuadorean *litoral,* where, according to anthropologist Norman Whitten, *"andar* means 'to strut' in the Black idiom" have similar behavior patterns. Whitten's description is strikingly similar to Johnson's:

> It is common to hear it said that a male must *andar y conocer* (literally "to walk [travel] and to know [learn])" before he becomes a man. . . . Walking in the manner prescribed for saloon giving, or for making sexual overtures to a woman, or for breaking the circling pattern described for the saloon dancing as an act of individual assertion is known as "walking," . . . *andar y conocer* also means to learn the ritual style for symbolizing cooperation, and attracting a woman, and to learn the proper styles for sexual intercourse.[36]

Such stylized walking patterns, connected to sexual success but not necessarily to pimping, are attested from New Orleans in the early twentieth century. The peculiar style described by Jelly Roll Morton in his Library of Congress conversations with Alan Lomax was called *shooting the agate.* Morton described it as "kind of a very mosey walk"—remember Johnson's "it's more of a stroll"—that the New Orleans swells had "adopted from the river." Morton remembered that "if you could shoot a good agate and had a red flannel undershirt" you could make an easy impression on "the real illiterate women": "You liable to be able to get next to that broad; she liked that."[37] Note that the red flannel undershirt, often worn under the overall shirt that Morton also attributes to the New Orleans swells, is made of the favorite material of the hoodoo doctors, whose special knowledge of love charms enables them to insure the favors of women.[38] Red flannel is, among other things, a favorite material for a mojo hand, which is one of the most effective love charms.

A red flannel undershirt under an overall shirt does not sound especially fashionable today, but Morton emphasized that the trousers and especially the shoes of these New Orleans swells were in the latest, most expensive fashion. Their dress was, in fact, in the flashily expensive taste that is presently associated with the inner city pimp. The shoes, which Morton identifies as "St. Louis flats" and "Chicago flats," were often especially made for the wearer and were elaborate in design. "They would," said Morton, "have different designs in the toes of the shoes—such as gambling designs, such as maybe a club, or a diamond, or a heart, or maybe a spade."[39] Gamblers share with pimps not only their unenviable position with respect to the law but also the extreme concern with flashiness of dress. At one time, either of them would have been likely to wear a *zoot suit*—

an Afro-American expression with a clear parallel in Liberian English.[40] And at one stage, at least a good zoot had to have a *gambler's stripe* in order to be "sharp."

In spite of the existence of these Black English terms, neither pimping nor gambling has any special connection with Blackness; the element that distinguishes Black language from white is not so much reference to such domains as the extensive use of conjure practices and a terminology based on them. As was noted in connection with terms like *trick,* the associations are not entirely lacking to the former trade.

As George J. McCall has pointed out, the numbers racket, perhaps the most specifically Black form of gambling, would not have been nearly so successful if it were not for the Black predilection for divination.[41] The numbers appeals to lower-class Blacks for perhaps the same reason that the red flannel undershirt appealed to what Morton called "illiterate" women—the function of each in conjure. Insofar as numbers are concerned, the appeal is possible because conjure itself uses numbers symbolically—369 for feces, 769 for death, and so on. The evangelical Black sects and cults, despite a certain amount of kinesic carry-over from hoodoo in their ceremonies, find it their greatest rival and often preach against it in terms of its bad influence in leading people into such vices as playing the numbers:

> Lucifer fell into a world of darkness and that's the world the spiritualists penetrate. They set you against your best friends, lead you into the numbers racket. Use dirt and filth: dead man's finger, grave dirt.[42]

There is a fairly standard methodology associated with the numbers. The winning number is, by tacit agreement, that appearing in some widely disseminated source whose authors may not be aware that they are being so used. In Washington, D.C., they are said to be derived from the payoff figures of certain daily horse races.[43] In Robert Dean Pharr's *The Book of Numbers,* the winning number seems to come, by telephone, from a central authority; even the pads used by numbers men in different cities are uniform in nature. In any case, the chances of "hitting" are about 1 in 1,000; the payoff is something like 600 to 1, with extra "handling charges." *Numbers runners* are available at certain places and times in the ghetto to take the bets, which can be very small. Sources like Pharr's novel make it clear that the possibility of betting with a small stake, plus the excitement intruded into a generally boring life, are the factors that make the numbers so popular in Black sections: "A Negro's social and recreational life is so limited that at times he has a yen as avid as a junkie's, for a tale of make believe to satisfy his needs."[44] Therefore, waiters and housemaids seem eager to make their bets with the runners, who collect so much that they pass their accumulations on to *numbers bankers* or *bagmen.* There are dangers, however, to the operators of the game. Hunches (see below) about the numbers run in cycles; if everybody in the ghetto is playing 711, it may possibly come up, and there could be a great loss. According to Hannerz, "to prevent this, the agent may declare that the number has to be 'cut.' "[45]

Books like *Policy Pete, The Rajah, Lucky Day Workout,* and *The H. P. Dreambook*[46] guide the players through the process of making hunch bets. These hunch bets are possible because certain activities, objects, or events, especially as dreams or forming part of some vivid experience, are supposed to be correlated with the number that will win. Without consulting an expert—or at least one of the supposedly authoritative books—the potential bettor has no way of translating the dream of, say, a wedding into the numbers he should play. On the other hand, many have become so familiar with those books that they have virtually memorized them, like these characters from Toni Morrison's *Sula:*

> Neither one bothered to look it [dream of a wedding in a red dress] up for they both knew the number was 522.[47]

Hannerz reports that such bets are "sometimes a question of idiosyncratic attachments."[48] Someone born on May 3 may play 503; others may play the street number of their residence or their apartment number. Consultations with "spiritualists," "readers," and dream books play an even more important role. One of Hyatt's informants gives an enlightening description of the process:

> To find de lucky numbahs, take de Bible. Now, ah want chew to read de ninth chapter of Psalms—read it ovah three times befo' goin' tuh bed. When yo' read it ovah three times befo' goin' tuh bed, *open de Bible an' sleep wit* it—sleep with dat Bible right under yore pillah an' yo'll dream of dat lucky numbah. When yo' git up de next morning yo' kin till a person exactly about dat numbah. An' if yo' throw dat numbah den dey'll ketch it.[49]

Otherwise, advice may be sought from a real or metaphorical "Gypsy."

Richard Wright's brilliant ghetto novel *Lawd Today* has an extended passage in which an aged female expert consults *King Solomon's Wheel of Life and Death Dream Book*[50] to find out the number associated with the "Steprow" (i.e., a dream about steps), which turns out to be the numbers 6, 17, 26; Runningrow (a dream about running up some steps): 11, 15, 37; Snakerow (dreaming about snakes): 16, 32, 64; Deadrow (a dream about a dead man): 9, 19, 29; Pregnantrow (dreaming that one is with child): 11, 22, 50.

Other writers tell us of other symbolisms, like the Washerwoman's Number: 4–11–44.[51] (There is also some indication of covert phallic symbolism associated with this number.) In fact, according to Hughes and Bontemps, there are "numbers for every dream, for every hunch." They give an example:

The other night I dreams a tall and handsome brown man was making love to me.
I played sixteen for his color, seven for his height and forty-two for the age he looked
to be.[52]

Although they do not explain the number symbolism in any detail, they give the
following associations:

316—a woman without a husband but with three children
212—a girl wanting clothes
530—a man paying his household debts
728—a Harlemite wanting luxury
471—the pastor of Lamb Holiness Church wanting a church site

References to the numbers are extremely frequent in Black fiction and in the
blues. Iceberg Slim's presumably nonfictional *Mama Black Widow*, which nevertheless uses elaborate devices like dialogue usually associated with fiction, reports
incidental events like the following:

Hattie Greene, who had been playing the dead man's row [9, 19, 29] of figures since
Ralph's death, hit Lock Jaw's policy wheel with a back bet for eight hundred and
sixty dollars [the sum mentioned in Pharr's *Book of Numbers*].[53]

Pharr's *The Book of Numbers* is, as the title suggests, built on the lore of the
numbers racket. Dave, the romantic hero of the novel, and his friend and foil
Blueboy, introduce the numbers game into a large southern ghetto and meet with
a series of adventures that represent almost a microcosm of Black life. Transitions
in the action are regularly marked by reference to the winning number of the day:

. . . 021 played the day the two men knifed each other to death. Nobody hit it.
                        . . .
The number was 244 the day that Blueboy sent for Makepeace Johnson.[54]

The function of the numbers in the blues is not so transparently obvious, but
they do come in handy for purposes of double entendre. British blues scholar Paul
Oliver has written:

. . . the singer played a game with the censor. . . . Sometimes a more specific code
would be used—the number combinations of the "policy racket"—a kind of
"housey-housey"—in which the figures 3–6–9 would mean excreta or 4–11–44 would
mean a phallus.[55]

The folk typology and the stereotype persistently attribute a special fondness
for gambling to working-class Blacks, and there may be some foundation for those
beliefs. We find frequent reference to gambling in blues lyrics:

> Becky Deem had the gamblers all on the ground,
> She win all the money the skinners laid down.[56]

Gambling was far from unknown in Africa, and the circumstances of slavery made it likely that the venturesome would be willing to risk their scant belongings either out of boredom or in the slight hope of augmenting them. Jelly Roll Morton's Library of Congress conversations with Alan Lomax give some indication as to how important gambling on pool and card games was to Blacks in the southern city at the turn of the twentieth century. Among the games he mentions is the *Georgia skin game,*[57] which is also mentioned by Zora Neale Hurston,[58] who thinks it worthy of special mention as a characteristic game of rural Blacks. There is no clear indication of how the name may have come about; it could be either Black or white in origin.

Rather more likely to be Black in origin is *cooncan,* the term for a rummylike game. The etymology is unknown; Spanish *con quien* ("With whom?"), suggested by the *Dictionary of Americanisms,* is more than faintly ridiculous. The first entry given by the *Dictionary of Americanisms* is from the *Century Magazine* for 1889, which turns out to be from a story by one Frederic Remington entitled "A Scout with the Buffalo Soldiers." *Buffalo soldiers* was a familiar, if somewhat racist, term on the frontier for Blacks in the U.S. Army. Although there is no suggestion of the fact in the material quoted in the *Dictionary of Americanisms,* the whole article stresses the importance of gambling for Black soldiers. Furthermore, they are represented as speaking the Black English vernacular:

> The men got out a pack of Mexican cards and gambled at a game called "Coon-can" for a few nickels and dimes and that other soldier currency—tobacco. Quaint expressions came from the card party. "No I'se a goin' to scare de life outen you when I show down dis han'," said one man after a deal. The player addressed looked at his hand carefully and quietly rejoined, "You might scare *me,* pard, but you can't scare de fixin's I'se got yere."[59]

The same card game was reported by Zora Neale Hurston, in *Mules and Men,* among rural Blacks in Florida. Hurston found it necessary to gloss *coon-can* "a two-handed card game popular among Southern Negroes."

The popular belief (sometimes substantiated) that Blacks have a special fondness for gambling has motivated some doubtful etymologies, however. Paul Oliver, for example, guessed that *the dozens* is named from "the dice throw of twelve, the worst in crap-shooting."[60] Oliver is a fine scholar of the blues, but his etymologies have always seemed questionable. There is rather more likelihood of accuracy in Lee's *Beale Street, Where the Blues Began,* which explains the origin of *gravy train.* Lee asserts that a lucky gambler would be followed by a line of those who had seen him win, a "train" eager to share in his "gravy." The gambler was supposed to buy drinks and other favors for such people until his winnings were exhausted. One who had located such a lucky, and generous, gambler was truly *on the gravy train.* The suggestion seems more than plausible, although further probing might reveal a deeper layer, in somewhat the same way that the prostitute's term *trick* can be determined to have conjure associations. The *Dictionary of Americanisms,* which offers no etymological explanation, cites as the first occurrence of the term a work by B. A. Botkin, which in turn cites Lee's book.[61] It is not immediately clear why someone on the dictionary staff did not take the trouble to follow up Botkin's reference, which is quite clear and unambiguous.

Neither in prostitution nor in gambling is there the impressive kind of evidence for originally Black terms that can be found in music, sex, and religion. Nor is there very impressive evidence that the terminology of narcotics is any more "Black" historically than the other two, although it is authoritatively reported that there are "a number of terms that originated with or were adapted by Negro addicts."[62] The Black American has been largely the victim of the narcotics trade, and he has probably taken most of the terminology from outside pushers. A great deal of addiction terminology seems to have been used by jazzmen, but it is highly doubtful that any large amount of it originated with them. The same is true for the preponderance of narcotic terms in "jive talk" or in street slang.

Folb's study of urban argot showed that "only three of eleven marijuana items were known exclusively by Black subjects": *gunny, skoofer,* and *stencil.*[63] The first of these is "an old word which identifies a particularly strong form of marijuana found in Jamaica and Africa." Another form, *Black Gungeon,* is listed as related. Although the phonological relationship is not absolutely convincing, according to the *Dictionary of Jamaican English,* this word may come from the same source as Jamaican *ganga,* "the plant *Cannabis sativa* . . . introduced to Jamaica by East Indians." This dictionary also points out that the term "has entered into local combinations." Folb says that the term has generalized, changing in meaning from "a particularly strong form of marijuana" to "marijuana in general." She also says that the term is "particularly race-bound," being known to the majority of the Blacks interviewed but not known by even heavy marijuana users among the whites interviewed. The term represented, in short, a major exception to her principle that the shared experience of drug usage constituted a bond that caused vocabulary sharing between different ethnic groups.[64]

Another interesting marijuana term studied by Folb is *black moat* "a particularly potent form of marijuana." Because of the phonological process of "weakened" articulation of a final voiceless stop, the term tends to be something like *black mo* for the Negro population of Los Angeles. For the Spanish-American population studied, the term had been adapted to Spanish grammatical processes and had become *black mota.* The whites who knew the term at all called it *black mole* or *black mold.* As Folb points out, the whites must have gotten the term from the Blacks since their form represents a faulty correction (misanalysis) of the Black pronunciation: They are aware that Black dialect simplifies or deletes final consonant clusters or consonants but lack a base form upon which to model their "restoration" of the lost sounds. Nevertheless, there is no reason to believe that the Spanish-speakers took it from the Blacks; ultimate origin would seem to be very much in doubt.[65]

Marijuana has been used in the Black musical community (as well as by their white associates like Mezz Mezzrow) since at least as early as the 1920s, and terms like the now old-fashioned *viper* "marijuana user" are fossilized in song titles from the period. Tunes like "The Viper's Drag," "Viper's Dream," and "You'se a Viper" were recorded by Black orchestras during the twenties. In some cases, however, the accompaniments, as in the case of Cab Calloway's "hep, hep" choruses, seem like pure put-on. Bessie Smith recorded "Reefer Man" in the 1920s.

Whitney Balliet, a typical writer on jazz matters, has asserted that "Jazz musicians have smoked marijuana since the twenties, and they have created endless euphemisms."[66] Neither Balliet nor any other such writer, however, has offered any proof that the jazzmen "created" such terms, although they do offer abundant evidence that the musicians have *used* the words. Balliet gives a typical list:

charge
weed
Mary Jane (cf. Spanish Mari(a) Juana)
muggles
mootch
boo
hemp
gage
panatela
pot
vonce
tea
stash
grass
reefer
stuff
roach

While earliest use by jazz musicians could be an argument in favor of Black origin of the terms, earliest use by pimps could not. (I.e., it can be argued that the first jazz musicians were Black but not that the first pimps were.) A text like Iceberg Slim's *Pimp* contains quite as abundant a list of narcotic terms as anything contained in the jazz works. Although the work is quite recent, the terms appear to have been around long enough in the vocabulary of prostitution to have been completely naturalized. As undoubted co-members of the "rackets" or "hustles"—where jazz and the blues are arguably only accidentally associated with them at all—the narcotics trade and prostitution have a kind of commensal relationship. Robert Beck ("Iceberg Slim") claims a certain benefit from cocaine: It was being constantly under the influence of that narcotic that allowed him to acquire his reputation for an "icy" demeanor, apparently a requisite for survival in the world of whores and pimps. His earliest mentor in "the life" bluntly informs Iceberg Slim that a pimp cannot be always smiling.[67]

There are, in the glossaries to Beck's *Pimp* and Milner and Milner's *Black Players,* as in the "jazz" glossaries, a fairly large number of terms relating to narcotics. The Glossary to *Black Players,* for example, has *jam* "cocaine" and *joint* "marijuana cigarette," in a quite short list. *Pimp* contains constant references to *girl* "cocaine," a term not frequently encountered in any of the glossaries, along with a great many of the more commonplace terms. None of these turn up in Gonzales' Gullah glossary, in the lists provided in Harrison's 1884 "Negro English," or in E. C. L. Adams' Glossary to *Nigger to Nigger.* Under the circumstances, there seems to be no reason to believe that these terms, or any of those for heroin *(smack, shit, horse)* originated either with jazz musicians or with pimps who happened to be Black. They came to both groups through general inner city argot.

The reason why such terms are so readily adopted into ghetto argot seems obvious. Both the Black community and the narcotics pushers had, for very different reasons originally, a pressing need for a wide range of disguise terminology. The Blacks' need stemmed from resistance to slavery and its sequel, the pushers' from evasion of legal authorities. Although the two groups of terminology did not have the same origin or exactly the same function, they mixed rather easily because the social functions overlapped to a great extent and because both population groups (Blacks and hustlers) were experienced in picking up whatever argot happened to be around. Each group found some value in "dramatic low status assertion," including the use of what certain authority figures would regard as "bad" English.[68]

A phrase like *turn on* "engage the attention of, incite the enthusiasm of, make an addict of" (if it was originally of the narcotics trade as Robert Gold asserts in *Jazz Talk*) had a more useful musical life than some of the other terms that either originated with or could be associated with drugs. To be *turned on* to, say, Charlie Parker could be the most important event in a musician's or fan's life. The opposite is *turned off,* which perhaps (as Gold claims, with as little real evidence) came from a radio dial but which acquired a deeper meaning as the antonym to *turned on. Shit* "heroin" was widely used by addicts, but *shit* in a metaphorical sense has a long and diverse history in English, and it would be hard to prove that all of them came from the narcotics trade. *To get your shit together* "to achieve a desired set of professional patterns or behaviors" was useful in the language of the jazzmen (and of the pimps, although the latter seem to have preferred *get your game together*), but there is no proof of anything more than parallel development, with later coalescence, to the use of the term in the narcotics trade.[69]

For reasons like these, it seems that the world is oversold on the importance of the hustlers' terminology to the Black lexicon. Especially among rural Blacks, there may be very many who speak Black English without being proficient in this vocabulary. This is not to deny the importance of the lexical items for those Blacks in inner city situations who are thoroughly familiar with them. Herbert Foster's claim that "the heavy thing in the Black community is the con and conversation"[70] is true for the kind of inner city teenager who is a "problem" in the schools—and Foster's reiterated recommendations that the teacher learn to communicate in the argot are well founded. It should not, however, be assumed that the dictionary of Black English would be formed exclusively, or even primarily, of such elements.

We do not expect, a priori, the Black population to have any large store of expressions for techniques of architecture or of engineering, all that is technical and not "folk" about those fields having been acquired from whites. (It is probable, too, that there is little African influence on terms for building houses since the owners often dictated the styles. It is striking to look at the French housing on Martinique and the Dutch styles on Curaçao and to realize that the "intimate" folklore of the two populations has a great deal in common.) We forget all too easily that the Black initiation into vice and the rackets came from whites, at least insofar as its New World manifestation is concerned. We may have been solicited by a Black prostitute on Times Square, or we may have read a fascinating book about a Black pimp. This does not mean that those are characteristically Black occupations. The "folk" Black of rural America is much more likely to have an acquaintance with the root-work conjure terminology or that of the church than he is to know the words treated immediately above. Where the terms are in his active vocabulary, there is a strong chance that they are reinforced from some other domain.

6

The Problem of "Slang" Versus That of a Genuine Black Lexicon

IT HAS become a matter of general, international knowledge that Black Americans have their own characteristic words and expressions and that those usages have strongly influenced the language of American teenagers. Such knowledge makes virtually obligatory a discussion of those words and phrases. It is necessary to consider, also, the most familiar statement of all about that vocabulary: It is "rapidly changing" and therefore "cannot be captured on paper." This would be a severe misfortune for one proposing a dictionary of the Black English vernacular, but it does not seem to me an irrefutable argument.

In the first place, what changes so rapidly is generally the argot of the rackets, "Black" only because of the socially disgraceful coincidence that American society has forced a disproportionate number of Blacks into such activities. That is what changes virtually from month to month so that, in one famous statement, the policemen trained to infiltrate vice gangs can be spotted because they use last month's—or last week's—slang. Even in that domain, however, change is not absolute either in meaning or in speed of operation. To take one simple example, *man,* as a term of address, may be a reaction against the hated appellative "boy." When *man* has been adopted by the teenyboppers, *dude* comes in. Now that every teenager is saying *dude,* the really hip Blacks probably have some other term of address. It is safe to predict, however, that they will never get back to *boy.* Thus, there are some limitations to what will happen, and some hope for the descriptivist.

In a recent book, Herbert L. Foster has stressed the importance of the Black lexicon—essentially lower-class usage or "argot" as far as he is concerned. Combining the approach to discourse strategies of Labov and Kochman and the ethnic slang approach well known to certain inner city studies since the days of Dan Burley,[1] Foster finds many possibilities of misunderstanding. In fact, he sketches out dozens of what he calls "Realities" involving such failures in communication between inner city public school students and their non-Black teachers. His assertion about the function of slang, based on his own experience in inner city schools and on the research in his own dissertation, is strong enough to merit repeating:

In the main, linguists have concentrated on studies dealing with phonology and syntax in their investigation and research of Black English. Studying phonology and syntax may be important for reading materials and certainly an accepted scholarly endeavor in its own right. However, in the primary area of communication in general, and of classroom communication in particular since it so vitally influences the affective domain and teaching and learning, this author argues that lexicon is of equal if not primary importance as an area of study.[2]

Foster goes on to report:

Indeed, Black males scored highest in my Jive studies and are the group with whom the schools are having the greatest discipline problems. And remember, in crisis, just when communication is necessary for resolution of differences, the principals often revert to their more familiar and secure language code.[3]

"More familiar and secure language code" is not, however, what we usually mean by "jive" or "argot." While Foster's test results may not be in doubt, something about the interpretation is.

At the opposite pole, in a sense, to the collectors of argot are a group of writers on Black usage who depend heavily on their intuitions (usually expressed in terms of *soul*) as members of the Black community. These assertions generally are in the nature of statements about semantics as opposed to external form. Probably the most famous of all is LeRoi Jones's claim about a Black preacher:

I heard an old Negro street singer last week, Reverend Pearly Brown, singing "God don't never change!" This is a precise thing he is singing. He does not mean "God does not ever change!" He means "God don't never change!" . . . He is telling you about the extraordinary order of the world.[4]

This statement is quoted with strong approval by a more academic writer, Geneva Smitherman, who objects to the omission of lexicon from linguistic studies of Black English and asserts that "language does not exist in a vacuum but in the sociocultural reality."[5] As conventional as Smitherman's statement is, it remains a just criticism of such works as my *Black English.* The trouble is, as always, with the exact nature of what has been left out and how it can be handled. Jones, particularly, is entitled to speak with authority about the language, culture, and feelings of Blacks. There is a strong inclination to believe what he has said about *God don't never change* and *God does not ever change*—that is, to grant the point that more than Labov's negative concord rule differentiates the two utterances.[6] But a lexicographer of any degree of formality needs something more definite to go on.

With Richard Long's " 'Man' and 'Evil' in American Negro Speech"[7] we begin to get onto firmer ground without, as it happens, loss of in-group intuition. Long demonstrates that the two terms actually function differently in Black English.

Man actually serves for direct address (a now-commonplace fact not so well known in 1959), although not "in the speech of women, except for the déclassée." The "déclassées" women, we would say, are the relatively unassimilated speakers of "deeper" Black English vernacular. But Long contributes more to our understanding when he points out that *evil,* applied to persons, means not "sinful" but rather "unpleasant, disagreeable, sullen" when used by Blacks and that verbal *she was evilling* can mean "she was brooding."

From Long's two words to a lexicon, however, is a very long jump. It would appear that some principles of lexical organization would have to be developed if the valid point is to be made that the Black English vernacular has a vocabulary store not dependent upon the argot of the inner city street hustler. Since I have frequently rejected the principle that Black English simply represents archaic white speech,[8] it is obviously incumbent upon me to develop some other characteristics of the lexicon. There appear, at this writing, to be two such characteristics: (1) compounding patterns peculiar to Black English among American English dialects but closely resembling processes among West Indian and West African English varieties and (2) vocabulary items relatively miscellaneous in nature but cognate to West Indian and West African words.

It happens that probably the best of the in-group intuitive writers about the Black lexicon, Zora Neale Hurston, has led the way in coping with the most peculiar form of compounding:

> So we have "chop-axe," "sitting-chair," "cook-pot" and the like because the speaker has in mind the picture of the object in use. Action. Everything illustrated. So we can say the white man thinks in written language and the Negro thinks in hieroglyphics.[8]

Obviously, Hurston has led us only part way toward a lexical explanation. The interpretation in terms of "written language" and "hieroglyphics"—not mutually exclusive terms, in the first place—cannot account for the relativists' principle that the "illiterate person or society thinks too—and, so far as we know, quite as well as the literate."[9] But we must not lose Hurston's insight completely simply because her linguistic and anthropological techniques are not perfect.

In the list *chop-axe, sitting-chair,* and *cook-pot,* the last seems to me out of place because it is less redundant: Chairs are "universally" or at least "basically" for sitting, and axes are for chopping (i.e., in some way *axe* = instrument for chopping) in the same way, but pots are no more for cooking than they are for storing or for carrying away waste. These intuitive judgments are, however, those of a speaker of ordinary English and not of Black English. For such a speaker, the first two seem "redundant."

The "redundant" compound is well-known in Afro-Creole varieties. West Indian English, as noted by Collymore and others, has "quite a few of these unusual formations. . . . boar-hog . . . ram sheep . . . fowlcock . . . boychild (male child), doll-baby (doll), gate-door (gate), hare-rabbit (hare), sow-pig (sow), sparrow-bird, rockstone (stone). Also deserving of mention are: too besides (besides), back-back (to go back), out-out (to extinguish), play-play (make-believe), wee-wee (tiny, wee), etc."[10] Ellipses in the preceding quote indicate omissions of irrelevant remarks that are Anglocentric or even puristic in import.

These "redundant" compounds can be found in all the Afro-American English varieties. Krio, according to Canadian Krio-ist Ian Hancock, has *bo-kyat* "male cat," *ramgoat* "ram," and *doll-baby.* Cameroonian Pidgin English has compounds like *sikru-nel* "screw" (literally *screw nail*). The Virgin Islands *Dictionary* lists *ram buck* "a male goat" and *rockstone* "rock." C. R. Ottley's *How to Talk Old Talk in Trinidad* has *boy child* "a boy," *certain sure* "very certain," *fowl cock* "cock," *goat-kiddy* "a kid," and *sow-pig* "a sow."

These kinds of impressionistically redundant (for a nonspeaker of the Black English vernacular) compounds are found throughout Black English in the United States. *Dry drought* may happen to come from a Gullah text,[11] but from Washington, D.C., we get *reading books,*[12] and from the general Black community many others like *photograph pitchure, incense temple, candle sponge, hut house, stickin' pins,* and *ink pen* (not distinguished from a ballpoint). We find hundreds of these redundant and semi-redundant compounds like *mare horse,*[13] *biscuit bread,*[14] *watah bath,*[15] *farmer woman,*[16] *lookin' mirror,*[17] *stove-heater* (not something that heats a stove!),[18] *doll baby,*[19] *infant baby,*[20] *gin liquor,*[21] *urinate water* (probably a hypercorrect derivation for the expected *urine water*),[22] *stick broom,*[23] *straw broom,*[24]—all of these quite quickly assembled from a few representative collections of Black speech.

Although these "redundant" compounds are much more abundant in the Caribbean Creoles and in West African varieties, where the Pidgin-Creole characteristics are more concentrated, there are some direct parallels between Gullah (the Creole of the Georgia-South Carolina Low Country) and the Black English vernacular elsewhere. Gonzales' *The Black Border* lists, for example, *yalluh yam tettuh,* in which *yam* and *potato* would seem at least partly redundant to most speakers of American English, in which yams are most often known as *sweet potatoes.*[26] Since they are, at least when ripe, yellow within, the term *yellow* is rather a lip-smacking kind of appreciative comment rather than a restrictive identifier. It just happens that a Negro folksong collected in Texas has the title "Yellow Yam Pertaters."[27]

That there is no really sharp break between Gullah and the generalized Black English vernacular of the United States has been a matter of folk wisdom for a long time, but the scholars have never been willing to listen. Robert Deane Pharr's *The Book of Numbers* traces the English of the plantations to Pidgin English and differentiates Gullah from other American Negro dialects because "unlike the rest of the confederacy, they were never reconstructed."[28]

Something of the process by which these doublet forms were developed is made clear through Gullah. There is the famous case of *done fuh fat*, wherein Gonzales (Glossary to *The Black Border*) regarded as a picturesque expression of the Gullah idea that an overweight person was "done for." Lorenzo Dow Turner provided, however, a sounder explanation when he found a clear African etymology for *dafa* "fat."[29] The doublet form was bizarre or "picturesque" to no greater degree than a Frenchman saying to an English-speaker *"demain*—tomorrow." Doublet forms tend to be generated in bi- or multilingual situations, as in the famous case of the Rio Grande River in Texas or the obscure one of Nido's Nest (*nido* means "nest" in Spanish), a bar in Santurce, Puerto Rico. On the multilingual early plantations, where the Pidgin English contact language was just beginning to become the native language of the slave group ("Creolize"), there would be reason to grope for a word that a speaker of some indeterminate other African language might understand, to gloss the same word in another language.

Misunderstandings like that of "done for" for *dafa* joined to the different derivational processes of the Plantation Creole that resulted from the nativization of the pidgin contact language produced a great many forms that seem "ungrammatical" to the speaker of ordinary English. Because he was in a prestige position, the user of those forms seemed to join in the conspiracy to label them as "wrong" or "bad"—or, condescendingly, "picturesque." Reed Smith's *Gullah*, for example, lists nineteen "popular etymologies" including *locus preechuh* "local preacher," *Saa'bint Day* (a "confusion" of Sabbath Day and Servant's Day), *muffle-dice* for "hermaphrodite," *nutten-aigs* for "nutmegs," and *Florida lime* for "chloride of lime." These were complicated by the fact that Gullah has a few words like the word for bullfrog that sounds like *bloody noun* (although it could not possibly be a substantive that somehow got blood on it!), and racist southern whites, placed in a superior position by the systems of slavery and color caste rather than by any multilingual abilities of their own, easily formulated the notion that the Blacks were simply poor managers of language. Paradoxically, as often is the case, they also described the Negroes as loquacious; southern white racist folklore is full of stories of how the Black can talk one into anything if one listens.

One southern white joke had it that an attractive young Black woman found herself in court but could have no respect for the judge, who was too aware of her charms. Fined for contempt of court, she explained to her friends that she had had to pay "fo' temptin' de cou't."

While most such anecdotes are probably inventions, and malicious ones in many cases, there is a certain basis for them in the actual linguistic situation. In tapes made by my University of Puerto Rico students in Samana, Dominican Republic, where a group of freed slaves went in 1840 and their descendants have been ever since, forms like *paragolized* "paralyzed" do turn up—not frequently, but they do turn up.

That not all these "malapropisms" are the inventions of malicious whites seems to be indicated by the fact that the same ones keep turning up from widely divergent sources. In a vocabulary of many thousands of words, the chances that one "incorrect" meaning would converge, accidentally, with the same word from several independent sources would seem small. There is, for example, the word *peruse*. Claude G. Bowers' *The Tragic Era,* a study of Reconstruction sympathetic to the South, put it this way:

> For under the patronage of new friends from the North, the negro had already become the equal of the white in blue and the potential master of the man in gray. Even their vocabulary had expanded in the light of freedom. "Where are you going?" asked a white man of a neighbor's former slave as he was striding militantly down the road. "Perusin' my way to Columbia," he replied, for "peruse" had a royal sound.[30]

Ambrose Gonzales' Glossary to *The Black Border* suggests another interpretation: *peruse* is a verb, at least in Gullah, meaning "to saunter, walk in a leisurely manner." Gonzales, often cursed for a racist because a few casual passages in his books can be interpreted as examples of "thick lips" theory, turns out to be more of a linguistic relativist than his detractors allow.

Neither Bowers nor his source suggests that this "perusing" Black was a Gullah, however. If one believes that Gullah is and always has been completely separate from the Black English vernacular outside the Low Country, then the relativism is vanquished, and this *perusing* becomes a malapropism again.

Fortunately for those of us who are temperamentally unable to give in to linguistic absolutism even when it is authoritatively advocated, there are many scraps of Gullahlike usages in the Black English vernacular far from the Sea Islands—enough to give some strong support to the theory that Gullah is no unique creation but the survivor of a generalized Plantation Creole. A perhaps trivial example can be found in the case of "Do!" as an interjection:

> "Do?" This one word was the huge man's [named Makepeace, and not a Gullah] masterpiece of a catchall. It served as exclamation and assent, epithet and word of encouragement.[31]

Do is, of course, the workhorse of English auxiliaries and has become linguistically famous in the do-support rule of the transformationalists. This is, however, a usage quite different from any generated by that rule, and it proves to be something more than a casual aberration on the part of a character in a novel (or of the novelist).

In Gullah, the form seems to constitute an extrastrong reinforcer for an imperative:

> "Do, Buh Wolf come lif' dis yuh log fuhm puntop me."[32]

And it occurs in the negative:

"Do, Buh Wolf, do don't trow me in de briar patch. . . ."[33]

This negative imperative is especially bizarre to ordinary English ears, but it is corroborated in the works of bilingual (or, if you will, bidialectal) novelist Julia Peterkin:

"Do, Jedus! Don' let Joy dead!"[34]

"Do, Jedus!" is, of course, one of the familiar interpolations of the congregation at a Black sermon (almost as widely used as "Sho nuff!"), and Peterkin's use of the term for a character who has just been engaged in an emotionally religious conversation lends credence to her use of the term.[35] Peterkin further attests a purely exclamatory use of "Do, Zeda!" where the phrase is a reply to a satirical thrust but is not an imperative.[36]

Another Pidgin/Creole grammatical structure preserved as an expressive tag in the Black English vernacular is the one embodied in Louis Jourdain's popular song of the 1930s, "Is You Is or Is You Ain't My Baby?" A double emphatic, double negative question, the structure would be rare under any circumstances, but several Black American informants have vouched for its authenticity, and it occurs in a line by Don Lee:

> change: is us is or is us ain't. now change.
> for the better change.[37]

Apart from the complexity of the double emphasis, the structure is very well known in Creole varieties. Jamaican has:

Is *dye* dem *dye* it 'They *dyed* [very emphatically] it!'[38]

And from Trinidad we get:

> Calypso gal is good a lot,
> Is what you see is what she's got.[39]

With preposed *na* rather than *is* (which must have replaced it during de-Creolization), the construction is very widespread in West African Pidgin English.[40]

Bits of Gullah- or Creole-like vocabulary occur rather frequently in special vocabularies of inner city groups, or occurred there in the recent past. Dan Burley attests *yam* "eat" as Harlem jive, but it clearly has some relationship to *nyam* or *nyam nyam,* the most strikingly West African of the terms of the Caribbean Creoles and Gullah.

An even more striking case of lexical bizarreness (from the point of view of other English dialects) is in the Black use of *soon* as a modifier of a noun, even, sometimes, of a human noun. Joel Chandler Harris' stories attest Brer Rabbit was *a mighty soon man,* and Gonzales glosses *soon man* as "a smart, alert, wide-awake man." *Wide-awake* is virtually equivalent, of course, to *early;* with a nonhuman noun, the modifier does mean "early"; an 1891 article reprinted by Jackson reports:

> . . . on the tongue of a . . . darky . . . an early breakfast is "a soon brekkus."[41]

Harrison's 1884 "Negro English," in a generally dismal collection of "Specimen Negroisms" that could not possibly be all Black English, reports:

> De soones' nigger on the plantashun 'the cleverest' etc.[42]

The *Dictionary of Jamaican English,* which cites Harris (almost its only comparison to continental Black English), has *suun-man* "clever, smart +man." In the blues, the meaning "early" seems to predominate, although not in exactly the ordinary English distribution:

> Soon in the morning, you'll get scrambled eggs.[43]

Phrases like *cut he eye* (sometimes *yeye*) and *suck he teeth (teet')* are exceedingly common among Afro-American dialects, including those in the United States. The *Dictionary of Jamaican English* records *cut-eye* "The action of 'cutting' one's eyes at someone as an insult or mark of scorn," and the *Brief . . . Dictionary of the Everyday Language of Virgin Islands Children* calls *cut eye* a verb, "an indirect insult effected by looking at a person from a sharp angle." Zora Neale Hurston supplies the Black American English vernacular use in an equivalent meaning:

> . . . gave him a top-superior, cut-eye look.[44]

Suck one's teeth is an even more widespread phrase for indicating one's scorn. The *Dictionary of Jamaican English* glosses it "The action of 'sucking' one's teeth at someone as an insult or mark of scorn" and gives no earlier citation than 1947—a strange fact since that dictionary proposes to limit itself to forms first attested in Jamaica (or current there after they were obsolete elsewhere), whereas *suck one's teeth* can easily be found both earlier and later than the Jamaican citation. It happens that Ambrose Gonzales' 1922 citation from *The Black Border* ("suck 'e teet':—a contemptuous gesture frequently indulged in by the fair sex") is earlier. Puckett's *Folk Beliefs* also constitutes an earlier attestation of the form than 1947.[45] A later attestation is provided by Toni Morrison:

Sula stirred a little bit under the covers. She looked bored and she sucked her teeth.[46]

The girl in this case is a promiscuous female confronted by the wife of one of her lovers and scornful of a woman who would get so upset over a mere man. Iceberg Slim has a character showing his contempt in a similar fashion: "He sucked his teeth noisily."[47] The term cannot be a Jamaicanism, *pace* the editors of the *Dictionary of Jamaican English,* since it occurred in Black English in the United States before their first attestation for Jamaica, and it cannot be an archaic form surviving in Jamaica alone because there are later attestations from the continental United States. Like many other such idioms, it is simply Afro-American.

One of the more interesting such idioms is a term familiar to those who have studied inner city slang, *ace boon coon. Ace* "the first, the greatest" poses no problem, and *coon* is a well known if now somewhat disreputable term of address,[48] but *boon* is a problem. The phrase is known, however, even in rural areas like Natchitoches Parish, Louisiana, where a lot of ethnic slang phrases are not in regular use. The context favors a semantic reading "good" for *boon,* and therefore a Romance language origin. The latter poses a small problem, but the former poses none at all. *Boen* (the same word, but with a Dutch spelling) means "good, well" in the Creole languages of Surinam, and the phrase is part of the Afro-Creole tradition. The Romance language look of the word can be explained by the theory that the nautical lingua franca that was the granddaddy of all the Creoles, Afro or otherwise, was Romance-based.[49]

In view of these continuities, the change in the Black lexicon has not been so rapid as the popular imagination would have it. There is, in fact, about as much stability as in any other language variety, if other than "argot" evidence is admitted. This point can be illustrated by many words and expressions, but the term *boss,* not an Africanism but in very early use in the language contact situation that made Pidgin English an important part of the verbal repertoire of West Africans taken to English-speaking islands and plantations. The 1854 *Kurzgefasste Neger-Englische Grammatik (Short Grammar of Negro English)* done by German missionaries as a tool for their workers in the field reports:

Auch drucken die Neger den Superlativ gern durch basi, Meister, aus z.B., da basi von dem dinaar, der erste Saaldiener.[50]

The phrase *a boss waiter* might seem strange to a hip inner city Black today because of the changes in attitude associated with militancy. But the Washington, D.C., Black who named his car Boss Bat[51] was expressing a superlative quite as surely as the plantation slaves were. *Basi* still performs the same function in the

English Creole of Surinam, attesting to the Afro-Creole background. For the plantation slave, as for some southern Blacks today, the employer tended to be designated not with the superlative *boss* but with *bossman*. Lee gives an example:

> Rev. Heck Mosby . . . pastor of one of these little store-front churches on Beale . . . had a way of opening with a prayer that began, "Oh Lord, Oh Boss man. . . ."[52]

Zero derivation, a process discussed primarily in Chapter One, is another Afro-Creole process that makes for subtle and confusing differences in the Black English vernacular word stock. The adjective *full* becomes the verb *full,* not *fill,* in the Black English vernacular basilect, the "deepest" form outside Gullah—as it does, of course, in Gullah. There is no verb *leave* in either Gullah or the basilect, *lef'* forming the verb base ("present tense," in some terminology that does not really apply to these varieties). This apparent marking for past tense confuses some investigators, who thus overestimate the amount of past tense marking made obligatory by the Black English vernacular grammar.[53] A Gullah sentence like:

> Him de gwine lefam 'He/she is going to leave him/her/it'

makes the relationship clear, in that variety at least.

Failure to understand about Black English grammatical and lexical differences has resulted in a large set of misimpressions in the folklore. Some of the forms that Americans, especially southern whites, believe to be Black may come from minstrel shows and their electronic successors, radio and television, but in many cases, that origin seems unlikely. Relatively technical usage seems about as free of that taint as anything could be. Dentists report, for example, that their poor Black patients speak of upper and lower *racks,* and optometrists say that the same kind of patient speaks of the frames of his glasses as having two *legs.* Both groups, quizzed further, typically assert that there are many such reportable usages but that they "can't remember them right now." Ethnic slang, or "jive talk," almost never figures in such reports.

For the person whose primary interest is social dialectology rather than the problems of the inner city schools, there is another reason for not giving exclusive attention to ethnic slang. Blacks in many parts of the United States (like, for example, Natchitoches Parish, Louisiana) use the zero copula, *be*-durative, non-redundant plural and past tense, and many other typically Black English vernacular structures—as well as having many of the lexical characteristics discussed in this book—without being such masters of jive talk as Foster's hip inner city teenagers. In a study by Sharon Douglas, with an arbitrary list of 680 terms from Major's *Dictionary of Afro-American Slang* and a few Natchitoches Parish informants, only 45 words were found to be both known and used by the informants; 234 others were known passively; and 401 were completely unknown. The slang words both known and used included words of doubtfully exclusive Black distribution like *blade* "knife," *bread* "money," *back off* "Stop!," *chick* "young woman." It also included *banjo,* an undoubted Africanism that has by now spread into General American English and is likely to be known by at least as high a percentage of whites as Blacks. The social dialectologist would like to consider the speaker whose language is recognizably Black, and who has the syntactic features but is not quite such a master of the ethnic slang, as still a speaker of the Black English vernacular.

This is not to contest what Foster has to say about the educational value of the teacher's knowing the slang if he must deal with inner city adolescents. But Black speakers in rural Louisiana and Mississippi have just as much right to special educational attention as those in inner city New York, Washington, and Detroit—even if the ethnic slang does not so abound in the rural areas. Furthermore, as Stewart has consistently pointed out, the greatest educational hope for pedagogical and textbook reform lies in the early grades, where children have not been preoccupied, so far, with slang. For these reasons, what will greatly benefit a teacher of inner city teenagers will not necessarily do so much for a teacher of rural southern first-graders.

I have already made the point several times that I consider a great deal of "Black" slang to belong to the rackets (pimping, prostitution, narcotics hustling, general underworld activities) rather than to the Black community as such. If that is true, then my historical claim in *Black English,* "Black English like any language deserves a dictionary of its own,"[54] seems to rest on shaky ground. The obvious reply is that the Black English vernacular lexicon, although overlapping in many areas, is by no means exclusively that "argot" or "ethnic slang." It is not quite the case that none of the inner city slang belongs in the historically justified Black lexicon. Words like *hip, cat, jelly (roll),* and such are, as Dalby has shown, probable Africanisms and should be included.[55] But most of the argument must rest on the demonstration that the Black English vernacular has its own word stock outside the terms that have become familiar to the general public from movies like *Super Fly* and from television programs like "Police Story."

7

Root Work and Conjure

IN ONE form or another, dozens of works on Black American folklore record this proverb:

> White man got the money and education;
> Black man got Gawd and conjuration.[1]

It is important to point out that this quotation comes from the work of an outstanding Black folklorist; otherwise, it might, with good reason, be suspected that it was one of the many racist statements about "superstitious darkies" that can easily be found. Not by any stretch of the imagination, of course, can *conjure* be called an Africanism; yet the importance of the term at the deepest level of Afro-American culture is great enough to make one feel that Harrison's "Specimen Negroism" *to conjure fokes* "to bewitch" in his 1884 article is in some sense accurate.[2] Numerous works testify to the importance of conjure and root work in Black American as in Caribbean behavior patterns. The terminology of this domain differs more from mainstream language than does that of any other activity.

The fragmentation of Afro-Creole culture in the United States, because of the long subjugation to European-derived culture, has resulted in the obscuring of certain semantic properties in Black American English that would otherwise be transparent. In both Haitian and U.S. Black intimate culture, for example, tale patterns (discussed in the next-to-last chapter) have close historical links to the systems of conjuration and root-work magic that are associated with the terms *voodoo, hoodoo,* and the like. Except for the two terms just cited, which may have been most immediately transmitted from Creole French in Louisiana, these terms seem to be gone. But the Caribbean *obia* or *obeah,* in the compound *obiah man,* is attested from 1763 and listed in the *Dictionary of Americanisms.*[3]

Anansi, the spider hero of Surinam, is linked in name as well as in more important characteristics to the web-god of West Africa who links earth and sky. Ti Malis in Haiti and Brer Rabbit in the United States do not share the name with Anansi, but even titles of blues lyrics like Bessie Smith's "Spider Man Blues" reveal that most of the links are still present in one form or the other.[4] Furthermore, the body of tale motifs and even of complete tales is strikingly similar. Anansi, in Jamaica, has a "strong" manifestation that reveals his religious origins in a way that the mildly diverting tales do not regularly do. (These manifest, of course, the "weak" side of his changing character—in a way strikingly like that of Dionysus in Greek myth.[5]) A few collections, like Owen's *Old Rabbit, the Voodoo,* show how clearly the religious linkage has always been and how readily it combines with other systems of mythology like that of one American Indian group.

Conjure was one of the African cultural survivals very early noted in the new world. James Grainger's 1763 poem "The Sugar Cane" reported, for example, that the early hoodoo, or obeah, men:

> . . . carried about with them a staff, which is marked with frogs, &c. The Blacks imagine that its blow, if not mortal, will at least occasion long and troublesome disorder. . . . As in all other countries, so in Guinea [the term, in eighteenth-century English, for Africa, especially West Africa], the conjurers, as they have more understanding, so are they almost always more mighty than the common herd of their deluded countrymen, and as the negro-magician can do mischief, so they can also do good on a plantation, provided they are kept by the white population in proper subordination.[6]

The conjure men were an important concern of slaveowners:

> Luckless he who owns
> The slave, who thinks himself bewitched, and whom
> In wrath, a conjurer's snake-marked staff hath struck!
> They mope, love silence, every friend avoid,
> They inly pine, all aliment reject.[7]

The poem goes on to tell how fern root, old teeth from the skulls of white men, lizards' skeletons, serpents' heads, all mixed with salt water from the spring:

> Are in a phial poured; over these the leach [i.e., doctor]
> Mutters strange jargon and wild circles forms.
> Of this possest, each Negro deems himself
> Secure from poison; for to poison they
> Are infamously prone; and armed with this,
> Their sable country demons they defy,
> Who fearful haunt them at the midnight hour,
> To work them mischief. This, diseases fly.
> Diseases follow: such its wondrous power!
> This o'er the threshold of their cottage hung,
> No thieves break in; or, if they dare to steal,
> Their feet in blotches, which admit no cure
> Burst loathsome out; but should its owner filch,

As slaves were ever of the pilfering kind,
This from detection screens; so conjurers swear.[8]

It is important to note how early these charms and other conjure practices were reported among the slaves, for it is easy to claim that the "superstitions" of the Black population are completely European in origin. Anthropologist and Afro-Americanist Norman Whitten, in an early statement that he might no longer support, even claimed that it was the symbolic system of the English language itself that prevented the carry-over of any African beliefs into the United States![9] As this book attempts to show, there is more complexity to certain varieties of the English language than Whitten's linguistic sources were willing to acknowledge. There is also, as this chapter will demonstrate, much that the Black English vernacular shares, especially in the domain of conjure, with French Creole of Louisiana. It is certainly arguable that the religious practices surviving from Africa (with, certainly, other admixtures) influenced the nature of the symbol system that is the Black English vernacular.

Despite the retention of the religious associations in Surinam and probably in Haiti, conjure in the United States (as in Puerto Rico and many other of the more "touristy" of the Caribbean islands) has been separated from religion and functions mainly as a kind of magic aimed at healing. Its practitioners may be revered, and some of them, like Marie Laveau in New Orleans, may be accorded relatively lasting fame. But one must look at the historical connections in order to realize how many similarities there are in this domain between the Black community in the United States and Haiti.

Since whatever is common to the two traditions (American and Haitian) may suggest derivation from Africa, rather than one of the two deriving from the other, it would not be surprising if there were virtually no direct verbal parallels. (Because, however, the same New World and maritime Pidgin English that figures in the history of the English Creoles of Surinam was used on the slave plantations of the United States, much more direct resemblance would be expected between those two.) Even between Haitian French Creole and Black American English, however, there are some semantic, if not phonological, parallels. Most notably, the Haitian voodoo celebrant is called the *chwal* "horse" of the spirit; his possession constitutes being "mounted" by the *loa*. American Negro conjure lore has a great deal about the riding of a possessed person as though he were a horse, with obvious syncretism to the European pattern of the incubus:

A witch is something that comes to your bed after you lays down and he rides you. . . . Some people call them nightmares now. When you are in bed asleep they get on you and bear on you. They ride horses too and tangle the manes.[10]

Because of the similarity to European witch lore, most investigators have dropped the matter—having discovered, probably, what they wanted to conclude from the very beginning. In doing so, they have overlooked valuable evidence from areas not so "deeply" Afro-American as Surinam and Haiti but not so completely assimilated as parts of the continental United States. In Trinidad, a "power" (about the same thing as a Haitian *loa*) manifests on a "horse" or "child."[11] In Surinam, of course, a similar term is used; the person possessed is called *asi* "horse."[12] In New Orleans, Hyatt found a Black informant who told of Saint Expedite (also Espedee, Espidee, Espedus), who "is in a horse with swords in his hand and a whole lot of snakes around him." Another New Orleans informant, who asserted that St. Michael "ain't good, St. Michael works with the devil," specified that the saint "rides a white horse."[13]

This particular feature has had an immediately obvious effect on the General American vocabulary. The concept of the deity as "riding" the worshipper, or simply as being essentially a rider, is the best explanation for the cry in church, "Ride on!" or "Ride on, King Jesus!" A phonological feature common to most nonstandard dialects (or even informal styles) of American English, the neutralization of *t* and *d* after a stressed vowel, leads to the reinterpretation "Right on!" the now almost universal call of approval and encouragement to a speaker, especially an aggressive advocate of a somewhat unconventional position. Andrews and Owen give a lively account of how the term "has been taken out of the church and put on the street," but characteristically ignore the conjure associations.[14] Carl Carmer recounts the secularization, in a context of dance, of the term in the form *rider:*

"Hey holy, hey holy," chanted the young buck and the rest replied, "Holy Rider!"[15]

The notion of the conjurer as the voodoo spirit's mount links even with the Negro folk belief that the blue-gummed Negro, conceived according to most accounts as being closer to the African source, is poisonous—that his bite will kill. Puckett quotes one old conjure doctor who said that such a Negro was "a 'Ponton,' a cross 'twixt a horse and a man, and ef he bites you het's shore death."[16]

In Haitian voodoo, a *loa* whose appearance at a given session is not desired is "tied" *(marré)* and therefore under control. Herskovits and Herskovits, in *Suriname Folk-Lore,* point out that a jealous woman may "go to a worker of charms to find out how she can 'tie his soul,' " that is, insure his sexual fidelity.[17] This same notion of "tying" in order to enforce sexual fidelity is prominent in root-work conjure, as in examples cited by Hyatt:

. . . you got him nailed down, he can't raise up. He'll have ideas but he can't do anything, see—not anything in this world.
An' tie it tight as yo' kin git it, and she'll be tied up. She won't be bothathed wit no othah man until he [her departed husband, or "man"] comes back.[18]

In Trinidad, roughly halfway between the United States and Surinam insofar as assimilation and syncretism go, Simpson reports that:

> . . . a person may try to prevent a power from possessing him. He attempts to "tie" the god by crossing two pins or using a needle with a black thread to fasten his shirt or undershirt.[19]

It seems reasonable to assume that the association of "tying" the possessing spirits and "tying" a potentially erring lover is generally Afro-American.

In Haitian voodoo terminology, not only does *marré loa* indicate the tying of a *loa* whose appearance at a given ceremony is not desired because his devotee would find possession inappropriate but *marré corde* means "to make charms."[20] Again, Trinidad gives an intermediate concept: *tie the god up.*[21] The tying concept occurs also in Black American folk medicine: A sore throat may be cured by "tying the palate," the idea being that the palate touches the tongue to cause the soreness. As usual, the tying depends upon symbolism for its value. In most cases, a small piece of cloth is used to "tie up" a bit of hair in the center of the head; by homeopathic action, it "ties" the palate and produces the desired result. A more dramatic form of tying, by the hoodoo woman protecting Aaron Harris (the "baddest" man known to Jelly Roll Morton), is described in Morton's Library of Congress conversations with Alan Lomax:

> He got out of jail, every time he would make a kill; He had a hoodoo woman, all he had to do was pay the bill.
>
> . . .
>
> Madame Papalouse, the lady that always backed him when he got in trouble . . . discourage[d] the judge from prosecuting, and all the different witnesses have all their tongues supposed to be tied. They're supposed to tie them by lambs' tongues, beef tongues, and veal tongues out of the markets and stick them full of needles . . . [and] pins . . . an' take some twine in order to make it real secure, and tie those tongues up an' that's supposed to have the prosecuting attorneys and the judges and the jurors have their tongues tied that they can't talk against [Aaron Harris].[22]

In Haiti, the *loa* (or "saints") demand to be fed—which means, of course, that the devotees must eat for them. In Trinidad, again, sacred "stones" and "powers" must both be fed. In the United States, the important conjure phenomenon called the *mojo* (see below) demands feeding upon occasion.[23] Feeding involves providing substances like whiskey, perfumes, urine, and other liquids—otherwise a certain type of *mojo* (or "hand") will "die."

The earliest attestations provide, in this case, less satisfactory results than in other historical studies, such as the grammatical development and "de-Creolization" of Black English.[24] Most early writers were, apparently, not familiar enough with the plantation Blacks to learn much about these relatively clandestine practices. As early as 1863, Gilmore, writing in *Southern Friends* under the pseudonym of E. Kirke, cited the "conjurer's bag of the Africans" and specified that it was called "waiter" or "kunger" by the Blacks of the South. While *kunger* may be simply a variant of *conjure,* the terms *conjurer's bag* (although a significance could be found for it in root-work magic) and *waiter* do not seem to play any important part.

Plant and Animal Lore, a book published in 1899, reported that a "conjure bottle" was an article that created "much terror among superstitious Negroes"; it localized the item in Alabama. The *conjure bottle* is, according to the many statements by Hyatt, extremely important today:

> You gets a black bottle—this black bottle. You places in the black bottle what they call a King Solomon—the root of King Solomon root, then you put the love root, then you put the devil's-shoestring root in there and that Conker what they call the Conkerin' John—it is known to be the Conker of the Earth. Then, to that, you take twelve—you starts on the officers. The first officer, you will say, is the clerk of the court, the judge, the attorney, chief juryman. See. Then you pronounce on the twelve jurymen, but you drap them in the bottle what [you call] these twelve square-head iron nails—down, that's down. And after they get the 18 in there, then you drap yourself with chure head up. But this bottle is bottled up.[25]

As suggested in the materials on "bottles," the particular form of conjure associated with Black Americans is closely bound up with root work. In fact, since witchcraft and conjure are such near universals, it may be the thing that is, in the long run, the most peculiarly Afro-American. Historically, the use of roots is no accident. The Haitian *loa* are earth "gods" in a sense:

> Magic in West Africa is not an isolated phenomenon, but is closely integrated with the other aspects of religion. In Dahomey magic charms are sold by professional workers of magic, but the derivation of the powers which actuate their charms are [sic] variously ascribed to Legba, the Earth gods, and, most importantly, the "little folk" of the forest.[26]

In the New World, the "little people" seem to be entirely missing. But the syncretic pattern here seems to have involved the substitution of European witch-animals, like the black cat and especially the rabbit—little animals, if not little people, of the forest. Brer Rabbit, notably in the Tar Baby story, inhabits the briar patch—a New World substitute for the African bush. No one who has not read Amos Tutuola's *My Life in the Bush of Ghosts* or a comparable collection can possibly understand the supernatural significance of that association.

With all this African mythic background, it is tempting to think of the practitioners of conjure as priests or priestesses. Yet the typical practitioner in the United States is more usually called "doctor," although he has spells and charms for sale rather than prescriptions to make and operations to perform.

Perhaps the most common name for the practitioner is *conjure doctor,* cited by the *Dictionary of Americanisms* as early as 1891. The term is obviously not one to attract any special attention: Although he holds no degree—not even a mail-order sheepskin—the healer has a designation common in American usage, which sees a "doctor" as a curer rather than a learned man. The Caribbean term *obeah man* (or *woman*) may not be in any kind of widespread usage, but it has a history of occurrence in the United States. The *Dictionary of Americanisms* recognizes that fact and, surprisingly, the connection between the slave population in the United States and that in the West Indies when it cites Grainger's *The Sugar Cane* of 1763 as the earliest occurrence. Grainger wrote most immediately of Barbados, but he did not exclude cane plantations of the other islands or of the continental United States. *Obear* [sic] *woman* is cited from Philadelphia in 1846, *obeah men* by *Harper's Magazine* in 1872, *obi power* in *Harper's Weekly* in 1885; the *Chicago Sun Book Week* called the *sacred order of "obi"* an "almost extinct cult" in 1947. Puckett's *Folk Beliefs of the Southern Negro* described an *obi-woman* in New Orleans, where it apparently coexisted with the more Gallic *wangateur.* Surinam *wisiman* may not have been attested from the continental United States, but I heard a storefront sermon in Washington, D.C., in 1967 in which the preacher told a radio audience of his return from South Carolina, where "Dey got some wise people" and hinted of what he might have available. Hyatt records *a wise man* for "a conjure man."[27] The *Dictionary of Americanisms* also reports *conjure worker* from 1900.

The most significant name, although not frequently recorded, may be *fixer.* Hyatt quotes one informant, "This girl's mother seemed to be one of these fixers, you know, and she put these spells on this boy."[28] For the relationship of conjure vocabulary to other phases of Black culture, there can perhaps be no more significant word (see Chapter 3). The *Dictionary of Jamaican English,* which wastes a lot of effort trying to demonstrate the supposed relationship between Jamaican Creole and British regional dialects and gives no consideration to possible connections with the Black English vernacular in the United States, lists *fix* "to put a person under the influence of obeah" as a Jamaicanism, although it finds no attestation earlier than 1942.

Knowledge and the ability to "fix" are the most impressive attributes of the conjure doctor. Blacks from the time of slavery have attested their faith in the power resultant from that knowledge, according to documents made primarily by whites; and it would be absurd to think that the field hands of earlier decades and centuries did not practice the religion and use the terminology just because they did not bother to inform any whites about it. Addressed as "doctor," the conjure man sometimes even performs operations:

I saw a root-doctor cut out of a man's leg a lizard and a grasshopper, and then he got well.[29]

But the *conjure doctor* or *conjuring doc,* as one is called in at least one source,[30] performs more typically through artifacts like John de Conquer root and graveyard dirt than with knife and scalpel:

> Only root doctors can git the graveyard dirt, they know what kind to git and when, the hants won't let everybody get it, they must git it through some kind of spell, for graveyard dirt works trouble 'til it gits back inter the ground, and then it wears off.[31]

This belief about his special knowledge often influences the name given to the doctor. He may, for example, be a *two-headed doctor.* In terms of semantic features, the Black notion of conjurers and magic workers obviously calls for something additive; the notion of the blind seer, such as the Greek Tiresias, where something is subtracted from the one with the supernatural power, is obviously foreign. The term *two-headed* has none of the ludicrous associations of, for example, *two-headed baby* in ordinary English. On the contrary, a *double-head doctor* is a specially skilled conjurer. Variants are *two-headed lady, two-headed person, double-sighted person, two-facer, four-headed people*—the context in each case making it clear that a worker of root magic is involved. David Cohn, describing the Black community of the Mississippi delta, refers to a *two-headed woman* who is able to counteract conjure because of her *secon' min'.*[32] Robert McKinney's WPA project transcript from Louisiana records the use of the term, here in a pejorative sense, at a Baptist preachers' conference: "I knows what I'se talkin' erbout an' don't need no two-headed man lak you to tell me nothin." This particular part of McKinney's transcript is full of expressions of scorn for the "lower" sects who want "hoodoo" rather than Christianity.

There are legions of names for these "doctors." The autobiographical account, *Cross Creek,* by novelist Marjorie Kinnan Rawlings, reported her Black servant using the rather plain term *root man.* More imaginatively, they may be *contact workers, practitional doctors, witchcraft people,* or *interpreters.* A man may want others to call him Daddy Snakelegs, Jack of Diamonds, Doctor Buzzard, the Jack Ball Man, or Havana Man—as well as just "Doc." Iceberg Slim's *Mama Black Widow* has a Prophet Twelve Powers, who, when he went to prison, left the eponymous "mama" with "a practicing knowledge of his craft and bountiful stock of oils, candles, incense, dream books, and, of course, "enemy destruct powder." A *three fo'k man* is "just startin' out in business." A *shield man* protects others against the effects of conjure, and those who acquire his services are *shielded.* The shield (in Haiti, *garde,* in Surinam *tapu* "stop") is the protector against the somewhat more sinister worker of evil magic and, as such, fits more easily into the system associated with Christianity. Richard Manuel Amerson describes it this way:

> I can preach the gospel, I can moan and groan, I can counteract conjure stuff, and I can play my mouthharp.[33]

A take-off man removes ("takes off") the spells *put on* by others.

A woman may be a *two-headed lady, Egyptian woman,*[34] or *Lady of the spiders.* She may also be a *granny woman* or just *granny. Seven sisters* is a term often associated with conjure women, and there is a report of a root-work woman known as *Seven Sister.*

Sister is a popular component of the name chosen for professional purposes: Sister Mary, Sister Rosalia, or Sister Carrie. She may be called Madame Pauline, Madame Barbara, or Madame Chakta. The mother in *Mama Black Widow* calls herself Madame Miracle when she takes over from the Prophet Twelve Powers. Male conjure doctors also frequently choose fancy names like Zorro the Mentalist (stressing, obviously, the special knowledge required), Root Seller, Doctor Julius P. Caesar, Dr. Frizzly, or Father Watson the Frizzly Rooster. The last two refer to the powers of a frizzled—or "frizzly"—hen. Hyatt's interviewees included a Prophet Warkie Sarheed "from Ghana, Africa, the Voice of Truth." Tallant's *Voodoo in New Orleans* has Doctor John or Jack (he shifts his name often and is also known as Bayou John, Jean Montaigne, etc.), Doctor Yah Yah (the term, in the local patois, means something like "constant talk"), and Doctor Cat. White Hoss Johnson, in Goodwin's *It's Good to Be Black,* seems a typical nickname not in any way diagnostic of a conjure doctor. It is characteristic, however, that his "work" (a "hand") is recognizable since the good conjurer puts his stamp on his product. "Lawd, I'd know it anywhere," is the comment of the conjure-wise Aunt Tempie of the last book.

The conjure doctor, like the numbers pusher or the prostitute, is involved in the performance of *tricks.* To *trick* the victim is the frequently recorded phrase, and Puckett has the phrase *layin' the trick.*[35] A character in Julia Peterkin's Gullah novel *Black April,* suspecting that he is the victim of hoodoo, claims that he has *been tricked.*[36] Elsewhere we read that "A colored man got angry at a woman and tricked her by the following complicated charm."[37] And the WPA field notes for Louisiana contain the following:

> "Another way to conjure people is to follow they tracks and take up they footprints an' bring 'em. They call that 'trickin', but they don't do that much like they useta," explained a hospital inmate.

Trick, as the common noun for a prostitute's encounter with a customer, is one of the conjure terms that most obviously applies in another domain. In the long poems ("toasts") associated with Stagolee, the term can mean the prostitute herself: "I seen this trick."[38] In the sense of "a task," the term has nautical antecedents. The reinforcing function of the conjure terminology, however, gives a dimension not usually understood to the usage: A certain element of control is present, which is why the prostitute may be a trick to the pimp. The "old Gullah saying" has been recorded: "De buckruh hab scheme, en de nigger hab trick, en ebry time de buckruh scheme once, de nigger trick twice."[39] The white man can also indulge in tricks, however; some Moslem (or "voodoo") cult members in Detroit in the 1930s blamed their plight on the white man's *tricknollogy.*[40] The Badman or Trickster of the Negro "toasts" specializes in *trickeration.*[41] In Jamaican usage, in which the obeah man, like the Surinam *wisiman,* is accompanied by two duppies, a good and a bad, the latter is "a trickify one."[42]

Without an understanding of the depth of such terminology, it is impossible to comprehend the allusiveness of an "in" novel like Ishmael Reed's *Yellow Back Radio Broke-Down.* Plagued by the Black Kid Loop Garoo (from *loup garou,* a supernatural character known in France but borrowed by New World Blacks, especially in Louisiana), the white antagonist complains:

> . . . he done gone ahead and got some strange magic he's whipping on me—even trying his hand at heraldry. I got to get the Old Woman in the valley to match him trick for trick.[43]

Reed uses such voodoo symbols as the snake freely; to the reader who does not see their function, part of the novel is a closed book.

The root doctor is able to perform his tricks because of his power over and from spirits; he is, therefore, a *spiritual doctor,* a *spiritual herb doctor,* or even a *Jesus Christ doctor.* The root doctors may not be orthodox Christians, but they certainly utilize the holy names of the Trinity along with those of other powers. Such doctors are described as *God-sent people*—note the identity to a term for a preacher—or as *spirit men.* Rather than being called an *'erb doctor,* one may be a *high man.*[44]

The word *high* plays an important part in the terms for the roots and other materials the conjure man uses. High John de Conquer, with its many striking variations, is perhaps the chief of these. Tradition links the name of this root to the trickster slave John of the "John an' Ol' Massa" tale cycle.[45] Given the permeation of Black culture by root-magic practices, it is not surprising that the tale cycles would reflect the importance of that relationship.

The name is, of course, subject to many variations. The phonology of the Black English vernacular virtually insures that the trisyllabic *Conqueror* (with two *r* syllables) will become disyllabic *Conquer (Conker),* but even that is subject to variation. The name may become simply John de Conker, or it may become Little John de Conker, American High John de Conker, Old Man John de Conquer Root, King of Roots, or even Rattlesnake Conquer. Tallant's *Voodoo in New Orleans* uses the form Johnny the Conqueror. The term may be a little bit suspect, especially since Tallant's authenticity of presentation has been scathingly questioned in a review by Zora Neale Hurston, but the statement of one of the informants has the ring of truth:

> There is Big John and Little John. High John is the same as Big John; that is the strongest.[46]

The *high* element may be preserved, while the *Conker* part is lost: *High John root* or *high man.* More often, perhaps, the *Conker* element is retained with interesting variations: Southern John de Conker, Man de Conker, or Conkerin' John. It can be expanded to Old Man John the Conqueror Root. The name John itself may be varied, as in Jack de Ruler, he Conker root, she Conker root. The conqueror/ruler motif may remain in King of Roots or King of the World. *White man's conker* seems more basic than *White man de conquer* since the two are used "to conquer the white man's mind."[47]

As early as Frederick Douglass' *Life,* we have a record of a root being used to help in coping with a slaveowner given to beating his slaves. Douglass seems skeptical of the power of the root and attributes the achievement of the desired result to his own courage and aggressiveness. It may be, however, that the root helped provide that confidence. At any rate, it is noteworthy that Douglass did keep the root given to him by Sandy Jenkins, a field hand knowledgeable about things African ("an old adviser" in Douglass' words) and did retain it on his right side as instructed until the desired result had been obtained; that is, the beating threatened by his white master was no longer a real possibility. Douglass also reported, in the same passage, that the belief in the root was very common among what he called "the more ignorant slaves."

Given the historical importance of slavery to the entire Afro-American community, it is not surprising to find that charms have served elsewhere to influence whites. Herskovits and Herskovits record a Surinam charm called *Bakra opo* "bought to secure a desired job from a white man."[48] One of Hyatt's informants tells how:

> ... you kin git High John de Conker and go anywhere to the boss to get a job, they put it in their mouth and chew it and spit, and walk up and talk to this boss and spit around, say if there airy job anywhere there the boss is goin' to hire you.[49]

One of the most prolific of Black researchers into Afro-American folklore, Zora Neale Hurston, made a heroic attempt to show how John de Conquer "had come from Africa."[50] In her intuition, as in others, Hurston was probably correct; nevertheless, we know nothing about what part of Africa either the root practice or its name may have come from, and the origin of the term remains in total obscurity. Judging from the many similarities in the root-conjure systems of the West Indies, we could probably say that there is some degree of common origin. Insufficient data on the names of the West Indian roots exists, however, to permit any confident statement about the linguistic relationships. The number of roots is legion, if not infinite, and their names make up almost an embarrassment of riches.

In Hyatt's record of interviews, [High] John the Conqueror [Root] remains vague botanically, but its superior qualities are as well agreed upon among his hoodoo "doctors" as they are in Hurston's short story:

> Actually, it is a mythical, at least a very uncertain, root, identified differently according to various persons in the root-selling business or according to the particular *root worker* who digs his own.[51]

Louisiana folklore researcher Sam Dickinson, however, has a more definite opinion about the exact root involved:

> From ancient times oriental and European cultures credited the forked root of the mandrake with human qualities.[52]

Dickinson believes that High John is the mandrake root. His article points out how a Louisiana Black ritual involves the *hand of glory,* a translation of *main de gloire,* which is in turn a corruption of the Latin *mandragoras.* (The last is, of course, the source of *mandrake.*)

In the many tales about John, the slave not only manages to trick his master concerning work but also gets just about any woman he wants. One of Hyatt's informants tells of how the root "works in love" as in the case where a man's wife had left him. He acquired a piece of the root and:

> . . . bit dat off and was standing up talking to his wife and ast her did she wanta come back to him. Well he had never, yo' know, went to chewing it. [She refuses at first to return to him.] An' he spitted 'bout two or three times, see, an' say, "Well, kiss me." An' she say, "Well, ah kin kiss yo' but ah ain't goin' back to yo'." An' she kissed him. An' 'fore dat man left dere she went back home wit' him.[53]

Perhaps the most effective love charm, however, is called the *mojo* or *mojo hand.* Blues singer Fred McDowell expressed the function of the charm thus:

> Lawd, I'm goin' down in Louisiana
> I'mon' buy me a mojo hand;
> I'm gonna fix my baby so she won't have no other man.[54]

The mojo "ties" the emotions (or, at least, the sex organs) of the lover whose fidelity is to be insured. If a woman who has been so tied attempts intercourse with another man, she may begin defecating or menstruating in the very act. A "fixed" male, on the other hand, is more likely to lose his erection when attempting to make love to a woman other than the one who has tied him. Blind Willie McTell made it a basic part of a blues lyric:

> Well I'd like to love you baby, but your good man got me barred.[55]

In some cases, however, the mojo apparently provides sex appeal for the one who has acquired it, an immediately practical way of attracting attention if not of insuring fidelity:

> Everybody says she's got a mojo
> 'Cause she's been acting that stuff
> She's got a way of tremblin' down and ooh babe
> I mean it's much too tough.[56]

Sometimes other charms, too, simply provide a great physical attraction to the wearer:

". . . no woman can get him from you as long as you have this goopher about you."[57]

Because of the power of these charms, it is important to be able to recognize that a member of the opposite sex has one:

> That's the reason you walkin' roun' here, smellin' so sweet,
> I been askin' you what you had on yo' head,
> You tole me you had Banberry [from] Walgreen drug store,
> You had been to that hoodoo, oh woman, don't lie,
> I know a hoodoo man fooled with you.[58]

If a person suspects that a hand or other charm has been put on him, he may go to a two-headed person to get a *walking boy* made. Sometimes just finding the charm will help:

> My mama she got a mojo, believe she got it hid.
> Papa Samuel got something to find that mojo with.[59]

Commercial dictionaries are beginning to list *mojo* as a "southern" expression, its frequent occurrence in blues and other popular music having brought it forcibly to the attention of a large segment of the public. When the *Dictionary of Americanisms* was being prepared, however, the academic world had apparently not heard of it. Therefore, there is no evidence to indicate how long the term has been current, even in fairly general American usage. African linguist David Dalby's important article "The African Element in American English" cites Fula *moca* "to cast a magic spell by spitting," hence *mocōre* "magic spell, incantation," and compares Gullah *moco* "witchcraft, magic." Turner's *Africanisms in the Gullah Dialect* (1949) had already compared Fula *moco'o* "medicine man." Dalby also calls attention to the current use of mojo for "narcotics"; since both conjure and drugs are ways of "fixing," the connection seems semantically reasonable. The literature of root-work magic is full of the designation of charms as *fixes.* Andrews and Owen, in *Black Language,* focus on the sexual aspects:

Today it is body magic and when your MOJO is working—on the dance floor or any other place of body excitement you better "Watch out!"[60]

In spite of Fred McDowell's expressed intention to go to Louisiana for his mojo hand and comments on Algiers as the hoodoo center in *It's Good to Be Black,* there seems to be no reason to associate this term with any limited geographic area. In fact, it does not have as many French or French Creole associations as terms like *gris gris.* Jackson quotes J. B. Smith, inmate of a prison in Texas, "We use the term *mojo hand* for a guy that seems to have something extraordinary or can do something the other fellas can't hardly do, or he holds out longer."[61] In Texas, the term can even, it seems, refer to stamina while at work. Puckett reported that it was used "by Mississippi Negroes to mean charms, amulets, or tricks."[62] He cited phrases like *to work mojo* (on another person) and *to carry a mojo.* He also reported that in New Orleans *tobe* or *toby* is used in the same sense. A variation of the term, and perhaps a disguise strategy, is provided by altering the vowels *(moojoo)* or by reversing the consonants *(jomo* or *joomoo).* Since *jomo* would be identical, in dialect pronunciation, to *Joe Moore,* that is probably the sense of *Joe Moore* "a piece of gamblers' lucky hoodoo."[63]

Whether in compound with *mojo* or not, the word *hand* is an important one in the vocabulary of conjure. Dickinson's unpublished article describes the hand as "a little ball of red flannel . . . [containing] yellowed blades of grass tied together." In Goodwin's *It's Good to Be Black,* the "hand" is described as "a tiny red flannel hand, complete to veins and fingernails . . . inside [were] the tiny shavings of the dried poisonous root of a mandrake bush and a sprig of Solomon's seal."[64] Other descriptions may differ, but the importance of red flannel as conjure material is beyond question. Compare the description of the "sexy" walk called *shooting the Agate* as used by Jelly Roll Morton (p. 91). Whistling Alex Moore, quoted by Paul Oliver in *Conversation with the Blues,* sings, "She had red flannel rags, talked about hoodooin' poor me."

Like the element with which it is frequently compounded, *mojo, hand* may be used alone not only in Louisiana but in the Low Country of Georgia and South Carolina. In Julia Peterkin's *Black April,* one character says (in internal monologue):

> If April mistreated her Joy now, she herself would put a "hand" on him; one so strong it would wither his hands and his feet![65]

A Tennessee informant told the Federal Writers Project how he bought a "hoodoo hand" from Old Bab Russ, a South Carolinian who "could talk African or some other unknown tongue, and all the young bucks and wenches was mortal 'fraid of him." The term is, in short, used throughout the American Black community. And it has acquired more abstract meanings, although the conjure source can probably be seen behind what Andrews and Owen report as a meaning of *hand:* "What someone is doing, or what they have. A brotherhood password used to help keep the people together."

There are many kinds of hands, for example a *talking hand.* Within Afro-Creole grammar, this almost automatically means not a hand that talks (as it would in ordinary English) but a hand to which one talks. The owner asks the hand questions, and if the hand "quivers," the answer is affirmative. It seems likely that the verb *hand* "deceive" used in the Virgin Islands comes from this source.

There are almost innumerable terms for the materials used by root men. Few of them are etymologically traceable; only in principle do they resemble the vividly picturesque terms for magic roots used by West Indians and residents of the South American coast in places like Surinam. Much of the terminology has undergone folk etymology so that tracing to sources would be an arduous and almost impossible task. Occasionally, someone sees through the process of adapting a root name to look like an American English word. Novelist Marjorie Kinnan Rawlings, in an account of her life in rural Florida, reported that she heard her maid Martha inquire if she were making "fumble dust." Having read a book on Haitian voodoo, Rawlings thought she saw a similarity to Haitian *fombé.*[66] Individual correspondences have been noted, but not much has been done about systematic relations. My graduate students at the University of Puerto Rico, for example, felt that the conjure practices of Loiza Aldeans and other Black Puerto Ricans were in some ways strikingly similar to the rites of nearby (English-speaking) St. Thomas. Translation of root names from Spanish, however, yielded no striking resemblances to the English names.

One reason why the etymological relationships are so easily obscured can be seen in the shortening of terms like *fumble dust* or *goopher dust* to just *dust.* Pops Foster, the New Orleans jazzman, tells in his autobiography how he frightened a fellow musician who owed him money by saying, "Man, I don't want you to pay me; but wait until we get to New Orleans where I can get some dust." When another interceded and wanted to force the debtor to pay, Foster demurred, "I'd rather get some dust and turn him into a lizard."[67]

Elsewhere, we find obviously related terms like *life everlasting leaves* and *live an' everlastin' leaves;* in this case, we are naturally predisposed to take the former as somehow original.[68] The same is true of *Adam and Eve root* and *Eve and Adam root.*[69] It would, however, be pretentious to say that we understand exactly how these led to *Holy Adam, Holy Idam, Holy Eden, Holy Idy,* and so forth.

This variability is an important factor in the association of these terms with the Black lexicon. The black cat plays an important role in folklores other than the Afro-American, but terms like *black cat bone, black cat lucky bone, black cat wish bone,* and *black cat powder* are so prominent in hoodoo lore, and descriptions of the exact method of acquiring a valid black cat bone so elaborate, that one is tempted to consider an important part of the process as originally Black in some sense.[70] Nothing in the familiar European lore prepares one for the wealth of detail resulting from close examination. Approximately the same thing can be said for the importance of graveyards in general beliefs about magic and for *graveyard dirt* as a hoodoo man's ingredient. Perhaps more characteristically Black than anything else is the variability that produces *graveyard sand* among many compounds.[71]

Powders and oils are important ingredients. Madame Miracle in Iceberg Slim's *Mama Black Widow* has "instant success oil" and "enemy destruct powder" as her mainstays.[72] In *It's Good to Be Black,* the "King conjurers" of Algiers, Louisiana, are said to all "carry a pocket full of John the Conqueror root and love powder." But the total list is almost infinite. There are attestations of terms like *disturbment powdah, confinement powdah, whirlwind powdah, get-away powdah, movin' powdah, hot foot powdah, waste away powdah, stay away powdah, get together powdah, never part powdah, business powder, Red Wash Powder, Lucky Bluing Powder, Yellow Wash Powder,* and others. Oils include *Holy Mammy oil, moving oil, confusion oil, Three Kings oil, Nozoo oil, Seven Eleven Oil and Perfume, Seven in One oil, Three way oil, Logger's oil, Black Cat oil, Drawing Oil, Queen Sita Oil, Controlling Oil, Swami Oil, Lucky Rubbing oil, Oil of Rose, Oil of Geranium, Oil of Lavender, Oil of Lemon, Oil of Bergamot, Oil of Cedar of Lebanon, Oil of Cinnamon, Oil of Wintergreen, Oil of Rosemary, Oil of Sassafras, Oil of Spirit, Oil of Van Van, Oil of Verbena, Oil of Amber, Oil of Orange, Oil of Fast Luck,* and *Bombay Lucky Oil.* Roots, besides those mentioned already, include *Snake Root, World Wonder Root, Prickly Ash, Poke Root, Sarsaparilla Root, Valerian Root, Five Finger Grass, Golden Rod Root, Orris Root Powder,* and *Queen Elizabeth Root.* More or less miscellaneous terms are *hog's hoof, red coon root, java water, grains of Job, waste 'way tea, van van, blood plant, war water, devil dust, hearts cologne, devil's huckleberry bush, luck success, palm of Christian seed, Queen delight, rattlesnake master, cruel man of the woods, Angel's turnip, Devil's shoe string, plant of peace, Samson Snake root, King of the Woods, Ten Fingers, Blood of Christ, shame weed, smart weed, jimson weed, Three Kings, Three Jacks, Jack of Clubs, Hindu Lucky Mystic Ring, Buds of Garden of Gilead, Berries of Fish, Lucky Beans, Juniper Berries,* and *Horse Shoe.*

Perhaps the most significant of all is, however, *goofer root.*[74] *Goofer* is, in fact, one of the most important and problematic of all the words of conjure. The *Dictionary of Americanisms,* usually cautious about such matters, calls it "of African origin," although neither the editor nor anyone else known to me has suggested a specific African source. The spelling *gopher,* which occurs frequently, may be based on a weak rationalization. The derivation from *goofy* or *goof* "an unintelligent person" seems even more far-fetched. Since the origin of these terms is by no means clear, it is not impossible that the etymology runs in the opposite direction—*goof* and *goofy* could possibly have originated as attributes of those on *goofer dust.* They occur, although the point has no real significance, in many of the dictionaries and glossaries of jive and jazz talk—as in the Glossary to Dicky Wells's autobiography. *Goof off* "behave irresponsibly, fail to achieve a fairly simple goal" is familiar in the inner city slang that includes a lot of Black-derived words like *hip, dig, funky, man* as term of address, *ofay,* and so forth. The air of irresponsibility could even be explained as the result of overconfidence on the part of one who has goopher dust working for him.[75]

The *Dictionary of Americanisms* lists *goofer* as early as 1899 and *goofer dirt* from 1943. (The latter is, however, attested from Montana, a state in which Black terms might ordinarily be assumed to have arrived late.) Earlier uses of the terms, however, can easily be found in works like those of Black novelist and civil rights exponent William Wells Brown. His autobiographical *My Southern Home* (1888) has an elaborate terminology involving *goopher.* Dinkie, the conjure practitioner who is never actually called a "doctor," is presented as "immersed in voodooism, goopherism, and fortune-telling."[76] And Dinkie rubs himself all over with "goopher" in order to thwart a master who threatens to whip him. A wife is promised that "No woman can get him [her husband] from you as long as you keep dis goopher about you."[77] Brown's credentials are indeed impressive: He is probably the first Black author, for example, to represent field-hand dialect in fiction. Nevertheless, earlier examples may yet be discovered.

Puckett lists *goofering* and calls it a general term for conjure itself, like *hoodooing, handicapping,* or *tricking.* He points out that certain hoodoos "burn a kind of powder called 'goopher dust' " that represents the person being hoodooed, who is perhaps miles away at the time. This causes the conjured person to lose his personality and to become sick or insane.[78] A person is especially liable to being goophered when he walks over a *root-bag* or *goopher-bag,* which may weakly suggest the gopher (the rodent), but the etymological relationship is no stronger than in any bad pun. According to Puckett, *goofer* may also be a synonym for bad luck.[79] Hurston identifies dust of goofer with "dirt taken out of a grave."[80]

Of all the devices to protect one against conjure, one of the most interesting is the *frizzly* (sometimes formally *frizzled*) *chicken* or *hen.* Hurston reports that many persons "keep a frizzled chicken in the yard to locate and scratch up any hoodoo that may be buried for them."[81] She further speculates that the chicken's ugly appearance may have given it this reputation. She is quite enthusiastic, however, about the handsome appearance of one Father Watson, called "The Frizzly Rooster," and the explanation, in that context, sounds far from convincing. It seems much more apropos that the chicken used in Haitian voodoo rites is *frisé.* Thus, once again, cultural transmission seems a more attractive explanation than a simplistic judgment about adaptation and environmental factors.

One of the terms most widely used in Louisiana and in the West Indies is *gris-gris,* which occurs frequently enough in English texts, although it is usually considered to be a loan word from the variety of French spoken in the area in question. It is attested in Jamaica, although no earlier than 1925 according to the *Dictionary of Jamaicanisms.* Read's Louisiana French cites it in the noun form (*faire un gris-gris* "to make a charm") and as a derived verb (*elle m'a gris-gris* "she has bewitched me"). He cites the common association with voodoo, leading to the "belief" that it is of African origin. This belief is apparently supported by some evidence since Read cites Mandingo *grigri* or *girgiri* "to shake," ultimately Arabic *hirz acihr* "amulet of enchantment." It would, probably, have traveled independently through the Arabs, to Spain, and to the West Indies. It is quite possible that each of these routes may have brought the form to different parts of the New World, including the United States. In New Orleans, center of voodoo in the popular imagination, they were especially attributed to Marie Laveau, perhaps based on an historical person but imbued with many of the composite characteristics common to romanticization.

Also associated with French and held to be used primarily in Louisiana is *ouanga* or *wanga* "a charm." Read cites "Southwest African" *owanga* "witchcraft" and compares Angolan *wanga* "magic," western Zambesian *vuanga* "witchcraft," and Congo *mbwanga* "a charm consisting of a bundle of aromatic powder." Haitian Creole has *wanga* "charm, spell" and Cuban Spanish has *uangá* —obviously the same word. So far, all of these are African-Romance associations, and the form is popularly associated with Louisiana, especially New Orleans. But Turner's *Africanisms in the Gullah Dialect* cites a Gullah personal name Wanga derived (as are many of the names studied by Turner) from a West African common noun. Turner cites as possible sources Umbundu (roughly equivalent to Read's "Angola") *owanga* "charm, witchcraft," Kongo *mbwanga* "a bundle of aromatic and peppery powder used as a cure for headache"; Kimbundu *wanga* "poison, witchcraft," and Mende *vanga* "a war drum." The last is probably irrelevant, the associations of the others being so consistent. The existence of the term in both Louisiana and South Carolina, both "extreme" states insofar as the conditions of slavery were concerned but widely separated geographically, makes it likely that the term was distributed wherever the descendants of West African slaves remembered and practiced some of the conjuring religion of their homeland.

An in-depth study of the Black lexicon bears out the principle that language and cultural differences are closely related. Puckett had a significant insight when he wrote:

> ... the greater the departure of the Negro from the standard English in dialect the less the lore of the Negro is like that of the white.[82]

On the other hand, the greater the difference in lore, the greater the vocabulary differences. Nowhere, perhaps, is this principle so well borne out as in root-work conjure. And only in the context of realizing how much conjure has contributed to other domains like the church, music, dance, and sexual activity can we really appreciate the individuality of the Black lexicon.

8

Discourse Distribution and the Problem of Semantic Difference in Homophonous Items

> Iron is iron and steel won't rust;
> You' mama got pussy like a Greyhound bus.

A couplet like this, one of a type made familiar in justly popular studies of the past few years, is typical of what many people think about when they think of "Black language." It represents the rough-and-ready cynicism that develops from the hard life of the streets. It is characteristic of the kind of language facility now known to be possessed by the kind of inner city youth who has a lot of what could be called "street smarts," falling within the realm of what Herbert L. Foster calls "streetcorner behavior."[1] This looks like what Foster calls "lower class" or "streetcorner" culture, especially in its attitude toward sex and in its use of the typically inner city insult game pattern, and on the surface, it would seem that the "class" or "locale" attitudes are all that could be called distinctively Black about such utterances. There certainly are not any Africanisms—or even any Afro-Creolisms—among the fifteen or so lexical items represented.

Yet there are some important historical factors to be taken into account before the existence of rhymed insult conventions like the one above can be fully understood. That particular example comes from a discourse tradition that is known in parts of the continental United States as *lying;* it is, historically, a development of a typical ending formula for a *lie.* It will, however, take a lengthy demonstration to prove that historical connection. As a bonus, however, we may discover why *lie* used by a Black person does not always mean the same thing as *lie* used by a white (or middle-class Black).

Although the ending formula—to which class I am about to prove that the quoted rhyme begins—is a familiar device in many Afro-American cultures, especially in the West Indies, it is convenient to use the recorded examples made by Zora Neale Hurston in the Florida Black community that she wrote about in *Mules and Men.* These formulas, it is important to note, come at the conclusion of "lying" session tales. They look, it is true, very little like the inner city couplet quoted by Labov and his associates. The first, especially, is innocuous:

[I] Stepped on a pin, de pin bent
And dat's de way de story went.[2]

The second, at least, has some suggested sexuality:

Biddy, biddy, bend my story is end,
Turn loose de rooster and hold de hen.[3]

Reading Hurston's magnificent collection of folklore material, one is struck by the way in which the tales, most of which have clear analogues in the Anansi stories of the West Indies, are characterized as *lies*. This is, unlike the use of the same term in most white society, a good-natured use of the term that no informant takes as an insult. Asked for tales, the Florida Blacks promised Hurston "lies above suspicion," and one asserted, "ah'm gonna lie up a nation."[4] A reader might pass by this "natural" use of the term *lie,* categorizing it as a spontaneous development, if there were not so many parallel occurrences in other Afro-American language varieties.

Haiti, from which much was drawn for the discussion of root-work conjure in the preceding chapter, is again the most convenient source for comparison. In Haitian tale lore, *mensonge* (French, of course, for "lie") is used in a strikingly similar way. In Haitian, the term is present or implicit in the formula that ends most tales:

Sé sa m-t-alé wé
Yo ba-m ti kou-t-pié
Voyé-m isit
Di-ou ti mensonge la.[5]

That's what I went to see.
They gave me a little kick
(and) sent me here
(to) tell you this little lie.

The term must be said to be implicit in the Haitian tale ending because the formula, like other Afro-American tale-ending formulas, is highly variable, and most parts of it can be omitted. That is, the Haitian storyteller can merely conclude with *Yo ba-m ti kou-t-pié,* or a St. Vincent tale can end *The story end and the pin bend.* These reductions are, however, perfectly understood as marking the conclusion, at least for the acculturated listener.

Is the correspondence between *lie* and *mensonge* as tale-ending and tale-descriptive terms coincidental, or is there some key to the relationship between Black American English and Caribbean Creole? Since there are many idiomatic correspondences between the Black American English vernacular and the Caribbean varieties, the matter seems worthy of investigation. This is particularly true since insistence upon labeling the fables as "lies" in the United States and in Haiti has interesting African parallels like the Ashanti beginning formula, "We do not mean, we do not really mean, that what we are going to say is true."[6]

Within the Americas, the notion that some transmission (i.e., between Haiti and the United States, particularly Louisiana) has taken place or that there is borrowing from a common source is reinforced by the striking functional similarities of the tale-ending formulas themselves. That relationship, superficially a far-fetched one, becomes obvious when an adequate amount of data relating the formulas of the West Indies to those of the United States has been amassed. In many English- or Creole English-speaking parts of Afro-America:

> I stepped on X
> X bended
> The story ended

is observable. There is, of course, the trivial variable that the verb of the second element may be either *bent* according to Standard English grammar, *bend* according to Creole grammar (where the familiar dominance of aspect over tense makes past marking superfluous), and hypercorrect *bended.* The immediately significant factor is symbolized by X above.

This particular X is a noun, and it belongs to the subclasses of count nouns (like *man* and *desk,* rather than mass nouns such as *flour* and *milk*), inanimate nouns (like *street* and *stone,* rather than *girl* and *dog*), and nonhuman (like *sky* and *grass,* rather than *child* and *father*). For purposes of consideration within these narratives, we can add another characteristic that grammar books would not usually take into account: bendability.[7] This X must be bendable (like *rope* and *putty*) rather than unbendable (like *city* or *diamond*). In the transmogrifications of the ending tag, this X can become a large number of other nouns: *bow, tin, pin, wire.* Significantly, it can also be replaced by a compound or phrase. But the noun must always be something that is nonhuman, inanimate, and countable. It must also be bendable, even though it sometimes becomes a noun bendable only with great difficulty, like *iron.* Perhaps it would be better, when *iron* enters the formula in examples cited later, to consider that the new variation is a replacement for the one with *pin* or *tin* and that "metallic" has replaced "bendable" in the inventory of features.[8]

By the provisions above, the most familiar Africanisms in American English *(buckra, banjo, cooter, pinder, goober, hoodoo* and *voodoo,* and *O.K.)* are excluded. In the most simplistic of historical terms—direct transmission or "substratum" influence—the tale ending itself is not West African at all. Elsie Clews Parsons, one of the most important workers on Caribbean folklore, traced it to the British "nominee" formula:

> Be bow bended,
> My story's ended.[9]

That form is not, however, attested in the Caribbean folktale or in the materials from the continental United States recorded by Hurston, Fauset, or others. The most obvious changes—in a formal sense, which is not necessarily chronological, the first—are grammatical, morphological:

> De bow bend,
> De story end.

Phonological changes occur also since the usual pronunciations are *ben'* and *en'.*

The Creole verb morphology is illustrated in these grammatical forms. A verb does not have to be marked for past tense if another in its immediate environment is so marked. Looking at the Haitian ending formula again, we see five verb forms (*alé* "go," *wé* "see," *voyé* "send," *di* "say"). All of these have past-time reference, but applying the somewhat ethnocentric standards of European grammar, we could say that two of them *(wé and di)* are used as "infinitives" and would "naturally" not be marked for past tense. Of the reduced inventory of three, *alé* is marked for tense (the preverbal *t,* a "shortening" of *té,* which may well be from French *était*). The other two are not marked; or, we can say, the entire unit is *nonredundantly* marked. This characteristic of nonredundancy is striking in the grammar of Afro-Creole language varieties. It is, among other things, the source of much confusion on the part of teachers of inner city youth: "They *know* the past forms—they use them some of the time —but then sometimes they'll just refuse to mark a past tense!"[11] We can realize that the inner city child is not reflecting any kind of urban pathology when we compare lines from a Calypso by Trinidadian Sparrow like "I was thinking that I fin' " or when we look at Blue Lu Barker's blues lyric "I grabbed my clothes and ran and hide."[12]

Semantically more significant changes, however, took place in the original British "nominee" formula as it became assimilated to Afro-American culture. Perhaps the most significant was the impersonal business about bending a bow, all in the passive voice (not a very prominent Creole grammatical category, anyway), which gave way to a more personal statement:

> I stepped on a bow
> De bow bend
> De story end.

This is, obviously, much closer to the concluding tags of the "lies" reported in Hurston's *Mules and Men.* This personal approach is, moreover, strikingly characteristic of Afro-American communities; folklorist Roger Abrahams has referred to it as the "intrusive I" phenomenon and has noted its occurrence in a variety of Negro folklore games.[13]

It might be noted that the X of the formula (first represented by *bow* in the British version) must not only be bendable but, perhaps redundantly, step-on-able. We have many variations in the wording, but all of them meet this constraint:

> I step on a pin
> De pin ben'
> De story en'.
>
> I step on a wire
> De wire ben'
> De story en'.[14]

Phonologically, the first example above, with rhyme, is more typical than the second, rhyme being a regular characteristic of the ending formula. *Tin,* which will rhyme with *bend* in most Afro-American dialects) is a minimal substitution. Larger-scale replacements occur:

> And I hang my shirt on a wire,
> Until it ketch afire,
> An' dat story end.[15]

These are piddling variations, true, but more significant ones do occur. Among the materials collected by Arthur Huff Fauset in the southern United States, we get much more extreme variations relating the formula more closely to known facts in the personal histories of the users. We can get, in fact, a kind of recapitulation of the Negro migration up the Mississippi to Chicago after World War I. A Natchez, Mississippi, informant gave Fauset:

> And at that time I stepped on a pin;
> The pin bent and that's the way the thing went.[16]

A little further up the Mississippi, a Black informant from Vicksburg gave tag-ending evidence of a later stage in the migration:

> Den I stepped on a piece of tin and went to Memphis.[17]

For the last, we have no identification of the informant and place collected—a rare failing in the materials provided by Fauset. But the tag itself seems convincing:

At dat time I stepped on a piece o' tin and went to Chicago.[18]

The migratory motif in these endings from the continental United States is not unknown in the West Indies. In the Parsons collection, an informant from Montserrat is reported as ending a story:

And he hit me to one of the sidewalk [sic] of London, and fling me to Montserrat to tell this story.[19]

Once we know what kinds of variation are possible within this framework, we can recognize the same formula in a Black folksong of protest celebrating the death of Georgia Governor Eugene Talmadge:

> Old iron is iron,
> But tin it never last;
> So we come to the end of our story,
> Cause that's all I has.
> He's gone, poor man, he's gone.[20]

Iron, which is perhaps not bendable but shares the feature *metal* with tin, has entered the formula, and we find it elsewhere. In the early short story "My Brother Went to College," by popular Black novelist Frank Yerby, one of the Georgia Black children quotes:

> Iron is iron, and tin is tin,
> And that's the way the story end.[21]

The two young boys in this story are very conscious of another Afro-American tradition with strong Caribbean and West African analogues, the dozens.

The dozens is, however, supposedly a tradition of the highly sophisticated inner city. The "lies" told by the rural Florida Blacks studied by Hurston and the Anansi stories of the southern plantations are more like the Brer Rabbit stories of the southern plantations than anything to be found in the big city ghettoes. Or so, at least, we have been conditioned to think. One of the reasons we tend to think so is that we first became familiar with the Brer Rabbit stories in the works of Joel Chandler Harris. Now, Harris was a pretty good amateur folklorist, as Brooks has demonstrated.[22] But Harris bowdlerized the Afro-American tales, taking out all the sex and scatology. Put those elements back (the Surinam informants quoted in Herskovits and Herskovits' 1936 study never took them out), and you have something like the rhymed "toasts" of the inner city—which have titles like *Pimping Sam.* Or you have rhymed couplets like:

Iron is iron and steel won't rus',
You' mama got pussy like a Greyhound bus.[23]

To link this couplet used in playing the dozens to a West Indian tale ending is to play a historian's trick, and the inner city youths would probably not be impressed. In fact, they would probably be disgusted. The couplet has lost one element and no longer has the meaning "end of a tale." The element that it has lost is, obviously, inclusion in a discourse pattern that can be labeled "an Anansi story" or "a tale."

Only by following through the historical sequence, somewhat as above, could we link this inner city "sound" (another term for the dozens) to the allegedly simple, rural tales to which the ending tags are attached. The Black teenager who gave Labov the couplet would probably have been extremely scornful if asked to tell a Brer Rabbit story—or any part of one. It does not seem to have been pointed out before that direct verbal echoes of the animal tales may be found in "hip" ghetto talk, but anthropologist Ulf Hannerz has seen that the characteristic trickster like Brer Rabbit (southern United States), Anansi (Caribbean and West Africa), and Ti Malis (Haiti) is still represented in the ghetto ideal:

> Although Brer Rabbit is no longer very important, the traditions of today still deal in characters who in one way or another oppose, circumvent, or ignore the order imposed on them. The "gorilla" type of ghetto man is idealized in long elaborate rhymes (known as "toasts") about legendary "bad niggers". . . . Other toasts still revolve around an animal trickster, the monkey, but he and his opponents, the elephant, the lion, and the baboon, live in a very urban jungle with pool rooms and card games, and the monkey is identified as a pimp, very concerned with male clothing and fashion.[24]

Transforming the surface features to match those of the mainstream culture is a frequent device among Afro-Americans. Crowley was able to perceive that Bahamian "Boy Nasty" was just another name for Anansi only after he recognized the tale pattern.

Sophistication is, therefore, no guarantee that "archaic" cultural features will not persist without conscious intent on the part of those who practice them. This unconscious West Indian linkage, stemming from the general Afro-American tradition, exists even for a Harlem resident whose attitudes might be summed up in graffiti importing that the islander was an "Uncle Tom."

This disappearance of the tale ending—or its absorption into other patterns—was not a sudden and unanticipated development in the movement away from the plantation. The rabbit tale lasted longer in the South, but its gradually weakening traces are to be found along the routes of the northward migration. In Calvin, Michigan, Richard M. Dorson collected tales from one family consisting of a mother and two daughters. The mother, guardian of the conservative tradition, insisted that the girls—who were obviously a bit reluctant to use the old-fashioned tale devices, especially in the presence of outsiders—complete the tales by adding the ending formula.[25]

However that may be, the linkage to Haiti is still incomplete. The Haitian *mensonges* have formula endings (like the ones quoted above), and those tags are to some degree variable—particularly in that only a line or two may stand for the entire thing. Even in translation, however, the Haitian ending tags are by no means identical to the stepping-and-bending pattern of the tales from the English-speaking Caribbean and the United States.

In order to establish any kind of comparability, it is necessary to look at more abstract relationships. When the Afro-American culture assimilated the British "nominee" formula, it will be recalled, several factors were added:

1. The text was realized in a "Creolized" grammar.
2. The formula was personalized, the teller being introduced as "I."
3. A misfortune occurred to the teller (i.e., he stepped on a pin, his shirt caught on fire, etc.).
4. The narrator established a direct association with his audience.

The reality of the third factor emerges convincingly once a great many different formulas have been compared. In the Bahamas, for example, Parsons reported:

Boukee he started back, an' de reins broke an' hit me an' cause me to tell dis storee.[26]

The persistence of Afro-American factors across the artificial lines of European-based languages is easily illustrated in the occurrence of Boukee (usually thought of as the Haitian dupe for Ti Malis) in an English-language tale. His name also occurs in tales from Louisiana, where *lapin* (rabbit) easily gets into the English tales, but is at least once misunderstood as *La Pain*.[27]

The second factor is striking in the context of the complete tales, which are not told in the first person. The tag ending marks, in most cases, the first occurrence of English *I* (*me* in some of the "deep" Creole varieties), Haitian Creole *mwẽ*, Louisiana Gumbo *mo*.[28] The same is true of certain tales collected by Andrade in the Dominican Republic, where Spanish is spoken. Direct translation from Haitian Creole to Dominican Spanish gives *y a mi me dieron una patá* [*patada*] from *yo bam-m ti kou-t-pié;* in one particular realization, *me dejaron sentao* [*sentado*] "They left me sitting there."[29]

Since the Haitian-Dominican formula, in spite of its complete difference in terms of words and phrases, also contains the four abstract features shown for the English Creole tale endings, a kind of genetic relationship seems far from impossible. Since these cross-language resemblances do not belong to the word or sentence-syntax level (there being no apparent similarity in those respects except where translation is involved), it would appear that they belong to the level of discourse. More precisely, they belong to the underlying matrix from which a portion of the discourse (i.e., the ending formula) is generated.

Any tracing back to putative African sources must, it would seem, depend upon such abstract criteria rather than upon simplistic word-for-word equivalences (even allowing for translation). Not every African tale-ending formula agrees with that four-step pattern; the Ashanti traditional ending seems to lack the third feature of the inventory:

> This, my story, which I have related, if it be sweet or it be not sweet, take some elsewhere and let some come back to me.[30]

(Since the formula is translated from Ashanti, the factor of Creolization of the grammar—the first on my list—would not be relevant.) Herskovits, however, recorded a Dahomeyan tale-ending pattern that shares all the abstract features of the general Caribbean and U.S. pattern:

> . . . and that is why one never asks Monkey "Where is Nana Lolwe?" If you did, he would point to his chest and you would die.[31]

The misfortune is obviously here. So is the personalization (the second of my features), although the narrator is not introduced as "I."

Variation and combination with other ending formulas seem to be characteristic of the Dahomeyan endings. A second formula attested by Herskovits is:

> The words I told, which you now have heard,
> tomorrow you will hear a bird tell them to you.[32]

The first person feature is present in that version, and there is evidence that the features combine in a number of different variations:

> Tomorrow morning you will hear the same story told you by a bird, but you had better not listen. If you hear it told by a bird, you will die.[33]

In addition to these concluding formulas, there are other structural features that the Afro-American groups who call their tales *lies* have in common. Most obvious among these features are, of course, the beginning formulas. Although it might have seemed logical to start with those formulas, they are less elaborately developed than the ending tags and therefore perhaps not so worthy of extended treatment.

Haitian Creole beginning formulas, for example, are extremely simple. Jules Faine, among others, specifies that the potential teller announces his intention by saying "Cric?" and the audience, if also willing, answers "Crac!" For the French Creole-speakers of Louisiana, Lafcadio Hearn reported a more elaborate procedure:

> In the old days the Creole story-teller would always announce his intention of beginning a tale by the exclamation "Tim-tim!" whereupon the audience would shout in reply "Bois sec"; and the story teller would cry again, "Cassez-li," to which the chorus would add "dans tchu (bond) macaque." Thus the story teller intimated that he had no intention of merely "joking" but intended to tell the whole truth and nothing else—"a real good story"—*tois fois bonne conte.*[34]

The phrase "the whole truth and nothing else" seems superficially contradictory to matters under consideration here, but it is obviously Hearn's own and does not represent the tradition.

These French Creole beginning formulas from the Caribbean and from the continental United States have a meaning primarily in terms of inaugurating a tale. Their lexical meaning, apart from that function, is negligible.

In the English Creoles, there is an equally strong tradition of tale beginnings. Herskovits and Herskovits point out the two most popular beginnings for Sranan Tongo tales told in Paramaribo: "Er, tin, tin," and "Kri, kra, all men on their kra-kra." To the former, the willing audience answers, "Tin, tin, tin."[35] In the Caribbean and Bahama islands, as in the continental United States, there is another very popular beginning formula that has no significance other than being a beginning:

> Once upon a time, a very good time,
> Monkey chew tobacco and spit white lime.[36]

In addition to this formal marking of beginning and ending, Afro-American tales typically incorporate transitional phenomena. Interruption is common in Sranan Tongo tales and is not resented by the teller. In fact, a man of status may feel insulted and refuse to continue if there is no listener interaction. A typical "interruption" may be *"Bato! Mi ben dape."* "I was there [and I saw it happen that way]." Unlike most European tale-telling styles, the Afro-American stresses the familiarity of the tale rather than its originality; such emphasis frees the audience to concentrate on the skill of the teller rather than on the novelty of his material. Herskovits compared the shouted encouragement (expressing, among other things, the fact that the speaker was producing well-known ideas and therefore had not departed from orthodoxy) of an American Negro storefront congregation to the preacher.[37]

The tales denominated "lies" by various Afro-American groups have, then, a great deal in common structurally. The similarity of their content, especially in terms of folklore motifs, has long been a matter of common knowledge.[38] It appears, therefore, that we have good reason to suspect that the semantic features shared by *mensonge* and *lie* (also, coincidentally, by Sranan Tongo *laytori*) are the result not of any accidental correspondence but of true cultural transmission.

The word *lie* can be a crucial one in Black texts. What, for example, did Pops

Foster mean when he said that Jelly Roll Morton "did a lot of lying on his [Library of] Congress records." Jazz historians seem generally agreed that, while some of Morton's claims are obviously exaggerated, there is an element of what Lomax called "symbolic truth" in all of them. In some places—like a long narrative of his travels with a character significantly named Jack the Bear— Morton obviously drew on traditional lore. Could Foster's statement mean that and not outright falsehood?

The use of *lie* to designate the tale is very widespread within the continental United States. From Texas, the Black folklorist John Mason Brewer reports the case of a young man who, asked for "one dem good ole Arkansas stories," responds:

> ... my mama allus tol' me to not tell no lies, to allus tell de truf, so ah'll be glad to tell you a true story.[39]

The point of the insistence that this is truth rather than a lie is that the young man's tale cues a cuckolded husband in on the location of a lover hidden under his wife's bed. The story is thus an *exemplum* in function. Paul Oliver, in *The Blues Fell This Morning,* tells how the Black workman (presumably everywhere) "when there is nothing else to do joins his fellows to tell 'lies'."[40] And a Natchitoches Parish, Louisiana, informant explained the relationship to me in these terms:

> The first [case in which lying may be excused] is when telling a tale. Without the humorous sense that a lot of people have, we could almost forget to try to be happy. We hear jokes almost every place we go. Sometimes the joke, or the lie told, makes up the better part of the occasion.

Although this informant was self-consciously aware of the cultural differences between Black and white in her town and preoccupied with the Standard English meaning of *lie,* the existence of the other meaning in her verbal repertoire is obvious.

This particular use of the word *lie* clearly comes from the Afro-American tradition. It may be obsolescent in relatively assimilated Black English vernacular contexts. A group of young Blacks, asked by Neil A. Eddington why they never "got up and told *lies,*" dismissed the subject with "That's dead." Eddington interpreted this reaction as *"de facto* recognition of the superior story-telling ability of the older males"; but acculturation—leaving the older tradition to the older generation—is also obviously involved.[41] In the older Afro-American culture, the tale had some deep significance beyond any simple "predilection for stories," although the slaveowners who wrote most of the plantation literature seldom if ever saw beyond that "personality" characteristic. In Charles S. Johnson's great sociological study, *The Shadow of the Plantation,* an informant says:

In those days [i.e., of the "old" church] people had to go to the graveyard, and 'less'n you told a great long tale about a dog or something else you couldn't be let in.[42]

The geographic spread of these usages is, as hinted above, extremely great. Some of the terminology is obviously common to the Bahamas:

One of the most amusing devices of the Bahamians is what they term "a double lie," wherein an impossible statement is made as if the truth, followed by a sanctimonious, "If I was going to tell you a lie (or story)," and then by another even more impossible statement.[43]

This virtual interchange of *lie* and *story* (i.e., fictional or traditional narrative) has other implications for the lexicon of Black English. In Black dialect, *story* often substitutes directly for *lie,* even when the subject is lack of veracity rather than the telling of a tale: *You a lie,* or *you a story.* In Gullah, also, *story* is often used for *liar,* the phonological feature of lack of articulation of final *r* making for homophony between *lie* and *liar.*[44] In the Black English vernacular, as in southern white English, *story* is also used as an intransitive verb meaning "to utter a fiction or a prevarication."

In Gullah, *lie* includes the meaning "riddle" as well as "tale."[45] According to *Creole Drum,* a collection of Surinam Creole materials edited by Voorhoeve and Lichtveld, *laytori* in Surinam refers almost exclusively to riddles or to stories "extremely short. They can hardly be considered folktales."[46] Voorhoeve and Lichtveld are not very clear on this point, however, and it may well be that specialization has taken place in Sranan Tongo. It would be tempting to reconstruct a composite Proto-Creole form (virtually identical to the Sranan Tongo form since the pidgin stage would not have *s-* of *story*) that split in different English Creole varieties. There is, however, hardly any documentary evidence to support so extreme a statement.

It appears, then, that the word *lie* in the Black English vernacular, while virtually identical in form to *lie* in ordinary English and even phonologically almost equivalent to the pronunciation in some other nonstandard dialects, is not semantically an exact duplicate of that form. The difference will be missed, however, unless careful account is taken of the most characteristic discourse from Afro-American culture that serves as a referent for *lie.* Very many differences will also be missed if comparisons are not made to other Afro-American varieties, even though they may not be geographically contiguous to the United States, and even in some cases to non-English varieties like Haitian Creole.

There are more profound implications, however, for the misunderstandings that are acknowledged to occur between speakers of Black English and other varieties of English. The problem may not be basically in the syntactic pattern, as Stewart says,[47] or in the lexicon, as Foster says.[48] The most pervasive communicative mismatches between Black English and other varieties may be in discourse pattern. Linguists have done very little with discourse, although it is well known that it, rather than the sentence, is the ultimate unit of language structure. There is some evidence, at any rate, that Afro-American varieties (for this purpose, English and French are considered exclusively since I have no data from other Creoles) have a kind of anticipatory prestatement of one of the principal themes of a discourse, as a folktale, that seems bizarre to speakers of other varieties. The scheme would be:

Afro-Creole varieties	*"ordinary" varieties*
B	
A	A
B	B
C	C
etc.	etc.

On January 1, 1962, Abner Haynes, halfback and team captain of the Dallas Texans (now the Kansas City Chiefs) stood at midfield after the game had ended in a tie to call the coin toss for the overtime period. Haynes was Black, and Dallas was still a racist town; but he knew his football so well that he was the obvious choice for captain. He knew the advantage of having the wind at one's back in pass-minded professional football, and a hard wind was blowing from the west end of the Cotton Bowl that day. The team with the west goal would have a perhaps overwhelming advantage. The offense-minded professional football teams of the era also wanted the ball as soon as possible. It was expected that the winner of the toss would choose the west goal, with the wind advantage, and the loser would compensate by choosing to receive.

The coin flew in the air, and Abner Haynes called it—correctly. The Dallas fans confidently expected the advantage of having a strong wind at their backs.

It is not clear exactly what happened, but the opposing team lined up at the west goal—with the wind advantage—and the Dallas team prepared to kick off. Apparently, Haynes had somehow managed to choose neither of the two advantageous kickoff procedures. It seems, however, that he used his own discourse pattern to put over his choice of the west goal: "We'll kick from the west goal" (i.e., if Dallas took the west, they could expect to have to kick). The other captain, however, interpreted the statement in terms of the dominant Standard English discourse pattern. Below, *A* marks the prevailing choice, *B* a subsidiary one that is not really within the province of the team captain making his choice:

	Black English		*ordinary English*
B	"We'll kick	A	"We'll kick"
A	from the West goal	B	NOT RELEVANT
B	(we'll have to kick)"		

Luckily for the sheriff's department of Dallas, which would have had to enforce the antilynching laws, the Texans won the game and the American Football

League championship, outscoring their opponents in the overtime quarter even with that double disadvantage. But the tale is still told in football circles in Texas, and the racists still adduce it as evidence of the Blacks' supposed lack of intelligence.[49]

This BAB discourse pattern is not the AAB pattern of the traditional blues lyric (see Chapter Four), but it may be what Lee meant when he wrote about an outstanding Negro orator, Roscoe Conkling Simmons, who "set the blues to oratory . . . the same over-and-over backward movement that characterizes blues songs."[50] If discourse distribution is the ultimate determiner of meaning of a word and if many American Blacks have retained different discourse patterns from their Afro-Creole heritage—both of which statements I obviously regard as being true—then it may be expected that semantic differences between Black and white usage in American English will persist for many years to come.

9

Can We Trust Literary Sources?

WHAT WOULD seem to be the greatest possible advantage to the student of the Black English vernacular, especially one interested in the history of the variety, has proved to be a great handicap. That is, writers since about 1770 have given profuse examples of the speech of Black Americans. Perhaps the seeming paradox can be resolved by the frequently stated hypothesis that the first writers of Black dialect faked the attestations and that the subsequent writers copied that fakery. Since most of the early writers were white (slaves were usually prevented from learning to read and write), the whole problem has been complicated by the issue of racism. But pure incompetence has also been alleged.

One of the most famous criticisms of another writer's use of dialect was Mark Twain's witty attack on "Fenimore Cooper's Literary Offenses."[1] Himself a user of Black dialect in the well-known *Huckleberry Finn* and the relatively neglected *Puddinhead Wilson,* Twain excoriated Cooper for inconsistent usage attributed to a single speaker. He asserted that one of Cooper's characters at one point talked like an educated man and at another talked like a Negro minstrel. Thus, he spotlighted the primary offender against accurate literary representation of Black speech—the use in caricature—and strongly hinted that Cooper had been influenced by that false tradition.

Taken in the context of trying to interpret reports of eighteenth-century speech, the trouble with Twain's criticism is that he was apparently not aware that in multilingual or multidialectal societies—as frontier America seems to have been—people do switch language varieties in the course of a "paragraph." They often switch from "corrupt" or "broken" (i.e., pidgin or Creole) English to the standard language, or vice versa, within the same conversation. In Haiti, the most learned citizens of Port-au-Prince change from French to Haitian Creole to tell a joke; on Dominica, ordinary citizens switch from English to French Creole and back again within one sentence—for no reason that the occasional visitor can discern. Certain Jamaicans do the same with Jamaican Creole and West Indian Standard English. On a worldwide scale, this practice is so commonplace that sociolinguists have a name for it: *diglossia.*[2]

If we look at parts of Africa such as the West Cameroon today, we do find switching, Englishmen using standard English in some contexts and switching to a variety of the same language that they learned from Africans in another. A reasonably good representation of the process can be gotten from British naturalist Gerald Durrell's books like *The Bafut Beagles* and *The Overloaded Ark.* Durrell, who writes in ordinary English prose, represents himself as saying things to Cameroonians like, "Now for true, you savvy dis beef?" which, translated into ordinary English, means, "Are you really familiar with this animal?" The pidginism *beef* "any animal" (the Cameroonians in this conversation have actually brought in a rare frog) is, of course, not directly represented in the Black English vernacular. The knowledge that *simol-beef* means "bedbug" helps us to understand pidgin word-forming processes but is no more directly represented in the Americas than WesKos *sikin* (from English *skin*) meaning "body." We do, however, find some direct parallels like *handle some grammar* (reported in Hurston's *Mules and Men*) and *grammar* or *Latin grammar* for non-Pidgin English in the Cameroon.

We know, however, that Gerald Durrell has had direct contact with pidgin-speaking Cameroonians. Is it possible that Cooper took all his ideas about the speech of Blacks from caricaturing literary works and had had no real contact himself? A biographer reports, on the contrary, how Cooper had been served by Black slaves in his youth and had bought and sold them in his maturity.[3] A historian has enthusiastically praised "Cooper's realistic account of the annual festival held by the Negroes of New York in colonial times, known as Pinkster."[4] *Pinkster* is a Dutch-influenced form of *Pentecost,* and not everyone knows that the Dutch in New York kept slaves there, just as did the Englishmen who came after them. Cooper may have known something about the language of the Blacks. In fact, his Black dialect closely resembles that attributed, a few decades later, to Sojourner Truth by Harriet Beecher Stowe, no owner, buyer, or seller of slaves but a crusading abolitionist who sought out escaped slaves in order to learn how they had suffered under the conditions of bondage.

Cooper was, of course, not such an overwhelmingly important writer of Negro dialect to make his accuracy or lack of it the critical issue in a historical consideration of the Black English vernacular. Yet his use of American Indian Pidgin English along with Negro dialect, with his overt identification of Pidgin English as the frontier lingua franca, makes him a test case for the validity of literary sources. George Philip Krapp, perhaps the first historian of American English but by no means a pidginist or Creolist, inadvertently pointed up the relationship: "Similar crude Indian dialect is to be found which differs not at all from Cooper's Negro dialect."[5] Any interested reader is invited to examine *Redskins,* to which the Krapp passage refers, and to see for himself that there are marked differences. For our present purposes, the most significant evidence is that there are vocabulary differences. Susquesus, the Indian, responds to the salutation "Sago," one of the words that Cooper specified elsewhere as belonging to the frontier Pidgin

English. The Indian's Pidgin English has been mixed somewhat with ordinary English; Japp, the Negro in the novel (his name is also spelled Yop) speaks a variety of the Black English vernacular that is fairly well along in de-Creolization. Similarities would be expected in such a situation—the two varieties of English shared a pidgin in their ancestry. Differences are also to be expected: The Indian's English has probably not undergone Creolization as an intermediate stage. Since he speaks the Indian language with his own people, his English could not be expected to have "progressed" far toward Standard English. Other documentation supports Cooper's picture rather than Krapp's objection to it.[6]

How much of the literary representation is to be trusted is another matter. It would be interesting if we could be sure about J. Robinson's farcical play, *The Yorker's Strategem,* in which a Black servant uses the Africanism *trokey* "turtle": "Dem tan so, dem hab salt fish in one hand, and trokey in todder."[7] The setting for the play is the West Indies, although it was written by an American. Many of us would guess that the speech of West Indian and continental slaves was not all that greatly different at the time and that the servant's speech seemed natural to New York audiences. There seems to be no other attestation of *trokey* in the continental United States, however, so the issue will probably have to remain unresolved.

The evidence concerning Blacks like this West Indian and Cooper's Caesar is important since it bears directly on the putative geographical factors in Black English. Caesar specifically denies African birth and proclaims that he is "York nigger born."[8] Other evidence leads us to believe that, although the heaviest concentration of the Black lexicon can be found in the Louisiana-Mississippi basin and in the South Carolina-Georgia area, Negro dialect did not first come to New York when large research projects began to discover the "language of the disadvantaged" in the 1960s.

In the New York area, if we allow the evidence of Caesar to stand along with that of Sojourner Truth and the report of New York Supreme Court Justice Daniel P. Horsmanden,[9] the Black forms have existed since the eighteenth century, not just since recent migrations from the South. In more recent times, a realistic (or "naturalistic") writer like Stephen Crane has represented Black speakers in that area in his *Whilomville Tales,* most notably in "The Monster." One of the lexical forms prominent in Crane's representation of Black English is *projeckin'* "going about, undertaking." The same word with the same meaning is attested by Harrison and by Black author Charles W. Chesnutt:

"Kunnel Pen'leton did'n' neber hab no luck wid his hosses, ef he did keep hisself po' projeckin' wid em."[10]

It also occurs, in the same sense, in Paul Lawrence Dunbar's 1898 story, "Trial Sermons on Bull-Skin," in *Folks from Dixie.* The lexical evidence offers some support for the conclusion, readily formed from a consideration of literary sources, that Black English was widespread in northern areas long before the post-World War I migration—or even before emancipation.

These literary sources, even the nonfictional ones, are not, however, by any means perfect. Thomas Wentworth Higginson's *Army Life in a Black Regiment,* one of the best and definitely the work of a man with a lot of firsthand contact with Blacks, confused the language relationship between Blacks and Indians, tracing *unu* "you, plural," one of the most striking pidgin/Creole forms in Afro-American communities, to the Indians.[11] For a writer like Higginson, we may be able to believe that he heard more or less what he reported, but we cannot always accept his explanation of it. In fact, this is one of the basic conditions on the use of literary sources for language materials. The widespread use of *unu* today in Afro-Creole communities makes us quite confident that Higginson was wrong at least on that one point.[12]

One of the most widely quoted literary users of Black dialect, from a period slightly later than Higginson, was William Gilmore Simms, whose first recording of *cooling board* is discussed in Chapter 3. In his short story "The Loves of the Driver," for example, he represents the speech of two groups—Blacks and American Indians—whose acquisition of a form of English has some important historical connections.[13] His Black character in *The Wigwam and the Cabin* is Mingo (a name that probably came from the Indians), an aggressive, womanizing bully as unlike Uncle Tom as is possible. Cowing an Indian antagonist, he says:

> I make's the law for this plantation—all 'round about, so far as you can see from the top of the tallest of them ere pine trees, I'm the master. I look 'pon the pine land field and I say, "Tom, Peter, Ned, Dick, Jack, Ben, Teney, Sam—boys—you must 'tack that field tomorrow." I look 'pon the swamp field and I say to 'nother ten, "Boys, go there!"—high and low land, upland and swamp, corn and cotton, rice and rye, all 'pen' 'pon me for order; and jist as Mingo say, jist so they do.[14]

There is a minimal representation of dialect here (Simms has much "deeper" dialect elsewhere, of course), but the reader of this passage would suspect no Black lexicon in any kind of completeness—or even in the making. Those who know some Gullah might speculate about the frequent occurrence of *'pon* as representing a de-Creolization of the near-universal Gullah preposition *pontop,* but even that is not overwhelmingly convincing.

Mingo is aggressive, and his manner of talking may have some resemblance to rapping or sounding, the now well-known speech styles of the inner city. He certainly voices his scorn of any Indian who gets in his way:

> "Oh, go long! . . . How you talk, Knuckles! Who makes you better for fight more dan me? Ki, man! Once you stan' afore Mingo, you tumble. Ef I was to take you in my arms and give you one good hug, Lor' ha' massy 'pon you! You'd nebber feel

yourself after that, and nothing would be left of you for your wife to see, but a long greasy mark, most like a little old man, yer, 'pon my breast and thighs. I nebber seed the Indian yet that I couldn't lick, fair up and down, hitch cross, or big cross, hand over, hand under, arm lock and leg lock. . . . Nebber Indian kin stan' agen Black man, whedder for fight or work. . . . I woul'n't give tree snaps of a finger for any pusson that's so *re*-dolent as an Indian."[15]

Some of the grammatical forms *(for fight or work* "to fight or to work") and pronunciations ostensibly indicated by the spellings *(nebber, tree, pusson)* are familiar from nineteenth-century representations of Black plantation speech. (Mingo, remember, is a driver, a man of status, and would not speak like the ordinary field hand.) But the indications of lexical differences are scant indeed: *Ki!* is frequently represented as an interjection used by slaves in the plantation literature, and *re-dolent,* probably for *indolent,* seems like an example of what would usually be called malapropism. One would examine a very great deal of such materials before anything of importance is found for the history of the Black lexicon.

What does emerge from a consideration of such evidence is more nearly of negative value. Of the hundreds of authors who chose to represent the dialect of slaves working as field hands, Black sharecroppers, or modern ghetto residents, no one has consistently marked it as being identical with any white dialect, no matter how nonstandard the latter may be or how uneducated its speakers. Those who have represented the speech of Blacks have every conceivable level of credibility as of respect. They come from periods as early as the first few years of the eighteenth century and late enough that the first works of some of them may not yet be in press.[16] They utilize different trappings of spelling, punctuation, and so forth, to mark the differences from other dialects, but in the mass, they consistently differentiate Black speech from the speech of other groups. Some of them, like Thomas Wentworth Higginson and William Gilmore Simms, provide direct evidence of Black influence on the English of American Indians. Others show that southern white children were often influenced by their Black playmates. Not all of them handle their evidence with equal skill, obviously; perhaps even more importantly, not all of them utilize whatever skill they have to the same purpose. Therein lies a problem that cannot be ignored since it is vitally important to historical study.

It is easy to see why some members of the Black community have been angered by white writers' use of Black English: The fact that the most skilled practitioners, like J. W. Page, learned it from the slaves they owned and sold is enough to motivate anger. Even after the difficult task of factoring out slavery and its consequences, another objection easily arises: White writers of Negro dialect may write it for purposes of ridicule.

As a test case, the twentieth century's best parallel to James Fenimore Cooper might be Octavus Roy Cohen, a perhaps forgotten writer of humorous short stories and novels about "darktown" characters. He was the target of an attack by Earl Conrad in *The Journal of Negro Education* and has been referred to by Nelson in the following terms:

> . . . stories of Hugh Wiley or Octavus Roy Cohen, which borrow copiously from both minstrel show and previous works of fiction.[17]

Everyone knows that the minstrel shows used phony dialect, although some of the earlier ones might have been more nearly accurate.[18] But Cohen was in some ways a close student of the Blacks' culture and language. If he studied it from the outside, without empathy for the sufferings of the members of the economically undervalued culture, he nevertheless did study it. His wife, Inez Lopez Cohen, published a collection called *Our Darktown Press* at a time when most Americans did not know there were Black newspapers. Cohen himself, from whose collection his wife took the newspaper materials, had the archivist's, if not the reformer's, zeal. When we read his description, in *Polished Ebony,* of a numbers player selecting the "Washerwoman's Number," we can check Langston Hughes's *Treasury of Negro Folklore* and see that there really is such a number (4–11–44) and that Cohen had it right. The trouble is, of course, in the facility with which playing such a number lifts Florian out of his troubles—instead of plunging him even more deeply into them as it would be most likely to do in reality.

This is probably the one generally valid complaint about the use of Black English in literature. Its syntax is generally (or at least sporadically) correct, but its semantics leave much to be desired. Virtually every articulate Black critic has argued that the white writer ignores the *meaning* of the Negro's language, as well as of his experience in general.

Although the sartorially splendid, fast-talking, living-by-his-wits Florian is an objectionable stereotype, superficially there are such characters in any large Black community; however, if they maintain this flashy appearance with any consistency at all, they are likely to be pimps. That group is hardly to be found in the fiction of Cohen, who, writing for "family" magazines like the *Saturday Evening Post,* would hardly use terms like *whore, trick,* and *fuck.* That the tendency toward splendor of dress existed before Black men became pimps in the inner city seems to be indicated from other sources. Stephen Crane made a superficially Florian Slappey type into an impressive tragic figure in "The Monster." Cohen was not the inventor of the type; his character is, however, closer to the uncomplicated stereotype than are those of his more talented predecessors. Jamaican novelist Claude McKay, who thought "Octavus Roy Cohen's porter" was among an inaccurate example of the stereotype, himself presented a character named Strawberry Lips, "a type by far more perfect than any created counterpart." In McKay, of course, we are much more likely to find the true vocabulary of the Black inner city, terms like *fly* "excellent" and *living sweet.*

The trouble with Cohen's practices, of course, is the way he uses genuine lore for artificial and derogatory purposes— how he uses a winning hunch about the numbers game as a deus ex machina ending. We know a great deal about not only the terminology of the numbers racket but also about its social causes and effects if we read Robert Deane Pharr's *The Book of Numbers*. Even though, as Kaplan pointed out in *The Jewish Tribune* in 1927, Cohen's performance in writing the Black dialect is a bit above the level of the stereotype, the stories themselves are virtually as harmful to the picture of the Negro as the minstrel shows or Amos and Andy (Florian Slappey, who wants to marry a beautiful but fickle Black girl, tries to fake a marriage with an ugly old woman who is pursuing him and almost loses his freedom).

Sensitive observers of Negro life in the United States have always been aware of the gap between the minstrel show and Black reality. The most sensitive have made the distinction without making the sweeping assertion that there was nothing in Negro folk humor to furnish a model for such inferior imitations. Careful studies have shown that there was indeed a great deal.[19] One of those sensitive observers was Joel Chandler Harris. It is one of the crowning ironies that Harris has come to be taken as an extension of the minstrel show tradition. In an article in *The Critic* for 1883, Harris made it clear how much he detested that tradition:

> All her life, in common with the people of the whole country, including a large majority of the people of the South, she [a young lady who had written to the editor] has been accustomed to associate the Negro with the banjo, the bones, and the tambourine.
> . . . In the Negro minstrel show, which is supposed to present to us the Negro as he was and is and hopes to be, an entire scene is devoted to the happy-go-lucky darkey with his banjo.
> . . . The stage Negro is ground into the public mind, and he cannot be ground out.[20]

Far from being the sustainer of the stereotype, Harris actually tended to react too much against it. The banjo is a genuine instrument in Negro folk music, almost certainly an African invention; the word *banjo* is one of the few African-isms that even the most conservative dictionaries admit to American English.[21]

Nevertheless, one cannot by any means accept everything in the works of Joel Chandler Harris. The statement at the end of Harrison's "Negro English": "The author is much indebted to the writings of J. C. Harris, J. A. Macon, Sherwood Bonner, and others"[22] is in itself *caveat* enough that we cannot accept Harrison's lexical forms without checking them out in more reliable sources. Nevertheless, if we assume that forms are not Black simply because they occur in both Harrison and Harris, we will miss Afro-Creolisms like *er soon beas'* "a clever creature."[23]

Simple common sense is a trustworthy guide in some of these cases. In more cases, however, historical background is useful. If we know from reading collections like Herskovits and Herskovits' *Suriname Folk-Lore* and Harris' *Nights with*

Uncle Remus that some of the trickster stories in the latter are genuinely part of the Afro-Creole tradition, we may still doubt the accuracy of the saccharine framework in which a young white "master" comes to the cabin of a worshipful Uncle Remus and is gladly entertained with the rabbit stories. We might like it better if Amos Tutuola had been in the mid-nineteenth-century American South to record the tales, but he was not. By comparison to the Herskovits and Herskovits collection, however, we know that the Anansi/Brer Rabbit stories can be bawdy or scatological. We also have a quick, easy historical reason why Harris did not include any such materials: The bowdlerizing temperament of American literature in the late nineteenth century, which came close to castrating even the stories of Mark Twain.

How can the historical investigator find a substitute for—or, better put, a supplement to—the well-known sources like Joel Chandler Harris, William Gilmore Simms, and James Fenimore Cooper? The canons of literary criticism ought to be of some help: We know that Mark Twain and Stephen Crane are more responsible commentators on American life than Octavus Roy Cohen or Thomas Nelson Page—not to mention Freeman Gosden and Charles Correll, who wrote and played the parts of Amos and Andy. We know that Higginson's *Army Life in a Black Regiment* has a better claim to being a description of Blacks in the Civil War period than Thomas Nelson Page's *Marse Chan*. We know there is likely to be more lexical significance to the work of E. C. L. Adams, who fitted out his perhaps unfortunately titled *Nigger to Nigger* with a glossary, than to the works of the author of Sam Slick, who did not.[24] But there ought to be more reliable checks and safeguards.

In the long run, the best of these are probably acquired by giving strict attention to the works of Black authors, although it will not do to accord them a Crow Jim kind of omniscience. Balancing George Washington Cable's *The Grandissimes* with William Wells Brown's *Clotelle* will probably help, and the latter should certainly be considered before William Styron's *The Revolt of Nat Turner*. Better than any of them, perhaps, but regrettably limited in the amount of information it supplies about language, is Frederick Douglass' *Life*. The narratives of escaped slaves, published under the auspices of abolitionist societies, presumably reflect directly the sentiments of escaped slaves, but the super-Standard English in which most of them are written suggests some tampering with the text.

In spite of the value of *Clotelle* for its attestations of the Plantation Creole of field hands (and of the completely Standard English of the heroine, who although a slave has never been a field hand), the most important contribution by Brown is probably *My Southern Home,* originally published in 1880. The importance of the early attestation of *goopher* in his works has been discussed in Chapter Seven. Other terms, largely used by or in description of the plantation conjurer Dinkie, may not have their first occurrence in this text, but their early recording by a Black writer (and in a nonfiction context) is evidence for both their genuineness and their spread in time and space. Dinkie prays to his hoodoo deity:

I axe you to stand by me in dis my trial hour. . . . Continer dis power; make me strong in your cause.[25]

Other plantation Blacks assert that Dinkie "got de power." The occurrence of the term *power* in a technical conjure meaning collected in recent years by Hyatt corroborates this early evidence.

In the last year of the nineteenth century, Charles W. Chesnutt's *The Conjure Woman* gave us important evidence of the use of hoodoo vocabulary by southern Blacks. Chesnutt's primary interest was in fictional development and not in folklore as such; in mass, his conjure materials seem slight compared to those of Hyatt. But it helps, if one wishes to undertake the controversial project of asserting that the most deeply significant level of Black lexical distinctiveness is conjure, that a writer like Chesnutt left as extensive a record as he did. Although it is not the first occurrence, Chesnutt's use of *goophered* in "The Goophered Grapevine" and elsewhere is an invaluable guidepost to the investigator. The many references, in the collection, to "working conjure," "working [usually spelled *wukkin'*] roots," and "goopher mixtry" anticipate Hurston, Puckett, and Hyatt in a way that makes them all the more convincing.

Literary sources have long suggested a different distribution of Black English vernacular dialects than that described by official academic groups like the Linguistic Atlas of the United States and Canada. Even after Turner's *Africanisms in the Gullah Dialect,* a revolutionary work for 1949, had overturned the accepted idea of the dialect of the Georgia-South Carolina Low Country, the official point of view remained that Gullah was a phenomenon of "isolation," that the English Creole spoken on the Sea Islands was essentially unrelated to anything spoken elsewhere. Although popular sources provided grossly distorted descriptions of Gullah, they frequently reflected a general awareness that Gullah (or, at least, dialects greatly resembling it and probably influenced by it) was spoken far inland, notably in Charleston, and that many whites of the area were familiar with and probably influenced by that variety.

In 1926, twenty-three years before Turner's linguistic fieldwork on the Sea Islands became generally known to American linguists, DuBose and Dorothy Heyward published *Porgy,* a drama set in the Negro quarter (Catfish Row) of Charleston and featuring Gullah-speaking Blacks. They specified that the speech was "Gullah, the language of the Charleston Negro, which still retains many African words."[26] This was, remember, a time when the academic world officially denied the existence of the African forms in Gullah. In a supposedly authoritative statement, "The position of the Charleston Dialect," Raven I. McDavid pontificated, "Grammatically, the most old-fashioned Negro speech shows a lack of inflection of both noun and verb."[27] A certain "lack" of inflection, compared with English, is characteristic of the Gullah noun, pronoun, and verb, but there is a great deal more to it. There are phrases like *Him been dead* "he died" in which no one word has the grammatical function it has in ordinary English, and there are all those African vocabulary items. It makes a great deal of difference to the picture of English in the United States whether Gullah is confined to the Sea Islands or is widely spoken inland.

William A. Stewart, with whom I have long been associated in the so-called Creolist approach to American Negro dialects, has examined, in a large-scale research project funded by the National Science Foundation, the distribution of Gullah. He finds that writers like Dubose and Dorothy Heyward come much closer to describing the actual situation than any of the publications of the dialectologists. (The methods of the latter, incidentally, were scathingly criticized by Glenna Ruth Pickford in "American Linguistic Geography: A Sociological Appraisal," in 1956.) Stewart, like any other linguist, deprecates the occasional false and even racist statement, like a reference to "thick lips," to be found in *Porgy,* but he insists that much of the linguistic information is valid.

It would be ideal if we could rely upon descriptions of the Charleston dialect by Blacks, but there is a paucity—perhaps complete—of such materials. That being the case, we have to rely on writers like the Heywards, allowing for their exaggerations, faulty emphases, and possible distortions. There seems to be some value in checking their statements against those of other writers since frequently reported statements are less likely to be the products of one writer's imagination. It should be remembered, also, that the Heywards' *Porgy* is not quite the same as Gershwin's *Porgy and Bess,* which too many readers may assume is the last word on Catfish Row.

Porgy not only represents the Gullah grammatical forms (although the authors specify, in the stage directions to Act I, Scene 1, that the Gullah is to be "tempered to their [the audience's] ears") but also the folk beliefs (like conjure practices), distinctive naming practices (Mingo, Scipio, Sporting Life), and gambling behavior often held to be among the characteristics of "folk" Negroes throughout the United States. The play opens on a gambling scene, in which Crown (a longshoreman, Bess's "man") kills Robbins in a fight. The very last scene (Act Four, Scene Three) shows Porgy back from a week in jail, where he has won a lot of money shooting craps with the "lucky bones" he managed to smuggle in. This conclusion has too much of the deus ex machina about it, even if Porgy's triumph is made bitter when he discovers that Bess has been lured to New York (where there is a fairly large Gullah colony) by Sporting Life's *happy dust.* The Black man just out of jail with a lot of presents for all his friends bought with the money he made shooting craps reads all too much like one of Octavus Roy Cohen's Florian Slappey stories, and the play would undoubtedly have been a better one if the Heywards had resisted that oversimple development. Nevertheless, there are some authentic things, even in *Porgy* and the works of Cohen.

It would be better, I think, to use such literary works as a means to a general overview—not to make confident decisions about either lexical items or grammatical structures solely on the evidence provided by any writer of fiction. Luckily, we seldom have to depend on any one such writer, and we have a vast amount of comparative evidence from the English Creoles of the Caribbean and from West African Pidgin English. When, after such checks have been carefully applied, a Black English vernacular lexical form seems to be suggested on the basis of fictional materials, I see no reason not to assume that it is authentic.

None of these sources can compare, however, to the materials provided by a small band of field workers in folklore. Since about 1920, highly trained professional researchers like Arthur Huff Fauset, Zora Neale Hurston, Alan Lomax, and John Mason Brewer have given us transcriptions of Black texts collected in the field, primarily in the rural South. It is a stroke of almost unbelievable good fortune that Fauset, who collected many Brer Rabbit stories in the rural South, also published a volume on the folklore of the Blacks in Nova Scotia. The many similarities in those two sets of materials are the best argument I know against the too easily adopted viewpoint that Black folklore (or dialect) represents a survival of archaic white materials. I have drawn primarily from those folklorists and from a small number of anthropologists like Whitten and Price. Except for Lomax, those outstanding folklorists are Black; among other things, they should all be free from any accusation of racist bias.

Brewer was the least formal of those researchers and writers, and I have never felt quite so much at ease about citing him as some of the others. In spite of a convincing introduction by Chapman J. Milling to Brewer's *Dog Ghosts and Other Texas Negro Folk Tales* detailing the care that was expended upon the dialect, one cannot completely avoid the suspicion of an occasional humorous exaggeration. Or if I may be allowed to put it differently, all the argument about the distinctiveness of Black English is superfluous if Brewer's materials can be accepted in their entirety. Brewer, in that case, made the point all by himself— long ago.

Although my own ears and J. Mason Brewer attest some grammatical usages (like a fancifying *he am*), which she would deny,[29] Zora Neale Hurston's writings come close to being the ultimate source for a rural Black lexicon in the twentieth century. Her Glossary to *Mules and Men* is disappointing, but the materials collected (like *Joe Moore* as a gambler's variant of *mojo*—see Chapter Seven) are priceless. Footnotes call attention to:

don't pay X no rabbit foot	"ignore X"
bookooing	"loud talking, bullying"
woofing	"talking aimlessly"
chitterlings	"hog intestines"
bogish	"bogus"
conthartic	"cathartic"
spuddin'	"playing for small change" (cards)
playin' wid yo' stuff out de winder	"risking nothing" (cards)
fat 'roun' de heart	"scared"

power	"funds"
pickin' de box	"playing the guitar"
doodley squat	"nothing"[30]
spread my jenk	"have a good time"
buckra	"white person"[31]
Old Hannah	"the sun"
southern can	"hips"[32]
Shake-baby	"dress very tight across the hips"
skillet blonde	"black girl"
have de white mouf	"be hungry"
signify	"show off"[33]
Aunt Hagar's children	"Negroes"
Bookity book	"running"
Jook it	"play piano in a low dive"
High balling	"waving ahead" (of a train)
Have a cub	"have the cards stacked" (cards)
Let the deal go down	"play all the cards in the deck"
Shoo-shooing	"whispering"
Boody	"sex"[34]
Set hawses (horses)	"get along with"
Hasslin'	"panting"[35]
Froe	"damaged pocket knife"
Eat acorns	"I give you one point" (cards—Florida Flip)

These are in addition to the many others in Hurston's other books[36] and to the expressions already treated in preceding chapters. Hurston's folklore collections are of basic importance for the Black lexicon.

Within a professional folklorist's framework, Stella Brewer Brooks (a relative of J. Mason Brewer) has rehabilitated perhaps the most important of the amateur folklorists of the nineteenth century who dealt with Black materials, Joel Chandler Harris. Again, although I find Brooks's arguments persuasive, I have preferred to avoid direct use of Harris' materials. The traditional academic suspicion is, it seems, just too deeply ingrained.[37]

Aside from the very special case of Alan Lomax, there are several white folklorists of recent years who have done valuable service in the study of Black materials, especially blues and folksongs. The recordings by Lomax and Harold Courlander, for example, are as fully acceptable and as usable as tapes I might have recorded in the field. If they are faked, they are astonishingly good fakes— and a vast number of critics have been taken in. Bruce Jackson and Harry Oster have done very recent fieldwork, especially in prisons, which seems to corroborate conclusions made through the use of other materials.

The most encouraging fact of all is that the materials derived from many kinds of sources are so strikingly similar. When the same lexical items appear repeatedly in the works of writers of fiction and nonfiction, of Black and white fieldworkers in folklore, it would seem that those items are genuine. When these are corroborated by live informants—when the smiles of recognition come onto the faces of the Black students in a graduate course but not onto those of the whites at the mention of a term like *two-headed man* "conjure doctor"—then there does not seem to be much room for doubt.

Generalizations are always suspect, especially in a field like literary representations where so many writers of so many different orientations are involved. The same writer may conceivably be completely reliable in one domain and almost unworthy of attention in another. But something of a generalization now seems possible: Many white writers, especially those who grew up on southern plantations and were bidialectal, have managed the grammar of Black English rather well and have, insofar as ordinary orthography will permit, done a reasonably good job of indicating pronunciation. The vocabulary is not, however, to be found in their writings. For a historical lexicon of the Black English vernacular, the writings of a few outstanding Black authors are the best sources. After several years of studying the matter, I am firmly convinced that William Wells Brown and Charles W. Chesnutt represent that vocabulary best of all.[38] In recent times, in spite of my great admiration for James Baldwin, Ralph Ellison, and several other Black authors, the prize would have to go to Richard Wright. In my opinion, there is no other book in which the speech of adult Black migrants from southern rural areas into the city is so well represented as in *Lawd Today.*

The works of Wright mean much more to the reader who understands the full import of the typically Black expressions in his dialogue, although the one who does not is probably never completely lost. Wright does depend more on such comprehension than most of the other well-known Black writers. This passage would seem bizarre to a reader who did not know as much about *lie* in the Black English vernacular, as described in Chapter 8:

> "Zeke, this lie about Laura Green [Zeke's first sexual conquest]," Fishbelly began with a nonchalant, twisted smile, "is it a *true* lie or just a *plain* old lie?"[39]

Variation between the Black English vernacular and the English of wider communication gives the young man two referents, partly in conflict, for the word *lie* and makes possible this method of distinguishing the two by attributive modifiers.

Unlike Iceberg Slim and the authors of jazz histories, a literary artist like Wright scorns to provide a glossary. Nevertheless, his work is full of subtleties that the reader may easily miss if he is not thoroughly familiar with the Black English vernacular lexicon. His West African Pidgin English in "Man, God Ain't Like That" (from *Eight Men*) is not as good as that of Gerald Durrell. There is not the fictional recapitulation of the history of Black English to be found in Alex Haley's more recent novel *Roots.* But the accuracy of his contemporary Black speech is impressive. Finding a word or expression in Wright's works is perhaps the best possible corroboration of the hunch that it was genuinely Black.

Notes

1. ON THE SOCIAL SIGNIFICANCE OF A LEXICON FOR THE BLACK ENGLISH VERNACULAR

1. The classical sources for descriptions of these differences are Labov and Wolfram and Fasold (see Bibliography). For phonological materials more closely impinging upon vocabulary differences (e.g., *umbreva* for *umbrella* and homophony of *furry* and *fairy*), see Luelsdorff, "Dialectology in Generative Grammar," in *Perspectives on Black English,* ed. Dillard, and Luelsdorff, *A Segmental Phonology of Black English* (The Hague: Mouton, 1975). It would also probably be accurate to refer to phonology such nonce forms as *paragolize* for *paralyze,* elicited in fieldwork by researchers among the Blacks of Samaná, Dominican Republic (descendants of freed slaves who migrated from the Washington-Maryland area around 1840).

2. Although, as has been frequently pointed out, Irish dialect does have a *be -ing (be dancing)* form, it is almost always preceded by *do.* More significantly, it cannot co-occur with a past time adverbial expression *(he be dancing last Friday),* whereas the Black English vernacular form most emphatically can. See Loflin, Sobin, and Dillard "Co-occurent Time Adverbials and the Black English Auxiliary," *American Speech* 48 (Spring-Summer 1973). In the same issue, see especially Sledd's article, for a strong version of the opposing viewpoint, including an amusing and uncharacteristic editorial footnote.

3. This point is acknowledged by William Labov, the most important opponent of the idea that there are syntactic differences between Black English and ordinary English, in his *Language in the Inner City,* pp. 53–55.

4. David Dalby, "The African Element in American English," in *Rappin' and Stylin' Out: Communication in Urban Black America,* ed.

Thomas Kochman (Urbana: University of Illinois Press, 1972).

5. Internal reconstruction, especially prominent in nineteenth-century linguistics, was a method of recreating the prehistory of a language or (more normally) language family. As the name suggests, it assumed that internal developments were more important than contact with other languages. In many cases, this was making a virtue of necessity since scanty or no facts were available about the languages in contact.

6. See, for example, Carl Bereiter and Sigfried Engelmann, *Teaching Disadvantaged Children in the Pre-School* (Englewood Cliffs, N.J., Prentice Hall 1966), p. 113 et passim.

7. See William A. Stewart, "Sociolinguistic Factors in the History of American Negro Dialects," p. 11 and "Continuity and Change in American Negro Dialects," p. 3; also J. L. Dillard, *Black English.*

8. A strong case for this point of view is made in Joan C. Baratz and Roger W. Shuy, eds., *Teaching Black Children to Read* (Washington, D.C.: Center for Applied Linguistics, 1969), especially Stewart's contribution, "On the Use of Negro Dialect in Teaching Reading," pp. 156–219.

9. Alwyn Barr, *Black Texans,* p. 156.

10. Transcript made by Bengt Loman for the Urban Language Study, Washington, D.C., 1967, p. 3. These transcriptions are not exactly identical to those published under the title *Conversations in an American Negro Dialect* (Washington, D.C.: Center for Applied Linguistics, 1970), which were heavily edited.

11. Harry Middleton Hyatt, *Hoodoo—Conjuration—Witchcraft—Rootwork,* p. 1289.

12. Manie Culbertson, *May I Speak?,* p. 148.

13. Barr, *Black Texans,* pp. 100–101.

14. Sam "Lightnin' " Hopkins, "On Stage," IR LP 9180–A, Side 1, Band 5.

15. George P. Rawick, ed., *The American Slave,* 7:145.

16. Ibid., p. 147.

17. *American Journal of Sociology,* 1938.

18. Culbertson, *May I Speak?,* pp. 61–62.

19. Reprinted in Alan Dundes, ed., *Mother Wit from the Laughing Barrel,* 1973.

20. See, for example, James Baldwin, *Tell Me How Long the Train's Been Gone,* p. 138, and Richard Wright, *Lawd Today,* p. 182.

21. Martha Emmons, *Deep Like the River,* p. 57.

22. Federal Writers Project, *Alabama: A Guide to the Deep South* (New York: Hastings House, 1941), pp. 127–8.

23. Kenneth Clark is quoted on the dust jacket of Edwin Newman's wildly puristic *Strictly Speaking:*

> *Strictly Speaking* is an important, long over-due plea for those of us who love and respect the English language but who have been in-timidated into silence as we watch the many forms of linguistic vandalism. . . . Those of us who recoil at the attempts to make some educational virtue out of 'black English,' who listen passively as expletives, deleted and undeleted, become the fashion of com-munication, now have a civilized advocate and defender in Edwin Newman. We must support him. We have no 'viable alterna-tive'.

That a distinguished professional in one field (psychology) should be so ill-informed about an-other (linguistics) is regrettable but all too com-monplace—especially where the two fields men-tioned are concerned. See my attempt to cope with this situation in the Introduction to Section IV of my *Perspectives on Black English.*

24. Culbertson, *May I Speak?,* p. 128.

25. See Arthur R. Jensen, "How Much Can We Boost. . . ."

26. One of the best jobs of popularization ever done by a linguist is that of William Labov, "Ac-ademic Ignorance and Black Intelligence," a refutation of the ideas of Shockley and Jensen.

27. Elsa Roberts, "An Evaluation of Standard-ized Tests as Tools for the Measure of Language Development."

28. Robert Politzer, "Developmental Aspects of the Awareness of the Standard/Non-Standard Dialect Contrast."

29. A. S. Carson and I. A. Rabin, "Verbal Comprehension and Communication in Negro and White Children," in *School Children in the Urban Slum,* ed. Joan I. Roberts (New York: Free Press, 1967).

30. Lorene C. Quay, "Language Dialect Rein-forcement and the Intelligence Test Performance of Negro Children," pp. 5–15.

31. Boris Levinson, "A Comparative Study of the WAIS Performance of Native-born Negro and White Homeless."

32. William A. Stewart, "Foreign Language Teaching Methods in a Quasi-Foreign Language Situation," pp. 1–19.

33. Virginia Heyer Young, "Family and Child-hood in a Southern Negro Community," p. 280.

34. Ibid., p. 273.

35. Ibid. Both of these terms occur frequently in texts like Rosengarten *All God's Dangers.*

36. Ibid.

37. Ibid., p. 275. See Howard W. Odum and Guy B. Johnson, *Negro Workaday Songs,* p. 212, for folksong boasting of being "a bad man." In Julia Peterkin's *Black April,* a Sea Islander who has moved to town writes his relatives that he is "de baddest man at de town whe' e stay" (p. 116).

38. Young, "Family and Childhood in a South-ern Negro Community," p. 282.

39. Ibid.

40. This scornful term, perhaps intentionally ungrammatical (the more likely derivation would produce *bidialectism*), is repeatedly used by James Sledd. See his "Bi-Dialectalism: The Linguistics of White Supremacy," pp. 1307–15.

41. See the works of Stewart listed in the Bibli-ography and in the more comprehensive Ila Brasch and Walter Brasch *A Complete Annotated Bibliography of American Black English.*

42. Margaret Anderson, *Children of the South,* p. 137.

43. Ibid.

44. Ibid.

45. Bess Lomax Hawes and Bessie Jones, *Step It Down,* p. 24.

46. Culbertson, *May I Speak?,* p. 100.

47. Daniel N. Fader, *The Naked Children,* pp. 55–56.

48. Ibid., p. 79.

49. Ibid., p. 86.

50. Stewart, "Foreign Language Teaching Methods in a Quasi-Foreign Language Situa-tion," in Stewart, (ed.) *Non-Standard Speech and the Teaching of English,* p. 3.

51. See Ivan van Sertima, *They Came Before Columbus.* This book is a reconsideration of a thesis advanced by Leo Weiner in 1924.

52. David Dalby, in "The African Element in American English," pp. 177–178, draws attention to Ibo and West African Pidgin English forms.

53. "Old Time Negro Proverbs," in *Spur-of-the-Cock,* ed. J. Frank Dobie (Dallas: Southern Methodist University Press, 1965), p. 101.

54. Ibid., p. 102.

55. In the terminology of sociolinguistics, a language or a dialect may be socially "superposed" on another, although there is no structural effect from such a relationship. Speakers often feel, however, that the superposed variety is "better" than the other, and they will often express that opinion very strongly—even if they are native speakers of the "inferior" variety. (They usually reserve some special expressive power in personal domains for their native variety, however.) One of the basic diagnostic characteristics is that speakers of the other variety will accept correction from the superposed variety.

56. Jane C. Beck, "The West Indian Supernatural World," *Journal of American Folklore* 88 (1975):237.

57. Newman, *Strictly Speaking,* p. 14.

58. George O. Marshall, Jr., "You Know," *American Speech* 48 (Fall-Winter 1974) pp. 304–305. The article actually quotes a citation from a Bulwer Lytton novel discovered by Randolph Quirk, and would thus seem to document rather a white origin.

59. Hyatt, *Hoodoo—Conjuration—Witchcraft —Rootwork.* This collection (in five volumes) is, although extremely strange in some of its methods of presentation, perhaps the one indispensable work on the subject.

Folk typologies of the Black English vernacular, as of most other nonprestige varieties, tend to be essentially negative. In the Jamaican Anansi stories, the spider-hero who speaks the deepest form of Creole is stigmatized (albeit affectionately) with the explanation "Him tongue-tied." In various West Indian islands, using Standard English is characterized as *speaking,* whereas using the local variety ("Creole") is merely *talking.* Proficiency in talking more prestigiously was long characterized in Jamaica by the term *cutting English;* I have not, however, come across any attestation of the term in the continental United States.

Explaining to a Black English speaker what a speaker of other dialects means, or vice versa, is a process that is frequently necessary. Because of the feeling that the former is merely "bad" English, however, fancy terms like *translator* or *interpreter* would seldom be applied to a person skilled in the process, no matter how useful his talents might be. One Black woman in Washington, D.C. (a Language Arts teacher) once told me that her husband (a janitor at the railway station) was skilled in such activity and was called a "dentist" because of his talent. With its suggestion of oral proficiency, the term is not bad at all. Unfortunately, I do not have any evidence that it occurs in wider distribution.

2. TERMINOLOGY OF SEX AND LOVEMAKING

1. Robert William Fogel and Stanley L. Engerman, *Time on the Cross,* p. 133. Eugene Genovese, *Roll, Jordan, Roll,* writes, "The plantations hardly emerge from the statistics looking like the harems of abolitionist fantasy" (p. 415).

2. David L. Cohn, *God Shakes Creation,* pp. 78–79. Genovese, *Roll, Jordan, Roll,* points out that New Orleans, Louisville, and "a few other cities" maintained "fancy girl" markets. He suggests that, when blacksmiths were bringing $2,500 and field hands $1,800, a particularly beautiful girl or young woman might bring $5,000 (p. 416).

3. See the discussion of the term in my *Black Names.* White borrowings of some of these terms were frequent, and the changes of domain that the forms went through were almost infinite. Elderly white Texas informants tell me how *jelly* *roll* was the term for the "lascivious" part of a dance known as the buck and wing, often presented in the Southwest in the 1920s by the star Black dancer in a traveling minstrel show.

4. Cohn, *God Shakes Creation,* p. 112.

5. Guy B. Johnson, "Double Meaning in the Popular Negro Blues," in *Mother Wit from the Laughing Barrel,* ed. Alan Dundes, p. 266.

6. Bruce Jackson, "What Happened to Jody," *Journal of American Folklore* 80 (October-December 1967): 387–417. See also his discussion in *Wake Up Dead Man,* pp. 169–170. Clarence Major, *Dictionary of Afro-American Slang,* refers to "the real meaning . . . that Jodie is back home making love to the enlisted man's wife," but has no reference to *grinder.*

7. Bo Carter, "All Around Man," quoted in *The Blues Line,* comp. Eric Sackheim, p. 170.

8. "Playing the Dozens," in *Mother Wit from the Laughing Barrel,* ed. Alan Dundes, p. 308.

9. Bruce Jackson, "Circus and Street: Psychosocial Aspects of the Black Toast," p. 137.

10. This lyric, an extremely familiar one for blues enthusiasts, is quoted at length in Stephen Longstreet, *Real Jazz Old and New* (Baton Rouge: Louisiana State University Press, 1956), p. 52.

11. Howard W. Odum and Guy B. Johnson, *The Negro and His Songs,* p. 260.

12. This version is from a recording by Bob Wills and His Texas Playboys, "What's the Matter with the Mill?" Although it has never figured prominently in any studies, this band was often a pioneer in adapting musical styles like Black or Cajun for southwestern white audiences. In that context, it is amusing to read in Charlie Gillett's *The Sound of the City* that Bill Haley and His Comets drew the style of "Rock Around the Clock" from Blacks and "a group called Bob Wills and His Texas Playboys." Such a statement is tantamount to saying "Black and second-hand Black sources."

13. "What's the Matter with the Meal [sic]?" by Muddy Waters, Chess 5023. *Can't Get No Grindin',* Side I, Band 1. On Black influence on the "Anglo-American hillbilly tradition," see John Cohen "The Folk Music Exchange: Negro and White."

14. Bessie Smith, "Empty Bed Blues," *Empty Bed Blues,* Side 3, Band 6 Columbia G 3030. The original recording was made on March 20, 1928.

15. Guy B. Johnson, "Double Meaning in the Popular Negro Blues," in *Mother Wit from the Laughing Barrel,* ed. Alan Dundes, p. 261.

16. Jelly Roll Morton, "Low Down Blues," Riverside RLP 9008, Side I, Band 2.

17. Ibid., Riverside RLP 9002, Side 2, Band 1.

18. Maggie Jones and Louis Armstrong, "Anyone Here Want to Try My Cabbage?" with Fletcher Henderson, is another obvious example of the same symbolism (Max Jones and John Chilton, *Louis,* p. 226).

19. Richard Wright, *Lawd Today,* p. 93.

20. Peg Leg Howell, "Tishamingo Blues," from the Samuel Charters collection *Country Blues* Vol. II (RBF).

21. Edward Thompson, "Seven Sister Blues," quoted in *The Blues Line,* comp. Eric Sackheim, p. 303.

22. Zora Neale Hurston, *Dust Tracks on a Road,* p. 71.

23. On possible African language influence, see David Dalby, "The African Element in Black American English," pp. 170–188.

24. Harold Courlander, *Negro Folk Music, U.S.A.,* pp. 129–130.

25. See especially Harold Courlander's notes to Ethnic Folkways 417. Dicky Wells, *The Night People,* p. 107, represents the following as typical "dressing room conversation" among jazz musicians:

> "She's only the baker's daughter, but oh, how I'd like to nibble on her cupcakes."

26. Smoky Babe (Robert Brown), Scotland-ville Prison, February 6, 1960, in *Living Country Blues,* comp. Harry Oster, p. 357.

27. Sung by the Angola, Louisiana, prisoner Hogman Maxey, *Southern Prison Blues* Tradition LP 2066, Side I, Band 6.

28. Butch Cage and Willie B. Thomas, "Jelly Roll," in *Living Country Blues,* comp. Harry Oster, p. 354.

29. J. Frank Dobie, ed., *Follow de Drinkin' Gou'd,* p. 103.

30. Oster, *Living Country Blues,* p. 293.

31. Vera Hall, "Black Woman," Folkways Jazz, Vol. 2, *The Blues* (collected by Frederick Ramsey, Jr.).

32. Sackheim, *The Blues Line,* p. 44.

33. The line with *lovin'* is printed in Alan Lomax, "I Got the Blues," in *Mother Wit from the Laughing Barrel,* ed. Alan Dundes, p. 473.

34. "Mamie's Blues," in *Jelly Roll Morton in Piano and Vocal Solos,* Jazztone J–1211, Side I, Band I.

35. Marshall Stearns, *The Story of Jazz,* p. 11.

36. Sackheim, *The Blues Line,* p. 136.

37. Edmond Souchon, M.D., "King Oliver: A Very Personal Memoir," in *Jazz Panorama,* ed. Martin Williams, p. 23.

38. Robert Beck, *Mama Black Widow,* p. 148.

39. Big Bill Broonzy, "Big Bill Blues," Riverside SDP 11, Band 6, Side 3.

40. Sam "Lightnin'" Hopkins, "Jailhouse Blues," *Blues in My Bottle,* Prestige Bluesville BV 1045, Side B, Band 2. See also Muddy Waters, quoted in *Mother Wit from the Laughing Barrel,* ed. Alan Dundes, p. 268.

41. Sackheim, *The Blues Line,* p. 471.

42. Rabbit Brown, "James Alley Blues," Victor 20577, recorded March 11, 1927.

43. Roosevelt Charles, "Hard Time Lovin' Blues," in *Living Country Blues,* comp. Harry Oster, p. 65. The song is also reproduced as his no. 164, p. 369.

44. Robert Pete Williams, "Rock Well Blues,"

in *Living Country Blues,* comp. Harry Oster, p. 65. Also no. 194, p. 413.

45. Bruce Jackson, *Wake Up Dead Man,* p. 126.

46. Quoted in LeRoi Jones, *Blues People,* p. 169.

47. Georgia Bill, "Scarey Day Blues," in *Country Blues,* Vol. II (RBF), comp. Samuel Charters,

48. Johnny Lee Moore, "Levee Camp Holler," in *Roots of the Blues,* comp. Alan Lomax, Atlantic SD–1348, Side 2, Band 2.

49. Herbert Foster, *Ribbin', Jivin', and Playin' the Dozens,* p. 148.

50. "Characteristics of Negro Expression," in *Voices from the Harlem Renaissance,* ed. Nathan Irwin Huggins, p. 234.

51. Sam "Lightnin'" Hopkins, "Black Cadillac," Bluesville 1057, Side 2, Band 5.

52. Georgia Bell, "Scarey Day Blues," in *Country Blues II,* comp. Samuel Charters. Compare the line from New Orleans oldtimer Billie Pierce (*Blues in the Classic Tradition,* RLP 370, Side 1, Band 2: "Goodbye Daddy Blues"):
I got a movement just like a Cadillac eight.

53. Bessie Smith, "Put It Right Here," Columbia 14324D, recorded March 20, 1928.

54. Sackheim, *The Blues Line,* p. 271.

55. Roosevelt Sykes, "Satellite Baby," Prestige/Bluesville 1014, Side B, Band 4.

56. See Dalby, "The African Element in American English," p. 184. He cites Limba *puntung* "vagina" and "convergence" with French *putain.*

57. Marshall Stearns and Jean Stearns, *Jazz Dance,* p. 16.

58. Quoted in John M. Hellman, "I'm a Monkey: The Influence of the Black American Blues Argot on the Rolling Stones," pp. 370–2. 367–373.

59. Charlie Pickett, "Let Me Squeeze Your Lemon," in *Country Blues II,* comp. Samuel Charters.

60. Hari Rhodes, *A Chosen Few.* New York, Bantam Books, 1965. p. 129.

61. H. Rap Brown, "Street Smarts," in *Mother Wit from the Laughing Barrel,* ed. Alan Dundes, p. 354.

62. John Jackson, "Rattlesnakin' Daddy," *Blues and Country Dances from Virginia,* Arhoolie F1025, Side 2, Band 1.

63. "Black Snake," *The Rooster Crowed in England,* 77A 1201, Side 1, Band 7.

64. The version by John Jackson ("Black Snake Moan," Arhoolie F1025) is surely a Bowdlerization of the Jefferson lyric:

That mean ol' black snake suck my rider down.

65. Hellman, "I'm a Monkey." p. 373.

66. Elliot Liebow, *Talley's Corner,* p. 255.

67. Beck, *Mama Black Widow,* p. 250.

68. Brownsville Son Bonds, in *Country Blues II,* comp. Samuel Charters.

69. Charters, *Living Country Blues,* p. 64.

70. Sam Hopkins "How Many More Years I Got to Let You Dog Me Around," *Walking This Road By Myself,* Bluesville 1057, Side A, Band 3.

71. Jenny Pope, quoted in *The Blues Line,* comp. Eric Sackheim, p. 41.

72. Rosengarten, *All God's Dangers,* p. 67.

73. "Hear My Black Dog Bark," Tradition LP 1035, Side 2, Band 8.

74. Christina Milner and Richard Milner, *Black Players,* p. 229.

75. Ian F. Hancock, "Nautical Origins of the Krio Lexicon," *International Journal of the Sociology of Language* Vol. 7: 23–36. (1976): shows the probability of nautical transmission of many British dialect forms to Creole (especially Afro-Creole) varieties. What is involved is not merely the transmission by sea (a truism) but the existence of special sailors' varieties of English through which the forms were transmitted.

76. Lafayette Jarreau, *Creole Folklore of Pointe Coupée Parish,* Louisiana State University, thesis, 1931, p. 86.

77. Zora Neale Hurston, *Mules and Men,* p. 193, a "jook tribute to Ella Wall."

78. *Southern Prison Blues,* Tradition LP 2066.

79. Charlie McCoy, "Ham Hound Crave," quoted in *The Blues Line,* comp. Eric Sackheim, p. 166.

80. Jackson, *Wake Up Dead Man,* p. 19. This process is labeled "Rocking along easy."

81. Ibid., p. 18.

82. *A Dirty Fighter* RS 1046, Side 1.

83. Harry Oster, "Easter Rock Revisited: A Study in Acculturation," *Louisiana Folklore Miscellany* (May 1958): 21–43.

84. Charlie Lincoln, "Jealous Hearted Blues," in *The Country Blues* Vol. II, comp. Samuel Charters, RBF RF 9B, Side 2, Band 2.

85. Muddy Waters, "Hootchie Cootchie," quoted in Sackheim, *The Blues Line,* p. 432.

86. John Lee Hooker, *I'm John Lee Hooker,* Vee-Jay LP 1007, Side 1, Band 6.

87. Jackson, *Wake Up Dead Man,* p. 161.

88. Sam "Lightnin'" Hopkins, *Strums the Blues,* "Rollin' and Rollin'" Score SLP–4022, Side 2, Band 2.

89. Jackson, *Wake Up Dead Man,* p. 89.

90. Ibid., p. 91.

91. W. H. Thomas, *Some Current Folk-Songs of the Negro* (Folklore Society of Texas, 1912), p. 64.

92. Jones and Chilton, *Louis*, p. 197.

93. Hurston, *Dust Tracks on a Road*, p. 243, uses the term *make your love come down on you* in a context of brotherly rather than of sexual love.

94. Beck, *Mama Black Widow*, p. 127.

95. Bessie Smith, "Please Help Me Get Him Off My Mind," Columbia 14375–D, recorded August 24, 1928.

96. Milton Mezzrow, *Really the Blues*, p. 308.

97. Ibid., p. 217.

98. Jelly Roll Morton, Library of Congress Recording, Vol. 2, Riverside RLP 9002, *The Animule Ball* Side 2.

99. Wright, *Lawd Today*, p. 176.

100. Willie Lofton, "Dark Road Blues," quoted in *The Blues Line*, comp. Eric Sackheim, p. 165.

101. Mezzrow, *Really the Blues*, p. 32.

102. Muddy Waters, *Can't Get No Grindin'* Chess 50023.

103. S. A. Babalola, *The Content and Form of Yoruba Ijala*, 1966, p. 39.

104. Quoted by Herbert Foster, *Ribbin', Jivin', and Playin' the Dozens, op. cit.*, p. 121.

3. TERMINOLOGY OF RELIGION AND THE CHURCH

1. Tony Heilbut, *The Gospel Sound*, p. 15.

2. Benjamin Mays and Joseph Nicholson, *The Negro's Church*, p. 279 (emphasis added).

3. Joseph Holt Ingraham, *The Southwest by a Yankee*, 2:203.

4. Ibid.

5. Ibid., 2:265.

6. Frederick Law Olmstead, *The Cotton Kingdom*, 1861, p. 467.

7. Ibid.

8. William H. Pipes, *Say Amen Brother!*, p. 178.

9. Ira Berlen, *Slaves Without Masters*, p. 293. While every resource, like appeal to the influence of Whitefield, is generally exhausted to support the proposition that the Blacks were imitating—or at most selecting from—the religious practices of whites, the observation was made as early as 1819 in John Watson's *Methodist Error* that "the example has already visibly affected the religious manners of some whites" (quoted in *Readings in Black American Music*, ed. Eileen Southern, pp. 63–64).

10. Charles Lyell, *A Second Visit to the United States of North America* (London: Murray, 1849), 2:175.

11. Ibid., 2:15.

12. Leroi Jones, *Blues People*, p. 41.

13. W.E.B. DuBois, "The Religion of the American Negro," *New World* 14 (1900).

14. Alan Lomax, *The Rainbow Sign*, p. 119.

15. George Rawick, ed., *From Sundown to Sunup*, pp. 45–48.

16. Charles S. Smith, *The History of the African Methodist Episcopal Church*, 2:126–127.

17. Lomax, *The Rainbow Sign*, p. 162.

18. Mrs. Frances Trollope, *Domestic Manners of the Americans*, p. 170.

19. See Zora Neale Hurston's material on "Seeker, come" in *Mules and Men*, p. 248.

20. "Certain Beliefs and Superstitions of the Negro," *Atlantic Monthly* XLV III (1891): 286–288.

21. Lorenzo Dow Turner, *Africanisms in the Gullah Dialect*, pp. 274–275, the transcription and the transliteration on facing pages. The entire text is interesting from the point of view of Black religious terminology (e.g., "When you see the baby [i.e., your soul], you be on good faith—on a good foundation," from the transliteration on p. 275). I am in general agreement with Gullah expert and Creolist William A. Stewart (see Bibliography) that Gullah terminology is of basic significance for Black English Vernacular terminology—that Gullah represents the stage before partial assimilation to General American norms ("de-Creolization") introduced superficial differences from Gullah in most Black American dialects. As an operational procedure, however, I have chosen to include only those Gullah forms that are so strikingly like Black American English vernacular items as to be beyond serious controversy. When, for example, Allen, Ware, and Garrison, *Slave Songs of the United States*, p. xii, report of the Port Royal slaves that "to get religion with them is to 'fin' dat ting'," I am inclined to believe that other Blacks outside the Sea Islands used the same expression. This cannot be assumed, however, unless supporting documents from outside the Low Country contain the phrase.

22. Norman Eliason, *Tarheel Talk*, p. 114.

23. The citation is from Arthur Singleton (pseud. Henry C. Knight), *Letters from the South and North,* Boston, 1824. p. 75.

24. Tony Heilbut, *The Gospel Sound,* p. 33.

25. Joseph R. Washington, *Black Sects and Cults,* p. 88.

26. James Baldwin, *Go Tell It on the Mountain,* p. 148.

27. "Certain Beliefs and Superstitions of the Negro," pp. 286–288.

28. George Eaton Simpson, *Religious Cults of the Caribbean.*

29. Allen, Ware, and Garrison, *Slave Songs of the United States.* See also Robert Winslow Gordon, "Negro 'Shouts' from Georgia," in *Mother Wit from the Laughing Barrel,* ed. Alan Dundes p. 446.

30. Dock Reed, *Negro Folk Music of Alabama,* Ethnic Folkways P418, Side 1, Band 1. The term occurs even in a sophisticated song context like Aaron Copland's arranged version of "Zion's Walls" (Columbia MS 6497), but it is doubtful that many listeners recognize the "holy dance" allusion.

31. The narrative is related by Pat Franks of Aberdeen, Mississippi, in *The American Slave,* ed. George P. Rawick, 7:58.

32. Ibid., 7:151.

33. Eugene V. Smalley, "Sugar-Making in Louisiana" *Century Magazine* Vol. 35 (Nov. 1887 to April 1888), p. 107.

34. Alan Lomax, jacket notes to *Sounds of the South* (Atlantic SD–1346).

35. Howard D. Odum and Guy B. Johnson, *The Negro and His Songs,* p. 273.

36. Ibid., p. 131.

37. Rev. Cleophus Robinson, *Sweet and Stinky,* Randy's Spiritual RS 1046.

38. *Negro Folk Music of Alabama, Rich Amerson II* (recorded by Harold Courlander), Side 1, Band 4.

39. Dock Reed, "Low Down Death Right Easy," Ibid., Side 2, Band 2.

40. Randy's Spiritual RS 1046. The same member (apparently) shouts "Fix it!" throughout the sermon.

41. Blind Willie Johnson, quoted in *The Blues Line,* comp. Eric Sackheim, pp. 98–99.

42. *Negro Folk Music of Alabama II* (recorded by Harold Courlander), Side 2, Band 4.

43. Baldwin, *Go Tell It on the Mountain,* p. 84.

44. Francis Dillon, *Fanatic Cults,* p. 14.

45. Nancy Cunard, "Harlem Reviewed," in *Voices from the Harlem Renaissance,* ed. Nathan Irwin Huggins, p. 127.

46. Pipes, *Say Amen, Brother!,* p. 138. In a footnote, Pipes comments "Maintaining the rhythmical stride in preaching is compared to staying on a moving horse."

47. Rev. Cleophus Robinson *Sweet and Stinky,* Randy's Spiritual RS 1046.

48. Dillon, *Fanatic Cults,* p. 42.

49. Alan Dundes, ed., *Mother Wit from the Laughing Barrel,* p. 435.

50. James A. Harrison, "Negro English," p. 149.

51. John Storm Roberts, *Black Music of Two Worlds* (New York: William Morrow, 1974), p. 162.

52. WPA Archives, Louisiana, Northwestern State University, Natchitoches, Louisiana collection.

53. Lomax, *The Rainbow Sign,* p. 47.

54. Everett Dick, *The Dixie Frontier,* p. 284.

55. Mance Lipscomb, quoted in *The Blues Line,* comp. Eric Sackheim, p. 136.

56. Robert Beck, *Mama Black Widow,* p. 91.

57. Lomax, *The Rainbow Sign,* p. 161.

58. See Jones, *Blues People,* p. 49.

59. Jelly Roll Morton, *The Animule Ball* Riverside RLP 9002, Side 2, Band 4.

60. Ruby Berkeley Goodwin, *It's Good to Be Black,* p. 41.

61. Rawick, *The American Slave,* 7:86.

62. Dillon, *Fanatic Cults,* p. 21.

63. Ibid., p. 10.

64. Ulf Hannerz, *Soulside,* p. 147.

4. MUSIC, ESPECIALLY THE BLUES

1. Howard W. Odum and Guy B. Johnson, *The Negro and His Songs,* p. 169.

2. John Henry Jackson, "Tell Me Pretty Baby," *Southern Prison Blues,* comp. Harry Oster, Tradition Stereo 2066, Side 2, Band 4.

3. Odum and Johnson, *The Negro and His Songs,* p. 183.

4. T-Bone Walker, "The Sun Went Down," *Classics of Modern Blues,* Blue-Note Reissue, Side 2, Band 7. The different rhyming practices of Negro songs were observed and reported at least as early as 1832 by James Hungerford in *The Old Plantation and What I Gathered There in an Autumn Month* (New York: 1859), quoted in

Readings in Black American Music, Eileen Southern, ed. p. 73. Predictably, Hungerford, whose observations were made on his uncle's plantation in Maryland, saw these rhyming practices as verbal deficiencies.

5. Blind Lemon Jefferson, "Rising High Water Blues," Riverside SDP 11 (*History of Classic Jazz,* vol. 2, *The Blues*) Side 1, Band 5

6. Roosevelt Sykes, "High Price Blues," *The Honeydripper,* Prestige 1014, Bluesville Band 2, Side 5

7. Bessie Smith, "I Used to Be Your Sweet Mama," *Empty Bed Blues* Columbia 14292D, recorded February 9, 1928.

8. Mississippi John Hurt, "Nobody's Dirty Business," *They Sang the Blues,* Historical Records HLP–17, Band 1, Side 1, originally recorded February 14, 1928.

9. Max Jones and John Chilton, *Louis,* p. 240. Nat Hentoff, *The Jazz Life,* p. 81, reports that "Heroin . . . became the 'in' drug because it was so defiantly antisquare. . . ." This, however, would have been a general ghetto reaction, not an attitude specific to jazzmen.

10. Frederic Ramsey and Charles Edward Smith, *Jazzmen.* The illustration was entitled "Charles Dickerson's Orchestra, with Louis Armstrong and Zutty Singleton."

11. Norman D. Hinton, "The Language of Jazz Musicians," and Whitney Balliet, "Jazz: New York Notes."

12. Robert J. Gold, *Jazz Talk,* cites the 1811 *Dictionary of the Vulgar Tongue* London, 1785 for *square* "honest, not roguish." It is not immediately apparent what connection that would have with the hip-talk *square.* If F. Grose's *Classical Dictionary of the Vulgar Tongue* is meant (as seems likely), it is noteworthy that Grose (whose work first appeared in 1785) was the first lexicographer to cite many of the Black Pidgin English forms.

13. James D. Corrothers, *The Black Cat Club,* p. 69.

14. David Dalby, "The African Element in American English," p. 180.

15. Dalby cites the semantic opposition to *hot* "fast, energetic" and points out that Mandingo *suma* "cool" also means "slow" with respect to music and that *goni* "hot" also means "fast" in the same context. James A. Harrison's "Negro English," a spectacularly inept performance by any professional standards but one that does contain a few insights, lists as a "Specimen Negroism" *to look cool* "not to be afraid." This listing by no means proves the Negro origin of the term;

nevertheless, it does illustrate the historical existence of southern traditions about the word. (The citation, reprinted in my *Perspectives on Black English,* is on p. 177.)

16. Gunther Schuller, *Early Jazz,* p. 6, attributes such a remark, in the context of a definition of *swing* rather than of *jazz,* to Louis Armstrong. Almost every early jazzman has, however, been credited with some such statement.

17. Stanley Dance, *The World of Swing,* New York, C. Scribner's Sons, 1974, p. 13.

18. William Gilmore Simms, *Woodcraft,* pp. 396–397. An interesting description, including the observation that "the Whites soon find it impossible to sustain their parts, and they soon retire," is given by Lewis K. Paine, *Six Years in a Georgia Prison,* 1851 (quoted in *Readings in Black American Music,* ed. Eileen Southern, p. 89), but the term *swing* does not actually occur. It does occur, however, in Paul Lawrence Dunbar's poem "The Party" in *Lyrics of the Lowly Life:*
Oh, swing Johnny up an' down, swing him all aroun', Swing Johnny up an' down, swing him all aroun' [p. 202].
An' he spun huh 'roun de cabin swingin' Johnny lak de res' [p. 203].

19. See my *Black English,* p. 124.

20. This is, at any rate, the usual interpretation of *Jim Crow,* deriving from the "Jump, Jim Crow!" dance step popularized by "Daddy" Rice. (See Hans Nathan, *Dan Emmett and the Rise of Early Negro Minstrelsy,* pp. 50–52.) Melvin J. Herskovits and Frances S. Herskovits, *Rebel Destiny,* derive the term rather from *nyonkro,* in use in Surinam and coming from the name of a play given by the women on the coast of Africa. It is quite likely that the "proper name" interpretation represents an intermediate stage, rationalizing (or folk etymologizing) the African word. Zip Coon was a now-forgotten popular nineteenth-century minstrel show dance. *Zip* was the slaves' version of what was for the owners *Scipio,* but there may well be a deeper African relationship.

21. Hinton, "The Language of Jazz Musicians," p. 39.

22. Shapiro, Nat, New York, Rinehart, 1955 *Hear Me Talkin' to Ya,* p. 97. The expression "You low down alligator" ("Odetta Down in Hogan's Alley," *Odetta and the Blues,* Riverside RLP 417, Side 1, Band 5) supports the deprecatory interpretation.

23. Possibly "Rock Around the Clock," by Bill Haley and His Comets, was the first (1955–56) example of that commercialized (by whites) rock

and roll. "See You Later, Alligator" was a fol-low-up "hit." The routine dependence on Black models, without much regard for authenticity, linguistic or otherwise, is a characteristic of much—if not all—of this music.

24. Bureau Volkslectuur *Woordenlijst van het Sranan-Tongo* (Paramaribo: 1961), p. 34. See also Herskovits, in *The New World Negro*, ed. Frances Herskovits, p. 299. The testimony of Sidney Bechet (*Treat It Gently*, p. 63) is thus not to be accepted without reservations:

> Sometimes we'd have what they called in those days "bucking contests"; that was long before they talked about "cutting contests." One band, it would come right up in front of the other and play at it, and the first band it would play right back, until finally one band just gave in.

Bechet's New Orleans background is not in itself proof of the accuracy of his statement. In spite of the much-publicized primacy of "New Orleans jazz," many of the developments took place elsewhere—and quite as early. It may, of course, have been that *bucking* was the New Orleans term and *cutting* developed elsewhere, insofar as the continental United States was concerned.

25. Bureau Volkslectuur, op. cit., p. 34.
26. Danny Barker, "Jelly Roll Morton in New York," in *Jazz Panorama*, ed. Martin Williams, p. 15.
27. Library of Congress conversations with Alan Lomax, recorded on Riverside RLP 9003: *Discourse on Jazz*, Side 1.
28. Ibid. Martin Williams' later editorial work rearranged the Morton-Lomax conversations, but the original does seem to have contained a kind of "discourse on jazz."
29. Ibid., in the discussion of Morton's composition "Kansas City Stomp."
30. Gunther Schuller, *Early Jazz*, p. 38.
31. George Washington Cable, "The Dance in Place Congo," p. 354.
32. Rudi Blesh and Harriet James, *They All Played Ragtime*, p. 17.
33. Karl Reisman, "Cultural and Linguistic Ambiguity in a West Indian Village," in *Afro-American Anthropology*, ed. Norman Whetten and John Szwed, p. 135. Reisman quotes an impressive example:

Me no ca'e what me do	I don't care what I do
'Cause me big, mi bad, an' mi boas'	Because I'm big, I'm bad, and I'm boastful

An' mi jine di police force.	And I've joined the police force.

34. W. C. Handy, *Father of the Blues*, p. 93.
35. Elizabeth Udall, "[m?m] ETC.," has recently received strong support from Dalby's "The African Element in American English." Dialect geographer Raven I. McDavid, in "The Grunt of Negation," *American Speech* XXX (February 1955), p. 56, temporarily squelched that approach to it by placing some totally unreasonable geographic constraints on anything to be even considered as an Africanism.

For the whole business of ritual use of African languages in ritual contexts, no more completely understood by every participant than every Roman Cátholic celebrant understood all of the Latin mass or every Protestant knows exactly what is meant by *hallelujah,* most of the research remains to be done. There are strong indications of what is going on in works like George Eaton Simpson's *Religious Cults of the Caribbean,* pp. 262–270. Frederick Douglass, *Narrative of the Life,* pp. 36–37, reported of field hands on the plantation: "This they would sing, as a chorus, to words which to many would seem unmeaning jargon, but which, nevertheless, were full of meaning to themselves." Whether or not later generations, farther removed from African languages, repeated these choruses as "meaningless jargon" themselves is a question that cannot be answered a priori. Clarence Major's *Dictionary of Afro-American Slang* cites *Streevus mone on the reevus cone* "a jitterbug expression that has no specific meaning." Sometimes such expressions are presented rather as disguised communications, unintelligible except to the in-group and often with a "sexy" connotation, than as nonsense forms. Lyrics like Fats Waller's "Seafood, Mama" combined easily recognizable food-for-sex metaphors with scat phrases, apparently suggesting a level of sexual knowledge not open to everyone.

The eighteenth-century observer Dr. James Eights (reprinted in *Collections on the History of Albany,* ed. Joel Munsell [1867]) reports Black slaves in the state of New York "successively repeating the ever wild, though euphonic, cry of *Hi-a-bomba, bomba, bomba,* in full harmony with the thumping sounds. These vocal sounds were readily taken up and as oft repeated by the female portion of the spectators not otherwise engaged in the exercises of the scene, accompanied by the beating of time with their ungloved hands, in strict accordance with the eel-pot melody." Neither Munsell nor Douglass suggests, however, any "sexy" connotation for these repeated words and phrases. There can be observed, today, a great deal of linguistic experimentation in the Black community, much of it concerned with apparently meaningless variation. Jim Haskins, *The Psychology of Black Language,* p. 85, describes "pimp talk": "affixing of a nonsense syllable to certain syllables of words" and asserts that its origin was in Chicago. This seems like what a Southern Illinois University Black student described to me as "zip talk" in 1971. Although "pimp talk," especially, is often taken to imply recent innovation, on examination pimp behavior turns out to have a great deal that is traditional about it. Some of these practices obviously have to be taken into account in ascertaining the origin and function of something like "scat."

36. *Mr. Deeds Goes to Town,* with Gary Cooper, 1936. Symptomatic of the state of general American adaptation of Black patterns was "boogie woogie" drumming by Gene Krupa, enthusiastically approved by "hep" whites in the movie.

37. See Chapter Six for a more detailed discussion of the grammatical process (derivation) involved. For West Indian English, an excellent article on the subject exists in Frederic G. Cassidy's "Iteration as a Word-Forming Device in Jamaican Folk Speech," *American Speech* 32 (February 1957): 49–53.

38. Although there has been much discussion, pro and con, of this point, only a few extremists seem really to deny it. A well-presented "pro" argument can be found in Leroi Jones, *Blues People;* a somewhat more completely documented one in Southern, *The Music of Black Americans.* Southern's *Readings in Black American Music* assembles an impressive collection of documents.

39. John Storm Roberts, *Black Music of Two Worlds* (New York: Praeger Publishers, 1972), pp. 4–5.

40. Hari Rhodes, *A Chosen Few* (NY, Bantam Books, 1965), p. 22.

41. Some of the basic Creole problems of this type are presented in F. G. Cassidy, "Multiple Etymologies in Jamaican Creole." Such factors also figure prominently in the explanations by Dalby, "The African Element in American English."

42. Alan Lomax, liner notes to *Roots of the Blues,* Atlantic SD–1348. A more complete discussion, with comparison to Haitian songs and the Surinam *lobi singi,* can be found in Harold Courlander, *The Drum and the Hoe,* Chapter 12.

Courlander's Chapter 13 deals with political commentary in the Haitian songs, a topic easily paralleled in Calypso if not in the blues.

43. Paul Oliver, *The Blues Fell This Morning,* p. 28.

44. Lizzie Miles, "Yellow Dog Gal Blues," *Singing the Blues,* comp. Leonard Feather, RCA Camden CAL 588, Side 1, Band 2. As usual, this particular citation is for convenience; the traditional material can be found in many other places.

45. Robert Johnson, "Hellhound on my Trail," quoted in *The Blues Line,* comp. Eric Sackheim, p. 223.

46. Alan Lomax, *Mr. Jelly Roll,* p. 209.

47. Ibid. p. 244.

48. Ibid.

49. Texas Alexander, "No More Women Blues," quoted in *The Blues Line,* comp. Eric Sackheim, p. 121.

50. Tommy McClennan, "Brown Skin Girl," quoted in *The Blues Line,* comp. Eric Sackheim, p. 179.

51. Ibid.

52. Ed Bell, "Hambone Blues," quoted in *The Blues Line,* comp. Eric Sackheim, p. 294.

53. Martin J. Williams, *The Art of Jazz,* pp. 91–94.

54. Formally, the blues tends to have a stanzaic pattern AAB, with the repetition of A being subject to minor variations. The variations may be as trivial as

Ain't been to Georgia, but I been tol'
Say, I ain't been to Georgia, Mama, but I
been tol'

55. Jones, *Blues People,* p. 34. For a historical statement about the relationship between Catholic saints and voodoo "gods," see Jack Vincent Buerkle and Danny Barker, *Bourbon Street Black,* p. 13. See also Hyatt, *Hoodoo—Conjuration—Witchcraft* passim.

56. Big Bill Broonzy, "Big Bill Blues" *History of Classic Jazz,* Riverside RLP 12–1131, Side 3.

57. Harry Oster, *Living Country Blues,* No. 112.

58. Jelly Roll Morton, "Michigan Water Blues," *Jelly Roll Morton in Piano and Vocal Solos* Jazztone J–1211, Side 1, Band 2.

59. Bill Wilber's "My Babe My Babe," quoted in *The Blues Line,* comp. Eric Sackheim, p. 286, has the line "She give me cherry wine" in a description of an idealized girl friend who has all the (good) attributes of the hoodoo woman mistress: getting her boyfriend out of jail, giving him money, dispelling his "troubles" and "misery."

This is not to deny that references derogatory to states of the former Confederacy. Nina Simone's "Mississippi Goddam" (*The Best of Nina Simone,* Phillips 600–298, Side 1, Band 2) is as direct a statement as any. Being overtly political, however, these are not the most traditional of blues.

60. On this point, for example, see Hurston's *Mules and Men,* Puckett's *Folk Beliefs of the Southern Negro,* Hyatt's five-volume *Hoodoo—Conjuration—Witchcraft—Rootwork.*

61. Langston Hughes and Arna Bontemps, eds., *The Book of Negro Folklore,* p. 374.

62. Billie Pierce, *Blues in the Classic Tradition,* Riverside RLP 370, Side 2, Band 2.

63. Ibid., Band 2, Side 1.

64. Muddy Waters, "Louisiana Blues," Chess 1427. See also Otis Webster (Angola, Nov. 5, 1960), *Living Country Blues,* comp. Harry Oster, p. 274.

65. Muddy Waters, "Hoochie Coochie," quoted in *The Blues Line,* comp. Eric Sackheim, p. 432.

66. Quoted in *The Blues Line,* comp. Eric Sackheim, pp. 370–371.

67. On the importance of the term *snake doctor* in dialect geography, perhaps (as some of us would think) exaggerated by researchers, see for example, E. B. Atwood, *The Regional Vocabulary of Texas* (Austin, Texas University Press 1953), pp. 58, 84, 96, 100, 101, 109, 66, 196, 120, 250. This does not include Atwood's treatment of synonyms and dialect variants.

Ruby Berkeley Goodwin's autobiographical *It's Good to Be Black* reports a Black man called Snake Doctor in a Black community in Illinois that has the conjure practices but looks to the South (especially Louisiana) for the most effective practice of them.

68. Probably the most famous is from Bessie Smith's "Downhearted Blues": "I got the world in a jug; the stopper's in my hand."

69. Memphis Slim, "Gee Ain't It Hard to Find Somebody," *Broken Soul Blues,* United Artists UAL 3137, Side 2, Band 6.

70. Bessie Smith, "Please Help Me Get Him Off My Mind," *Empty Bed Blues* Columbia 14375-D, Side 4, Band 7 recorded August 24, 1928.

71. Joachim Berendt, *The Jazz Book,* p. 147, writes, "The blues is the secular form of spiritual and gospel song or the other way around: gospel song and spiritual are the religious forms of the blues. Thus it is not only in a relative, but in a literal sense that blues singer Alberta Hunter says, 'To me the blues are—well, almost religious. . . . The blues are like spirituals, almost sacred.' " Statements like this could be made much more impressive if the public expression of non-Christian religious sentiments was easier in the United States.

72. T-Bone Walker, opening lines to "I Got the Blues," Blue Note Reissue Series, *Classics of Blues,* Side 1, Band 1.

73. Schuller, *Early Jazz,* p. 46. Compare Southern, *The Music of Black Americans,* p. 334.

74. John A. Lomax, *Adventures of a Ballad Hunter,* p. 165.

75. See Cassidy and LePage, *Dictionary of Jamaican English,* p. 254. The much less formal *Dictionary of the Virgin Islands* lists the noun *jump up* "a street dance or tramp." It is doubtful whether there is any connection to American jazz talk *jump* "be lively or animated, dance animatedly" (Gold, *Jazz Talk,* pp. 150–1) or what the relationship of either is to the familiar hyperbolic *The joint is jumping* "This is a lively place." Certainly, however, all of these belong in the domain of (jazz or blues) music and dance.

76. Tony Heilbut, *The Gospel Sound,* p. 32.

77. Ibid.

78. Ibid., p. 81.

79. Allen, Ware, and Garrison, *Slave Songs of the United States,* p. x.

5. THE STREET HUSTLE: PROSTITUTION, GAMBLING, AND NARCOTICS

1. Christina Milner and Richard Milner, *Black Players,* pp. 145 ff.

2. Ambrose E. Gonzales, *The Black Border,* p. 326.

3. Susan Hall, *Gentleman of Leisure,* p. 86.

4. Milner and Milner, *Black Players,* p. 142.

5. See my *All-American English,* p. 163.

6. Herbert L. Foster, *Ribbin', Jivin', and Playin' the Dozens,* p 258.

7. Claude Brown, *Manchild in the Promised Land,* pp. 155–156.

8. Robert Beck, *Pimp,* pp. 38–40. See also p. 316 of that book.

9. Jelly Roll Morton, "Mamie's Blues," Jazztone J–1211, Side 1, Band 1.

10. Louis Armstrong, *Satchmo,* p. 73.

11. Howard W. Odum and Guy B. Johnson, *Negro Workaday Songs,* p. 211.

12. Ibid., p. 212.

13. H.C. Brearley, "Ba-ad Nigger," p. 81.

14. Quoted in *The Blues Line,* comp. Eric Sackheim, pp. 258–259.

15. Milner and Milner, *Black Players,* p. 297.

16. Ibid., pp. 41–43.

17. Julius Hudson, "The Hustling Ethic," in *Rappin' and Stylin' Out,* ed. Thomas Kochman, p. 420.

18. Milner and Milner, *Black Players,* p. 130.

19. Hudson, "The Hustling Ethic."

20. Hall, *Gentleman of Leisure,* p. 65.

21. Milner and Milner, *Black Players,* p. 61 et passim. See also Beck, *Pimp,* passim.

22. Hall, *Gentleman of Leisure,* p. 85.

23. Milner and Milner, *Black Players,* p. 110.

24. Robert Beck, *Mama Black Widow,* p. 281.

25. The first of these terms is found in Milner and Milner, *Black Players;* the second, in "Menhadin Chanties," by the Bright Light Quarter, Prestige International 25008.

26. Milner and Milner, *Black Players,* p. 298.

27. Ed Bell, "Hambone Blues," quoted in *The Blues Line,* comp. Eric Sack Reim, p. 294.

28. Beck, *Pimp,* p. 219.

29. Ibid., p. 206.

30. Ibid., p. 273.

31. Milner and Milner, *Black Players,* p. 71.

32. Ibid., p. 97, not included in the Glossary. The Glossary to Hall, *Gentleman of Leisure* lists *get down* "Have intercourse; also, to become serious about what one is doing." Gold, *Jazz Talk,* asserts that the phrase originated around 1955 and treats it as a kind of reduction from *get down with* and as somehow related to the notion of "getting to the bottom of things." No one of these assumptions seems to me to reflect any real "feel" for the term.

33. Pops Foster, *Pops Foster,* p. 32.

34. Kenneth Johnson, "Black Kinesics—Some Non-Verbal Communication Patterns in the Black Culture," *Perspectives on Black English,* ed. J.L. Dillard, p. 301.

35. Ibid., p. 302.

36. Norman Whitten, *Black Frontiersmen,* p. 125.

37. Jelly Roll Morton, *The Animule Ball,* Side 1, Riverside RLP 9002.

38. Harry Middleton Hyatt, pp. 2341–2509, *Hoodoo—Conjuration—Witchcraft* et passim are in Niles Newbell Puckett, *Folk Beliefs of the Southern Negro,* pp. 193ff et passim.

39. Jelly Roll Morton, *The Animule Ball,* Side 1 Riverside RLP 9002.

40. Warren L. d'Azevedo, *Some Terms from Liberian Speech,* p. 63, lists *zootin* "to be all dressed up; showing off; swaggering." The comment is that it is "obviously borrowed from American idiom." There is no explanation of where the "American idiom" got the word, however; d'Azevedo is explaining *ignotum per ignotius.*

41. George J. McCall, "Symbiosis: The Case of Hoodoo and the Numbers Racket," in *Mother Wit from the Laughing Barrel,* ed. Alan Dundes. Indications of the Black fondness for the numbers turn up as early as Coley Jones's recording made in Dallas on December 5, 1928:

I was feelin' lonesome, kinda blue,
Thought I'd play some numbers like most colored people do.
[Historical Records HLP–17, Side 2, Band 2]

42. Joseph R. Washington, *Black Sects and Cults,* p. 135.

43. Ulf Hannerz, *Soulside,* p. 140.

44. Robert Dean Pharr, *The Book of Numbers,* pp. 36–37.

45. Hannerz, *Soulside,* p. 141.

46. Pharr, *The Book of Numbers,* p. 153.

47. Toni Morrison, *Sula,* p. 74.

48. Hannerz, *Soulside,* p. 141.

49. Hyatt, *Hoodoo—Conjuration—Witchcraft* 2:1488.

50. From Hyatt's reports of Black "readers," and so on, who call themselves "Egyptian" or "Gypsy," it would appear that the term is taken from the stereotype of the Romanes woman. However, Ian F. Hancock, secretary of the Gypsy Literary Society, has assured me that genuine Gypsies do engage in such activities within ghetto communities. He has provided me with a very interesting group of handbills given out by such Gypsy advisors and readers.

51. See Langston Hughes and Arna Bontemps, *The Book of Negro Folklore;* there is considerable use of such materials in Octavus Roy Cohen's *Polished Ebony* and other such works. Paradoxically, Cohen has always been regarded as the epitome of phoniness in popular writing about the Negro. Some of his facts, however, are obviously correct.

52. Ibid., p. 206.

53. Beck, *Mama Black Widow,* p. 156.

54. Pharr, *The Book of Numbers,* There are many such transitional passages, like the following:

It was the morning after 088 came out. . . . [p. 157]
The next day everybody played Jim Penny's

address [he had been murdered], which was 890 Westend Avenue. But the number was 171. [p. 202]

It was the afternoon that 483 came out. . . . [p. 207]

It was the day after 518 came out straight. . . . [p. 212]

Let's make believe that Joe Louis comes to town tomorrow morning. When the ward lamps his license plate numbers they are gonna jump on it with both feet. [p. 217]

The day the number was 505, and Dave and Blueboy had to pay out over two thousand dollars in hits [after a raid by police]. [p. 221]

After the raid, everyone in the Ward played 000. Just why this number was preferred was a mystery but Dave guessed that three zeroes were picked because the Ward felt that his bank was doomed. [p. 222]

The number had been 030 the day Kelly graduated. [p. 287]

This conversation [about hiring a bodyguard] took place the same day that 967 came out. [p. 352]

Just after lunchtime on the winter day that 176 played. . . . [p. 371]

55. Quoted in Foster, *Ribbin', Jivin', and Playin' the Dozens*, p. 127.

56. Leadbelly, "Becky Deem," quoted in *The Blues Line*, comp. Eric Sackheim, p. 114.

57. Jelly Roll Morton, *Georgia Skin Game* Riverside RLP 9005, Side 2.

58. Zora Neale Hurston, *Mules and Men*, pp. 307–308. Note that Hurston considered the term worthy of inclusion in her Glossary.

59. Mitford M. Mathews, *Dictionary of Americanisms*, p. 120.

60. Paul Oliver, *The Blues Fell This Morning*, p. 130.

61. Benjamin A. Botkin, *A Treasury of Missis-*

sippi River Folklore, p. 82 (cited in *Dictionary of Americanisms* under *gravy train*).

62. David Maurer, "The Argot of Narcotics Addicts," in *Readings in American Dialectology*, ed. Harold B. Allen and Gary N. Underwood (New York, Appleton-Century-Crofts, 1971), p. 500–523.

63. Edith A. Folb, *A Comparative Study of Urban Black Argot*, p. 89.

64. Ibid., p. 89.

65. Ibid., p. 91.

66. Whitney Balliet, "Jazz: New York Notes," p. 101.

67. Beck *Pimp*, p. 66.

68. The phrase is used by Karl Reisman, "Cultural and Linguistic Ambiguity in a West Indian Village," in *Afro-American Anthropology*, ed. Norman Whitten and John Szwed, p. 135. Something of the same process operates, obviously, in "back to the roots" terminology like *funky* and even *Geechee*, used as terms of approval by jazz musicians.

69. On the use of *shit* in a nonscatological sense in Melanesian Pidgin English, see Robert A. Hall, Jr., et al., *Melanesian Pidgin English, Grammar, Texts, Vocabulary* (Baltimore, Md.: Linguistic Society of America, 1943).

70. Foster, *Ribbin', Jivin', and Playin' the Dozens* p. 117. It is noteworthy that the works by Andrews and Owens, Twiggs, and Major (see Bibliography) take this same approach. Glossaries by Mezzrow, Wells, and a few others, which do not reflect any special concern with language beyond the merely practical one of making their books intelligible to readers, also tend to be weighted heavily toward the "con" aspect of the Black English vernacular lexicon. None of these terms seems to be of especially wide currency, however, in rural areas where Black vernacular grammatical and lexical forms abound.

6. THE PROBLEM OF "SLANG" VERSUS THAT OF A GENUINE BLACK LEXICON

1. Dan Burley, *Dan Burley's Handbook of Jive* (New York: Jive Potentials, 1944).

2. Herbert L. Foster, *Ribbin', Jivin', and Playin' the Dozens*, pp. 167–168.

3. Ibid., p. 168.

4. Leroi Jones, *Home*, p. 171.

5. Geneva Smitherman, "God Don't Never Change: Black English from a Black Perspective," pp. 828–833.

6. William Labov, "Negative Attraction and

Negative Concord in English Grammar," *Language* 48 (December 1972):773–818. Labov's viewpoint would be, ostensibly, that the two utterances represent the same "deep" sentence but that the Black English vernacular has a "surface" rule of negative attraction that turns (roughly speaking) *ever* into *never*. William Labov and LeRoi Jones are thus directly opposed on this matter since the Labov rules could not allow for any semantic material to be introduced with the "concord" or "attraction" rule.

7. Richard Long, " 'Man' and 'Evil' in American Negro Speech."

8. See my books *Black English, All-American English,* and *American Talk.*

9. See Claude Levi-Strauss, *The Savage Mind,* Chicago, U. of Chicago Press, 1966, *passim.*

10. Frank C. Collymore, *Glossary of Words and Phrases of Barbadian Dialect* (Bridgetown, Barbados: Advocate Co. 1957), p. 34.

11. Ambrose Gonzales, *The Black Border,* p. 255.

12. Loman transcription, p. 132.

13. Harry Middleton Hyatt, *Hoodoo—Conjuration—Witchcraft,* p. 1521.

14. Zora Neale Hurston, *Mules and Men,* p. 93.

15. Hyatt, *Hoodoo—Conjuration—Witchcraft* p. 1521.

16. Ibid., p. 1741.

17. Ibid., p. 1782.

18. Ibid., p. 371.

19. Ibid., p. 398. The term is widely used in the United States, even among whites. Warren L. d'Azevedo, *Some Terms from Liberian Speech,* p. 14, reports *dollbaby* "any kind of figurine or stickdoll."

20. Hyatt, *Hoodoo—Conjuration—Witchcraft* p. 416.

21. Ibid., p. 615.

22. Ibid., p. 632.

23. Ibid., p. 674.

24. Ibid.

25. Gonzales, *The Black Border,* p. 92.

26. The fact that American sweet potatoes are not "yams," as the term is understood in some places (e.g., West Africa), is irrelevant here since *yam* and *sweet potato* are homonymous for at least most American users.

27. Gates Thomas, *South Texas Negro Work Songs: Collected and Uncollected,* No. 28, Texas Folklore Society, Austin, 1928.

28. Robert Deane Pharr, *The Book of Numbers,* p. 299.

29. Lorenzo Dow Turner, *Africanisms in the Gullah Dialect,* p. 191. Turner cites a source in Vai, of Liberia and Sierra Leone.

30. Claude G. Bowers, *The Tragic Era,* p. 299.

31. Pharr, *The Book of Numbers,* p. 74.

32. Duncan Emrich, ed., *Animal Tales Told in the Gullah Dialect by Albert H. Stoddard of Savannah,* p. 15. (This is a booklet of notes to the

Folklore Collections of the Library of Congress recordings AAFS L44, L45, L46.)

33. Folklore Collections of the Library of Congress, Record L44.

34. Julia Peterkin, *Black April,* p. 263.

35. Ibid., p. 187; the preacher recites the Ten Commandments to the congregation, who respond after each, "Do, Lord, help us to keep this law."

36. Ibid., p. 166.

37. Don Lee, "A Poem to Complement Other Poems," 1. 38.

38. Quoted (without the translation) in *Jamaica Talk,* F. G. Cassidy, p. 63.

39. Dot Evans, "Calypso Blues," *Beauty and the Brute Force,* Cook LP Record 1049.

40. See Gilbert D. Schneider, *First Steps in WesKos.* The poet John Figueroa of Jamaica cites (personal conversation) the Jamaican woman trapped in a narrow alley and shouting after the car that almost hit her, "Is *mash* you want fe *mash* me?" Popular sources like Gerald Durrell (Bibliography) are usually good for examples.

41. "Word Shadows," *Atlantic Monthly* 67 (January 1891):143–144.

42. James A. Harrison, "Negro English," p. 176.

43. Sam "Lightnin' " Hopkins, "Tom Moore's Farm," *A Treasury of Field Recordings* (77–LA–12–3), Vol. 2.

44. Zora Neale Hurston, "Story in Harlem Slang," in *Mother Wit from the Laughing Barrel,* ed. Alan Dundes, p. 223.

45. Niles Newbell Puckett, *Folk Beliefs of the Southern Negro,* p. 426.

46. Toni Morrison, *Sula,* p. 144.

47. Robert Beck, *Mama Black Widow,* p. 257.

48. In the nineteenth century, however, it was no insult. Certainly, mountain men used it to one another in the friendliest of conversations.

49. See Keith Whinnom, "The Origin of the European-Based Pidgins and Creoles," *Orbis* 14 (1965):509–527

50. *Kurzgefasste Neger-Englische Grammatik,* p. 11.

51. J.L. Dillard, *Black Names,* p. 71.

52. George W. Lee, *Beale Street,* p. 34.

53. This seems to be especially true of Ralph Fasold, *Tense Marking in Black English.*

54. J.L. Dillard, *Black English,* p. 242.

55. David Dalby "The African Influence on American English."

7. ROOT WORK AND CONJURE

1. J. Mason Brewer, *Dog Ghosts and Other Texas Negro Folktales*, p. 108. In Julia Peterkin's *Black April,* a Low Country (Gullah or "Geechee") character puts it this way: "White people leave money to their children, but Black people teach theirs signs, which is far better." The controversial nature of a domain like conjure is obvious; it is probably the major reason why "color blind" liberal scholarship has never dealt with the issue. It seems obvious, however, that a topic should not be proscribed simply because it can be approached irresponsibly.

It is difficult to draw the line between academic responsibility with respect to an inherently controversial topic and sensationalism. Where would we place, for example, Robert Tallant's *Voodoo in New Orleans?* Zora Neale Hurston's review accuses it of exoticism and irresponsibility. Her own *Mules and Men,* however, contains many materials of the same general type. We are on firmer ground with extreme oddities, like J. Justice, *The Black Apostle* (1946, privately printed):

> The present Black or Negro people today are credited with being the most superstitious people in the world regarding signs, yet they do not know why. [p. 75]

I shall proceed on the assumption that lexical information reported by Hurston, for example, is accurate unless contradicted by strong evidence from some other source, that Tallant's materials may be useful if corroborated by independent sources, and that a work like Justice's probably could be assumed to have no validity whatsoever.

2. James A. Harrison, "Negro English," in *Perspectives on Black English,* ed. J.L. Dillard.

3. James Grainger, *The Sugar Cane,* 4:37n.

4. Bessie Smith, "Spider Man Blues," *Empty Bed Blues,* Side 3, Band 5 Columbia 14338–D, recorded March 19, 1928.

5. See Melville J. Herskovits and Frances S. Herskovits, *Suriname Folk-Lore, passim.* For the magic powers of Anansi, often forgotten or swallowed up in the humor of the tales, see "Anansi and King's Son," the well-chosen example in F. G. Cassidy's *Jamaica Talk.*

6. Grainger, *The Sugar Cane,* 143n.

7. Ibid.

8. Ibid.

9. Norman E. Whitten, Jr., "Contemporary Patterns of Malign Occultism Among Negroes in North Carolina," in *Mother Wit from the Laughing Barrel* ed. Alan Dundes. Whitten lists a number of interesting "synonyms for the spell": *curse, trick, fix, conjure, root,* and *hoodoo,* as well as "other less common terms": *wuwu, hack,* and *under-worlded.* He also reports that a person under a spell is referred to as *carrying a dirty undermining point.* Whitten offers no evidence that these terms have been borrowed from whites, and I doubt that there is any. Nevertheless, he concludes that there are virtually no African survivals in these beliefs and submits "two factors greatly influencing the assimilation of European occult beliefs by eighteenth-century Negroes. These factors were the language spoken by the Negroes and the church attended by them" (p. 415). This is a classic case of begging the question, where it is not simply the output from a naive linguistic theory. An opponent of Whitten's viewpoint could still point out the different nature of the English spoken by Blacks (especially the slaves in the nineteenth century) and the different character of the churches they attended. (Even leaving aside the absurdity that churches were somehow agents of the transmission of European witch lore!) The conjure vocabulary itself—or so I have tried to argue above—is a strong exception to the facile assumption that the Blacks learned the English of the British colonists. It should be pointed out, however, that Whitten could draw only on the linguistic information of his own time (e.g., McDavid, "The Position of the Charleston Dialect"), which traced the forms in the Black English vernacular to archaic survivals from British English dialects insofar as it mentioned them at all.

10. Hyatt, *Hoodoo—Conjuration—Witchcraft* 136. It would be absurd to deny the similarity of some of this material to European witch lore, even in terminology. For example, this same informant told Hyatt, "I know a woman who was a *familiar hag*" (Ibid.).

11. George Eaton Simpson, *The Shango Cult in Trinidad,* p. 22.

12. Herskovits and Herskovits, *Suriname Folk-Lore,* p. 294.

13. Hyatt, *Hoodoo—Conjuration—Witchcraft* p. 864.

14. M. Andrews and P.T. Owen, *Black Language,* Los Angeles, Seymore-Smith, 1973. p. 50. Alan Dundes, in an editorial explanatory note to *Mother Wit from the Laughing Barrel,* p. 235, draws the connection to religious practices, but not to conjure.

15. Carl Carmer, *Stars Fell on Alabama,* p. 21.

16. Niles Newbell Puckett, *Folk Beliefs of the Southern Negro,* p. 204.

17. Herskovits and Herskovits, *Suriname Folk-Lore,* pp. 18–20. The authors use the phrase *tie his* [the man's] *soul* (p. 19).

18. Hyatt, *Hoodoo—Conjuration—Witchcraft* p. 309.

19. Simpson, *The Shango Cult in Trinidad,* p. 30.

20. Melville J. Herskovits, *Life in a Haitian Valley,* p. 147.

21. Simpson, *The Shango Cult in Trinidad,* p. 30.

22. Jelly Roll Morton, *Georgia Skin Game* Library of Congress Recording 9005, Side 1.

23. Hyatt, *Hoodoo—Conjuration—Witchcraft* 159.

24. See my *Black English* for the most complete account published to date.

25. Hyatt, *Hoodoo—Conjuration—Witchcraft* 2:1391. Much more material in Hyatt's collection is directly relevant to this meaning of *bottle:*

> Well, now, yo' gonna take de name of dis individual an' yo' gonna take a bottle an' yo' gonna write de names of dis individual. If it's a white person, use white papah and red ink; if it's colored, yo' use brown papah an' black ink. Now, yo' gonna take de names of dis individual nine times on dis papah an' yo' gonna put it into dis bottle—see, a black bottle or a brown bottle, if it's a colored person; a white bottle if it's a white person. [2:1379]

> Now, dat is tuh put a person down an' tuh make a person drag. Yo' take all dat an' yo' put it in a bottle wit de names of dose individuals. Now, der's sut in dis dog dirt, yo' see. Well, now, yo' gonna bury dat bottle upside down an' dat party's gonna drag—dey jis' gonna go down an' dey gonna drag. [2:1383]

There is a Louisiana French Creole tale (e.g., in Jarreau's LSU thesis) "*Les Chiens en Bouteille*" about some magic (and immortal) dogs who destroy witches. *Bouteille* here may mean "bag" rather than "bottle"—but so may *bottle* in most conjure texts. Compare conjurer's bag ("of the Africans") attested as early as 1863 ("E. Kirke," pseud. James R. Gilmore, New York, 1863, *My Southern Friends,* p. 153).

26. Herskovits, *Life in a Haitian Valley,* p. 31.

27. Hyatt, *Hoodoo—Conjuration—Witchcraft* 1132.

28. Ibid., p. 511.

29. Charles W. Chesnutt, "Superstitions and Folklore of the South," pp. 371–372.

30. Benjamin A. Botkin, *Lay My Burden Down,* p. 46.

31. Hyatt, *Hoodoo—Conjuration—Witchcraft* 309.

32. David Cohn, *God Shakes Creation,* p. 127.

33. Richard Manuel Amerson, *Negro Folk Music of Alabama,* Ethnic Folkways P471, Side 1, Band 3.

34. The terms are found in Hyatt, *Hoodoo—Conjuration—Witchcraft passim.*

35. Puckett, *Folk Beliefs of the Southern Negro,* p. 205.

36. Julia Peterkin, *Black April,* p. 38.

37. Lenora Herron and Alice M. Bacon, "Conjuring and Conjure Doctors," in *Mother Wit from the Laughing Barrel,* ed. Alan Dundes, p. 363.

38. William R. Ferris, "Black Prose Narrative in the Mississippi Delta," p. 120.

39. Quoted by Eugene D. Genovese, *Roll, Jordan, Roll,* p. 219.

40. Erdmann Doane Beynon, "The Voodoo Cult Among Negro Migrants in Detroit," p. 898.

41. Bruce Jackson, "Circus and Street: Psychosocial Aspects of the Black Toast," p. 119.

42. Frederic G. Cassidy and Robert B. LePage, *Dictionary of Jamaican English,* 1968.

43. Ishmael Reed, *Yellow Back Radio Broke-Down,* p. 82.

44. Hyatt, *Hoodoo—Conjuration—Witchcraft* p. 309.

45. This is a major point in Zora Neale Hurston's "High John de Conquer," in *Mother Wit from the Laughing Barrel,* ed. Alan Dundes. In an introductory note, Dundes argues against Hurston's theory.

46. Tallant, *Voodoo in New Orleans,* p. 229. Note the use of the same term in Hurston's *Mules and Men,* p. 233. In spite of Hurston's criticism of Tallant's book, it is striking how many elements it has in common with hers. One major objection (not necessarily Hurston's) to Tallant's work is that he romanticizes, making Marie Laveau a voodoo "queen" and the central figure in a novel of conjure. No such picture of domination by any one person emerges from studies like that of Hyatt *Hoodoo—Conjuration—Witchcraft.*

47. Hyatt, p. 665.

48. Herskovits and Herskovits, *Suriname Folk-Lore,* p. 100. See also Puckett, *Folk Beliefs of the Southern Negro,* pp. 227.

49. Hyatt, *Hoodoo—Conjuration—Witchcraft* p. 593.
50. Hurston, "High John de Conquer," p. 450.
51. Hyatt, *Hoodoo—Conjuration—Witchcraft* p. 593.
52. Sam Dickinson, " 'Hands' and Hands," pp. 7–8.
53. Hyatt, *Hoodoo—Conjuration—Witchcraft* p. 593.
54. "Fred McDowell's Blues," *Yazoo Delta Blues and Spirituals,* Prestige International INT 25010, Side A, Band 7. A lengthier and more hoodooistically complete version is sung by Muddy Waters, "Louisiana Blues," Chess 1427. The lyrics include specific reference to mojo, black cat bone, John the Conqueror Root, and luck oil.
55. "Talking to Myself," quoted in *The Blues Line,* comp. Eric Sackheim, p. 331.
56. This stanza from Robert Johnson's "Little Queen of Spades," Vocalion 04108 (recorded June 20, 1937) is quoted by John Solomon Otto and August M. Burns, "The Use of Race and Hillbilly Recordings as Sources for Historical Research."
57. William Wells Brown, *My Southern Home,* p. 81.
58. Harry Oster, *Living Country Blues,* p. 278. See also p. 36, Oster quotes Robert Pete Williams' "Hoodoo Blues": "Oh, darlin', the way you smell, darlin', I know you been with the hoodoo."
59. "Talking to Myself," quoted in *The Blues Line,* comp. Eric Sackheim, p. 331.
60. Andrews and Owen, *Black Language.*
61. Bruce Jackson, *Wake Up Dead Man,* p. 313.
62. Puckett, *Folk Beliefs of the Southern Negro,* p. 215.
63. Hurston, *Mules and Men,* p. 190: "I got Joe Moore in my hand," obviously a pun on "I got a mojo hand." The lucky player has just been told by an envious opponent, "You must be setting on roots."
64. Goodwin, *It's Good to Be Black,* p. 136.
65. Peterkin, *Black April,* p. 265.
66. Marjorie Rawlings, *Cross Creek,* p. 300.
67. Pops Foster, *Pops Foster,* p. 143.
68. The first appears in Puckett, *Folk Beliefs of the Southern Negro,* p. 341; the second in Hyatt, *Hoodoo—Conjuration—Witchcraft* p. 934.
69. Hyatt, *Hoodoo—Conjuration—Witchcraft* pp. 410, 222.

70. Ibid., p. 737 records *catbone wishers.* The prominence of the term in blues lyrics is an added reason. There are many like Blind Lemon Jefferson's stanza in "Broke and Hungry Blues":
I believe my good gal has found my Black Cat's Bone,
I can leave Sunday mornin', Monday mornin'
I'm sittin' back home.
[Oster, *Living Country Blues,* p. 273]
71. Hyatt, *Hoodoo—Conjuration—Witchcraft* p. 54, records *wicked graveyard dirt.*
72. Beck, *Mama Black Widow,* p. 290.
73. Hyatt, *Hoodoo—Conjuration—Witchcraft* passim, largely in Vol. I.
74. Puckett, *Folk Beliefs of the Southern Negro,* p. 232, gives an elaborate description of the goofer-root.
75. Maurice Harley Weseen, *A Dictionary of American Slang,* New York, Thomas Y. Crowell Co., 1934 gives *"Goof*—a foolish person. *Goofer* is a variant." There is a surprising lack of treatment, otherwise, of the term in dictionaries.
76. William Wells Brown, *My Southern Home,* p. 70.
77. Ibid., p. 81.
78. Puckett, *Folk Beliefs of the Southern Negro,* p. 215.
79. Ibid., p. 319.
80. Hurston, *Mules and Men,* pp. 244, 281.
81. Ibid., p. 265. Louis Maximilien, *Le Vodou Haitien, Rite Radas-Congo,* Port-au-Prince, n.d., p. 185: "Leur confection se realise au cours d'une ceremonie en l'honneur des dieux Simby et Carrefour. Les deux vevers sont tracés et le rituel est celui d'un service petro. Un coq (frisé) est sacrifie . . ." TRANSLATION: Their creation is achieved during a ceremony in honor of the gods Simby and Carrefour ("Crossroads"). The two *vevers* (ceremonial patterns) are traced [on the floor, with flour] and the ritual is that of a "petro" service. A cock, with frizzled feathers, is sacrificed . . . Cf. Genovese, *Roll, Jordan, Roll,* p. 217, on the use of the "frizzled hen" by southern Black slaves. The usual assumption would be that *frizzled* would become something like *frizzly* in casual speech. In view of the comparative evidence, however, it seems more nearly possible that *frizzly* is closer to the original condition and that *frizzled* represents a rationalization.
82. Puckett, *Folk Beliefs of Southern Negros,* p. 21.

8. DISCOURSE DISTRIBUTION AND THE PROBLEM OF SEMANTIC DIFFERENCE IN HOMOPHONOUS ITEMS

1. Herbert L. Foster, *Ribbin', Jivin', and Play-in' the Dozens,* p. 46; the term *streetcorner man,* widely used in the anthropological literature, was popularized in Elliott Liebow's *Talley's Corner.* A streetcorner man lacks the drive and perhaps the peculiar intelligence of the *hustler* and the muscle of the *gorilla,* although he imitates both, especially the latter, in some of his behavior patterns.

2. Zora Neale Hurston, *Mules and Men,* p. 54. A similar formula occurs on p. 160.

3. Ibid., p. 132.

4. Ibid., p. 37.

5. Robert A. Hall, Jr., *Haitian Creole,* p. 89. Many more examples, with a wide range of variants, can be found in compilations like Elsie Clews Parsons, ed., *Folk-Lore of the Antilles.* Harold Courlander, *The Drum and the Hoe,* suggests a slightly different distribution of norms for the tale endings. He points out that "These formula endings often provide a dramatic punch for the children who are listening." This tendency to relegate the tags to children, possibly as a kind of pretense because adults consider them old-fashioned and embarrassing, is a good indication of the obsolescence of the tags. For the relegation to grandparents rather than children alone, see below.

6. Paul Radin, *African Folktales and Sculpture,* p. 19.

7. This may seem ad hoc insofar as semantic features are concerned, particularly since the standard works on generative semantics have not concerned themselves with such a category. Such works are, however, far from exhaustive in their treatment of the lexicon, even when it is limited to nouns. It seems fairly clear that in a scheme like:

± Noun
± Common
± Count
± Animate
± Human

certain "branching" devices would be necessary in order to deal with subgroups below Animate. One branch would, of course, involve those + Animate nouns that were +Human *(man, boy, woman, grandmother, referee, senator)* rather than −Human *(typewriter, eraser, room, desk, river).* For the +Human branch, ± Male, ± Adult, ± English-speaking, ± American would obviously be necessary, whereas those +Ani-

mate nouns that were −Human would need no specification as to nationality or language. (I am following Bolinger, *Aspects of Language,* Second Edition, 1975, New York, Harcourt Brace, Jovanovich, Inc. here, and overlooking the very obvious fact that ± American- and ± English-speaking would be relevant only to a highly chauvinistic discourse. The fact that the −Human branch would also include ± Male and ± Adult may also mean that a simple flow chart procedure is far from adequate. These considerations are, however, largely irrelevant in the present context. They are offered, as they were by Bolinger, simply to illustrate the principles.) Among those nouns that are −Animate, some would include the feature +Metallic; presumably, ± Bendable would apply to that group at some point in the representation. (The same feature would, obviously, also apply to some nouns in the −Metallic class.) No treatment seems to have given serious consideration to the absolute number of features required.

8. Actually, it seems most likely that both ± Metallic and ±Bendable would be present, in a hierarchical order, in the representation and that the variation here would simply represent a choice at a "higher" level. If, however, ±Metal is a "higher" choice than ±Bendable, then the latter must also be associated with some −Metal items (especially *bow*). See the preceding footnote on the features ±Male and ±Adult.

9. Parsons, *Folk-Lore of the Antilles,* 2: 11.

10. Ibid., 2:407.

11. The occurrence of tense in the Black English vernacular would best be described by nonredundancy rules (i.e., past tense marking must show up in a past tense context, but not necessarily in every verb) in a discourse grammar. Thus, individual sentences containing two or three verbs often mark all the verbs for past tense—and thus confuse linguists like Ralph Fasold *(Tense Marking in Black English).* A sentence later, tense marking may be omitted from two of three verbs. The verb not marked for tense is thus a fact of the grammar of the Black English vernacular and not of its phonology. Some of the "dialect" readers that incorporate sentences like *He go yesterday* are, however, artificial and probably confusing to the Black children who have been told that this is "their dialect." A single verb, in an isolated sentence, will almost never be un-

marked for tense—assuming that the time reference is past.

12. Blue Lu Barker, "Trombone Man Blues," *The History of Jazz*, Vol. I, New Orleans Origins, Capitol T793, Side 2, Band 3.

13. Roger D. Abrahams, *Deep Down in the Jungle*, pp. 58–59.

14. Parsons, *Folk-Lore of the Antilles*, 2:11.

15. Ibid., 2:409. The tale was collected on the island of St. Martin.

16. Arthur Huff Fauset, "Negro Folk Tales from the South," p. 264.

17. Ibid., p. 222.

18. Ibid., p. 250.

19. Parsons, *Folk-Lore of the Antilles*, 2:303.

20. John Greenway, *American Folk Songs of Protest*, p. 120.

21. Frank Yerby, "My Brother Went to College," p. 165.

22. Stella Brewer Brooks, *Joel Chandler Harris.*

23. The report of this couplet, completely innocent of any of the tale-ending or Creole analogues (in fact, in a context rather tending to suggest that there are no such associations), is in Labov et al. *(A Study of the Non-Standard English).*

24. Ulf Hannerz, *Soulside*, p. 115.

25. Richard Dorson, *Folklore from Benton Harbor, Michigan*, passim.

26. Parsons, *Folk-Lore of the Antilles*, 3:30–31.

27. Fauset, "Negro Folk Tales from the South," p. 273.

28. The fact that *mo*, or a form somewhat like it, is used for *moi* in Cajun French is obviously irrelevant here, although it is almost certain to be cited in any discussion. The important point is not the phonetic shape of the pronoun but its use as a subject form, which is almost exclusively Creole. The use of *moi* as part of an emphatic form *"Moi*, je . . ."* in Standard French is more nearly relevant.

29. Manuel J. Andrade, *Folk-Lore from the Dominican Republic*, p. 44. Among many variations in the tag ending are *y entre mierda y cagá me dieron una patá* (p. 95), *y aquí se acabó me cuento con pimienta y ajo, y a mi me dieron una patá y me dejaron aquí sentá* (p. 72; this is a combination of the Haitian formula in translation with a more "respectable" Spanish formula, often given to me by middle-class informants in Puerto Rico), *y Grigrí fue dichosísimo y heredo todas las riquezas del principe, y a mi no me dieron ni una copa del brindis, ni porque fui yo que lo conté* (p. 139).

30. Radin, *African Folktales and Sculpture*, p. 19.

31. Melville F. Herskovits, *Dahomeyan Narrative*, p. 53.

32. Ibid., p. 54.

33. Ibid.

34. *Gombo Zhébes*, New York, 1885 p. 36.

35. Melville J. Herskovits and Frances S. Herskovits, *Suriname Folk-Lore*, pp. 142–143.

36. Ibid., p. 145. (See also examples of this formula, with many variations, in Parsons, *Folk-Lore of the Antilles*, passim.)

37. Ibid., p. 143. Heinz Eersel, former director of the Taalbureau, Paramaribo, Surinam, has given in public much more complete descriptions of this feature. Unfortunately, he seems never to have published that material.

38. This is frequently pointed out in Herskovits and Herskovits, *Suriname Folk-Lore*, as in Parsons, *Folk-Lore of the Antilles*.

39. John Mason Brewer, *Dog Ghosts and Other Texas Negro Folktales*, p. 66.

40. Paul Oliver, *The Blues Fell This Morning*, p. 152.

41. Neil A. Eddington, *The Urban Plantation*.

42. Charles S. Johnson, *The Shadow of the Plantation*, p. 171.

43. Daniel J. Crowley, *I Could Talk Old-Time Story Good*, p. 27.

44. For the Gullah material, I am indebted to William A. Stewart (personal communication).

45. Stewart also supplied this information. He has graciously provided me with many of the results of his National Science Foundation-funded research project.

46. Jan Voorhoeve and Ursy M. Lichtveld, eds., *Creole Drum*, p. 77.

47. William A. Stewart, "Foreign Language Teaching Methods in a Quasi-Foreign Language Situation."

48. Herbert L. Foster, *Ribbin', Jivin', and Playin' the Dozens*, pp. 117–178

49. Morris Siegel, "No Abner This Time," *The Dallas Morning News*, n.d.

50. George Lee, *Beale Street*, p. 145. Several people, including my wife Margie I. Dillard, (who made notes on the speech), have called my attention to these characteristics in a speech that Barbara Jordan made at the Democratic National Convention in July 1976. One noteworthy characteristic is that all these observers commented on the effectiveness of Ms. Jordan's speech, no one of them suggesting that such a pattern was the result of a lack of proficiency in speaking. Television commentator Bill Moyers

displayed typical ineptness in characterizing the style as "biblical." Such a classification is, however, a folk cliché and therefore need be given no special credence.

It would be astonishing if no one had noticed this discourse pattern, although those who have are, like Lee, more nearly folk reporters than professional analysts. The repetitive pattern of the first line of each blues stanza has often been commented upon, although the newspaper critics roughly attached to music criticism who have done most of the work on jazz have seldom if ever had anything insightful to say about it. Perhaps the most meaningful comment has come from a source that, on reflection, could be expected to have something sensible to say about the matter:

There's a lot of people can understand English, but you gotta talk very slow. So, the blues singers, they sing the same thing over twice. The same thing. Over and over again. No matter 'cause you're dumb, but simply to give you a chance to catch it the next time when they come around.
[Big Bill Broonzy, quoted in *The Sound of Surprise*, by Whitney Balliet, p. 178]

although there is an established American folk usage in which *understand English* is equivalent to "understand language," Broonzy's statement just might represent a more literal interpretation of the phrase. If, as suspected, the blues go back very far into Black history, there may well have been a time when some of the listeners were literally learning English and may have needed the repetition.

9. CAN WE TRUST LITERARY SOURCES?

1. Samuel Clemens, *Writings,* Author's National Edition, 1925 22:62.

2. The term was first used, in English at any rate, by Charles Ferguson, "Diglossia."

3. Tremaine McDowell, "Negro Dialect in the American Novel to 1821," *American Speech* 5 (April 1930): 291–296.

4. Jerome Dowd, *The Negro in American Life* New York, The Century Co. 1926 p. 263.

5. George P. Krapp, *The English Language in America,* 1:266.

6. See my books *Black English,* especially Chapter IV, and *Perspectives on Black English,* Introduction to Section II.

7. J. Robinson, *The Yorker's Strategem: or, Banana's Wedding* (New York: 1792), p. 9.

8. James Fenimore Cooper, *Satansoe,* p. 149.

9. Daniel P. Horsmanden, *The New York Conspiracy.*

10. Charles Waddell Chesnutt, *The Conjure Woman,* pp. 138–139.

11. Thomas Wentworth Higginson, *Army Life in a Black Regiment,* (1872), p. 234.

12. See, for example, Frederic G. Cassidy, *Jamaica Talk,* London, MacMillan and Co., Ltd. and works on West African Pidgin English by Gilbert Schneider (see Bibliography).

13. See Chapter IV of my *Black English.*

14. William Gilmore Simms, *The Wigwam and the Cabin* (New York, Wiley and Putnam, 1845), p. 197.

15. Ibid., p. 387.

16. Some idea of the fictional sources can be gained from the section "American Negro Dialect in Literature" in John Reinecke, et al., *A Bibliography of Pidgin and Creole Languages,* Oceanic Linguistics Special Publication No. 14, pp. 481–529.

17. John Herbert Nelson, *The Negro Character in American Literature* (Lawrence, Kansas, Dept. of Journalism Press, 1926), p. 121.

18. See Hans Nathan, *Dan Emmett and the Rise of Early Negro Minstrelsy.*

19. Ibid., Nathan discusses this point at great length.

20. Quoted in *The Negro and His Folklore . . .* ed. Bruce Jackson, pp. 178–80.

21. David Dalby, "The African Element in American English," cites Kimbundu *mbanza* "stringed musical instrument," whence also Jamaican *banja* and Brazilian and Portuguese *banza.* The European stringed instrument, the bandore, may have influenced the instrument, but it can hardly be the source of the word.

22. Dillard, *Perspectives on Black English,* p. 195.

23. Ibid., p. 183.

24. On the writings of Thomas Henry Haliburton, a Nova Scotian who wrote under the pseudonym of Sam Slick of Slickville, Connecticut, see Elna Bengtsson, *The Language and Vocabulary of Sam Slick,* Upsala Canadian Studies, Vol. 5, 1956.

25. William Wells Brown, *My Southern Home,* p. 74.

26. Stage directions to *Porgy,* Act I, Scene 1.

27. Raven I, McDavid, Jr., "The Position of the Charleston Dialect."

28. An indication of the state of previous studies can be gained from Nathan van Patten's statement ("The Vocabulary of the American Negro . . ." p. 24). Working from four books, van Patten pointed out, "Two of these books are by Negroes." It is no wonder that he missed most of the significant terms. This is not to assert that van Patten's choices (Claude McKay's *Home to Harlem,* Carl Van Vechten's *Nigger Heaven,* Eric Walrond's *Tropic Death,* and R. Emmet Kennedy's *Gritny People*) are not good ones. There could, however, have been better choices, especially since only four books were used.

29. "Characteristics of Negro Expression," in *Negro Anthology,* ed. Nancy Cunard (London: privately published 1934).

30. A more accurate gloss, at least of the usage of southern white children in my youth, would be "shit."

31. Correctly glossed as an Africanism, this word is in widespread use among whites, especially in the Georgia-South Carolina area. It is also a common Caribbeanism and has been attested in Nova Scotia in the nineteenth century.

32. Again, Hurston's gloss may be a euphemism. Use in blues lyrics suggests "arse" rather than "hips."

33. As a familiar discourse device from the inner city, *signifying* tends to mean "communicating (often an obscene or ridiculing message) by indirection." Hurston's gloss "show off," on the other hand, may be accurate for the rural Florida Blacks in her study.

34. Again, the term seems to mean, in the inner city and among southern whites, the female sex organs (or "ass") rather than "sex."

35. If this is connected with present-day teenage *hassle* "inconvenience" (the great fear of the modern American teenager!), the semantic development must have been an interesting one.

36. See C. Merton Babcock, "A Word List from Zora Neale Hurston."

37. I have a suspicion, however, that many of the academics who react with a sneer to the mention of the writings of Joel Chandler Harris are familiar with the Uncle Remus stories only through Walt Disney's movies.

38. Although neither of these would rate very high, perhaps, on the militancy scale of LeRoi Jones ("The Myth of a Negro Literature," in *Home*), neither of them was deficient in what would today be called Black Pride. Robert A. Bone (in Melvin Drimmer's *Black History* [Garden City, N.Y., Doubleday and Co., Inc., 1968.] pp. 408–410) has missed the point of Chesnutt's rather low-keyed protest. He writes:

> Chesnutt's hero, Dr. Miller in *The Marrow of Tradition* (1901) dislikes being made to share a segregated car with Negro laborers. "These people," Miller thinks, "were just as offensive to him as to the whites at the other end of the train." . . . Few novelists had their characters identify with the masses, and when lower-class characters were depicted, it was in the same condescending manner as used by Joel Chandler Harris or Thomas Nelson Page. . . . Negro intellectuals were still under the Booker Washington influence, which believed that the answer to the race problem could be found in an alliance between the better class of colored people and the quality white folks.

This is to condemn Shakespeare because of the sentiments ascribed to Polonius—or to quote one of Othello's speeches to prove that Desdemona was really unfaithful. The whole point of *The Marrow of Tradition* is how Dr. Miller loses that snobbish attitude toward "lower-class" Blacks and takes up the responsibilities of his ethnic identity. And Dr. Miller's past history plays an important part in the novel: It is his "white man's" accent that enables him to rescue some Blacks pursued by a lynching party.

The snobbery of "middle-class" Blacks toward "lower-class" Blacks was a theme that Chesnutt treated again in *The Wife of His Youth.* Anyone who reads that work as meaning that Chesnutt *condoned* such attitudes is missing all the irony of which a very skilled writer is capable.

39. Richard Wright, *The Long Dream,* p. 86.

Bibliography

Abrahams, Roger D. *Deep Down in the Jungle: Negro Narrative Folklore from the Streets of Philadelphia.* Hatboro, Penn.: Folklore Associates, 1970.

———. "Playing the Dozens." *Journal of American Folklore* 75 (1962): 209–220, reprinted in *Mother Wit from the Laughing Barrel,* ed. Alan Dundes, 1973.

A Brief History, Description, and Dictionary of the Everyday Language of Virgin Islands Children. Charlotte Amalie, St. Thomas: Office of Education (Draft), 1974.

Albertson, Chris. *Bessie.* New York: Stein and Day, 1972.

Alderman, Edwin Anderson, Joel Chandler Harris, and William Kent. *Library of Southern Literature.* New Orleans: The Martin and Hoyt Co., 1907–23.

Alexander, Captain J. E. *Trans-Atlantic Sketches: Comprising Visits to the Most Interesting Scenes of North and South America, and the West Indies. With Notes on Negro Slavery and Canadian Emigration.* London: R. Bentley, 1833.

Allen, William Francis. "Negro Dialect," *Nation* 1 (December 14, 1863):744.

Allen, William Francis; Ware, Charles Pickard; and Garrison, Lucy McKim. *Slave Songs of the United States,* 1867. New York, Oak Publications, 1965.

Alvarez Nazario, Manuel. *El Elemento Afronegroïde en el Español de Puerto Rico.* University of Puerto Rico Press, Madrid, 1961.

Anderson, Margaret. *Children of the South.* New York: Dell Publishing Co., 1967.

Andrade, Manuel J. *Folk-Lore from the Dominican Republic.* New York: American Folklore Society,

Andrews, Malachi, and Owens, Paul T. *Black Language.* West Los Angeles: Seymour Smith Publisher, 1973.

Armstrong, Louis. *Satchmo: My Life in New Orleans.* Englewood, N.J.: Prentice-Hall, Inc., 1954.

Armstrong, Orlando Kay. *Old Massa's People: The Old Slaves Tell Their Story.* Indianapolis, Ind.: The Bobbs-Merrill Co., 1931.

Arnold, Byron, comp. *Folksongs of Alabama.* Drawer: University of Alabama Press, 1950.

Atwood, E. Bagby. *A Survey of Verb Forms in the Eastern United States.* Ann Arbor: University of Michigan Press, 1953.

Babcock, C. Merton. "A Word List from Zora Neale Hurston." *Publications of the American Dialect Society*

———. "The Echo of a Whistle." *Western Folklore* 19 (1960):61.

Bailey, Beryl Loftman. "Toward a New Perspective in Negro English Dialectology." *American Speech* 40 (October 1965):171–177.

Baldwin, James. *The Amen Corner.* New York: Dial Press, 1968.

———. *Go Tell It on the Mountain.* New York: Alfred A. Knopf, 1953.

———. *Blues for Mr. Charlie.* New York: Dell, 1964.

———. *The Fire Next Time.* New York: Dial Press, 1963.

———. *Tell Me How Long the Train's Been Gone.* New York: Dial Press, 1968.

Balliet, Whitney. "Jazz: New York Notes." *The New Yorker,* February 23, 1976.

———. *The Sound of Surprise.* New York: E. P. Dutton, 1961.

Ballowe, Hewitt Leonard. *The Lawd Sayin' the Same: Negro Folk Tales of the Creole Country.* Baton Rouge: Louisiana State University Press, 1948.

Barabola, S. A. *The Content and Form of Yoruba Ijala.* Oxford: Clarendon Press, 1966.

Baratz, Stephen S., and Baratz, Joan C. "Early Childhood Intervention: The Social Science

Base of Institutional Racism." *Harvard Educational Review* 40 (February 1970):29–50.

Barr, Alwyn. *Black Texans: A History of Negroes in Texas, 1528–1971.* Austin: Jenkins Publishing Co., 1973.

Barth, Ernest A. T. "The Language Behavior of Negroes and Whites." *Pacific Sociological Review* 4 (1961):69–72.

Barton, William E. "Hymns of the Slave and the Freedman." *New England Magazine* 19 (1899):609–624.

Beach, Lazarus. *Jonathan Postfree: Or the Honest Yankee.* New York: David Longworth, 1807.

Beadle, Samuel A. *Adam Shuffler.* Jackson, Miss.: Harmon Publishing Co., 1901.

Bechet, Sidney. *Treat It Gently.* New York: Hill and Wang, 1960.

Beck, Robert (Pseudonym Iceberg Slim). *Pimp: The Story of My Life.* Los Angeles: Holloway House, 1969.

———. *Mama Black Widow.* Los Angeles: Holloway House, 1969.

———. *Trick Baby.* Los Angeles: Holloway House, 1969.

Benardete, Dolores. "Eloise," *American Speech* 7 (October 1931–August 1932):349–364.

Bennett, John Richard. *The South As It Is.* New York: The Viking Press, 1965.

Berendt, Joachim. *The Jazz Book: From New Orleans to Rock and Free Jazz.* New York: Lawrence Hill Co., 1973.

Berlin, Ira. *Slaves Without Masters: The Freed Negro in the Antebellum South.* New York: Pantheon Books, 1974.

Beynon, Erdmann D. "The Voodoo Cult Among Negro Migrants in Detroit." *American Journal of Sociology* (1939).

Billups, Edgar P. "Some Principles for the Representation of Negro Dialect in Fiction." *Texas Review* 8 (1923):99–123.

Blassingame, John W. *The Slave Community: Plantation Life in the Antebellum South.* New York: Oxford University Press, 1972.

Blesh, Rudi, and Janis, Harriet. *They All Played Ragtime.* New York: Grove Press, 1950.

Botkin, Benjamin A. *Lay My Burden Down: A Folk History of Slavery.* Chicago: University of Chicago Press, 1945.

———. *A Treasury of Mississippi River Folklore.* New York: Crown Publishers, 1955.

———. *A Treasury of Southern Folklore.* New York: Crown Publishers, 1949.

Bowers, Claude G. *The Tragic Era: The Revolution after Lincoln.* New York: Blue Ribbon Books, 1929.

Bradford, Roark. *Ol' Man Adam an' His Chillun.* New York: Harper and Brothers, 1928.

———. *John Henry.* New York: Harper and Brothers, 1931.

Brasch, Ila, and Brasch, Walter. *A Complete Annotated Bibliography of American Black English.* Baton Rouge: Louisiana State University Press, 1974.

Brearley, H. C. "Ba-ad Nigger." *South Atlantic Quarterly* 38 (1939):75–81.

Brewer, J. Mason. *Negrito: Negro Dialect Poems of the Southwest.* San Antonio: Naylor Printing Co., 1933.

———. *The Word on the Brazos: Negro Preacher Tales from the Brazos Bottoms of Texas.* Austin: University of Texas Press, 1953.

———. *Aunt Dicy Tales: Snuff-dipping Tales of the Texas Negro.* Austin: University of Texas Press, 1956.

———. *Dog Ghosts and Other Texas Negro Folk Tales.* Austin: University of Texas Press, 1958.

———. *American Negro Folklore.* Chicago: Quadrangle Books, 1968.

Brooks, Cleanth, Jr. *The Relation of the Alabama-Georgia Dialect to the Provincial Dialects of Great Britain.* Baton Rouge: Louisiana State University Press, 1935.

Brooks, Stella Brewer. *Joel Chandler Harris: Folklorist.* Athens, Ga.: 1950.

Brookter, Marie, with Curtis, Jean. *Here I Am—Take My Hand.* New York: Harper and Row, 1974.

Broonzy, Bill, as told to Bruynoghe, Yannick. *Big Bill Blues.* New York: Oak Publications, 1964.

Brown, Calvin S. *A Glossary of Faulkner's South.* New Haven: Yale University Press, 1976

Brown, Claude. *Manchild in the Promised Land.* New York: Macmillan, 1965.

Brown, Sterling A. *The Negro in American Fiction.* Washington, D.C.: The Associates in Negro Folk Education, 1937.

Brown, William Wells. *My Southern Home: Or, The South and Its People.* Boston: A. G. Brown and Co., 1880.

———. *Clotelle: Or, The Colored Heroine, A Tale of the Southern States,* 1867. Miami: Mnemosyne Publishing Co., 1969.

Buck, Joyce F. "The Effects of Negro and White Dialectical Variations upon Attitudes of College Students." *Speech Monographs* 35 (1968): 181–186.

Buerkle, Jack Vincent, and Barker, Danny. *Bourbon Street Black.* New York: Oxford University Press, 1973.

Bullins, Ed. *Five Plays*. Indianapolis, Ind.: The Bobbs-Merrill Co., 1969.

Burling, Robbins. *Man's Many Voices: Language in Its Cultural Context*. New York: Holt, Rinehart, and Winston, 1970.

———. *English in Black and White*. New York: Holt, Rinehart, and Winston, 1973.

Butler, Melvin A. "African Linguistic Remnants in the Speech of Black Louisianians." *Black Experience* 55 (1969):45–52.

Byrd, James W. *J. Mason Brewer: Negro Folklorist*. Austin: Steck-Vaughn Co., 1967.

Cable, George Washington. *Creoles and Cajuns: Stories of Old Louisiana*. Garden City, N.Y.: Doubleday, 1959.

———. "The Dance in the Place Congo." *Century Magazine* 21 (February 1886):517–532.

Campbell, James E. *Echoes from the Cabin and Elsewhere*. Chicago: Donohue and Henneberry, 1905.

Carmer, Carl Lamson. *Stars Fell on Alabama*. New York: Farrar and Rinehart, 1934.

Carson, A. S., and Rabin, A. I. "Verbal Comprehension and Communication in Negro and White Children." *Journal of Educational Psychology* 51 (February 1960):47–51.

Cassidy, Frederic G. "Multiple Etymologies in Jamaican Creole." *American Speech* 41 (1966): 211–213.

———. *Jamaica Talk: Three Hundred Years of the English Language in Jamaica*. London: Macmillan, 1961.

———, and LePage, Robert B. *Dictionary of Jamaican English*. Cambridge (England), at the University Press, 1967.

Charters, Samuel. *The Bluesman: The Story and the Music of the Men Who Made the Blues*. New York: Oak Publications, 1967.

———. *The Country Blues*. New York: Rinehart and Co., 1959.

Chesnutt, Charles Waddell. *The Conjure Woman*. New York: Houghton, Mifflin, and Co., 1899.

———. *The Marrow of Tradition*. Boston: Houghton, Mifflin, and Co., 1901.

———. *The House Behind the Cedars*. Ridgewood, N. J.: The Gregg Press, 1901.

———. "Superstitions and Folklore of the South." *Modern Culture* 13 (1901):231–235, reprinted in *Mother Wit from the Laughing Barrel*, ed. Alan Dundes.

Clemens, Samuel Langhorne (Mark Twain). *Writings*, Author's National Edition, 1925.

Cocke, Sarah Johnson. *Bypaths in Dixie: Folk Tales of the South*. New York: E. P. Dutton and Co., 1911.

Cohen, John. "The Folk Music Interchange: Negro and White." *Sing Out!* (December 1964–January 1965):.

Cohen, Octavus Roy. *Polished Ebony*. Freeport, N.Y.: Books for Libraries Press, 1970.

———. *Come Seven: A Negro Farce-Comedy in Three Acts*. New York: Longmans, Green and Co., 1922.

———. *Florian Slappey*. New York: Appleton-Century Co., 1938.

Cohn, David L. *God Shakes Creation*. New York: Harper and Brothers, 1935.

Cole, Bill. *Miles Davis: A Musical Biography*. New York: William Morrow and Co., 1974.

Connelly, Marc. *The Green Pastures*. New York: Farrar and Rinehart, 1929.

Conrad, Earl. "The Philology of Negro Dialect." *Journal of Negro Education* 13 (1944): 150–154.

Cook, Bruce. *Listen to the Blues*. New York: Charles Scribner's Sons, 1973.

Cooper, James Fenimore. *Satansoe: Or, The Littlepage Manuscripts*. New York: Burgess, Stringer, and Co., 1845.

———. *The Redskins: Or, Indian and Injin*. New York: Burgess Stringer, and Co. 1846.

Corrothers, James D. *The Black Cat Club*. London: Funk and Wagnalls, 1902.

Cotton, Jane B. *Wall-eyed Caesar's Ghost, and Other Sketches*. Boston: Marshall Jones Co., 1925.

Courlander, Harold. *Negro Folk Music U.S.A.* New York: Columbia University Press, 1963.

———. *The Drum and the Hoe*. University of Berkeley California Press, 1960.

Crowley, Daniel J. *I Could Talk Old-Time Story Good: Creativity in Bahamian Folklore*. Berkeley Folklore Studies, 1966.

Culbertson, Manie. *May I Speak? Diary of a Crossover Teacher*. Gretna, La.: Pelican Publishing Co., 1972.

Cuney-Hare, Maude. *Negro Musicians and Their Music*. Washington, D.C.: Associated Publishers, 1936.

Dalby, David. "The African Element in American English." In *Rappin' and Stylin' Out*. Ed. Thomas Kochman.

Dance, Stanley. *The World of Swing*, New York, C. Scribner's Sons, 1974.

Davis, Henry C. "Negro Folklore in South Carolina." *Journal of American Folklore* 27 (April–June 1914): 241–254.

Davis, John. *Travels of Four Years and a Half in*

the United States of America. London: T. Ostell 1803.

Davis, Reuben. *Butcher Bird.* Boston: Little, Brown, and Co., 1936.

d'Azevedo, Warren L. *Some Terms from Liberian Speech.* 2nd ed. Liberia: U.S. Peace Corps, 1970.

Dick, Everett. *The Dixie Frontier: A Social History of the Southern Frontier from the First Transmontane Beginnings to the Civil War.* New York: Capricorn Books, 1948.

Dickinson, Sam. " 'Hands,' and Hands." Unpublished manuscript.

Dickson, Harris. *Old Reliable.* Indianapolis, Ind.: The Bobbs-Merrill Co., 1911.

Dillard, J. L. *Black Names.* The Hague: Mouton, 1976.

———. "Black English in New York." *The English Record* Vol. 21, No. 4 (1971): 114–120.

———. "The Creolist and the Study of Negro Nonstandard Dialects in the United States." in *Pidginization and Creolization of Languages.* Ed. Dell Hymes, Cambridge University Press, 1971.

———. *Black English: Its History and Usage in the United States.* New York: Random House, 1972.

———. "On the Beginnings of Black English in the New World." *Orbis* 21 (1972): 523–536.

———. *American Talk: Where Our Words Came From.* New York: Random House, 1976.

All-American English; A History of American English, New York, Random House, 1975.

———. ed. *Perspectives on Black English.* The Hague: Mouton, 1975.

Dillon, Francis. *Fanatic Cults.* Unpublished manuscript, Louisiana Federal Writers Project Series.

Dobie, J. Frank, ed. *Follow de Drinkin' Gou'd.* Texas Folklore Society, 1928.

Dollard, John. *Caste and Class in a Southern Town.* Garden City, N.Y.: Doubleday, 1937.

Dooley, Mrs. Henry. *Dem Good Ole Times.* New York: Doubleday, 1906.

Dorson, Richard. *Folklore from Benton Harbor, Michigan.* Greenwich, Conn.: Fawcett Publications, 1967.

Douglass, Frederick. *Narrative of the Life of Frederick Douglass: An American Slave,* ed. Benjamin Quarles. Cambridge: Harvard University Press, 1960.

Dowd, Jerome. *The Negro in American Life.* New York: Negro Universities Press, 1968.

DuBois, W. E. B. *The Souls of Black Folk.* New York: New American Library, 1969.

Dunbar, Paul Laurence. *Folks from Dixie.* New York: Dodd, Mead, and Co., 1898.

———. *The Sport of the Gods.* New York: 1902.

———. *Lyrics of the Lowly Life.* New York: Dodd, Mead, and Co., 1912.

———. *The Uncalled.* New York: Dodd, Mead, and Co., 1898.

———. *In Old Plantation Days.* New York: Dodd, Mead, and Co., 1903.

———. *The Heart of Happy Hollow.* New York: Dodd, Mead, and Co., 1904.

Dundes, Alan, ed. *Mother Wit from the Laughing Barrel: Readings in the Interpretation of Afro-American Folklore.* Englewood Cliffs, N.J.: Prentice-Hall, 1973.

Durrell, Gerald. *The Bafut Beagles,* London, Rupert Hart-Davis, 1954.

Early Elementary Program, Southwest Educational Development Laboratory. *Black Girls at Play: Folkloric Perspectives on Child Development.* Austin: Southwest Educational Development Corporation, 1975.

Eddington, Neil A. *The Urban Plantation: The Ethnography of an Oral Tradition in a Negro Community.* Dissertation, University of California, 1967.

Eells, Kenneth; Davis, Allison; Havinghurst, Robert J.; Herrick, Vergil E.; and Tyler, Ralph W. *Intellectual and Cultural Differences.* Chicago: University of Chicago Press, 1951.

Elam, William Cecil. "Lingo in Literature." *Lippincott's* 55 (1895): 286–288.

Eliason, Norman. *Tarheel Talk: An Historical Study of the English Language in North Carolina to 1860.* Chapel Hill: University of North Carolina Press, 1956.

———. "Some Negro Terms." *American Speech* 13 April (1938): 151–2.

Emmons, Martha. *Deep Like the Rivers: Stories of My Negro Friends.* Austin: Encino Press, 1969.

Erickson, Frederick David. " 'F'get you, honky!' A New Look at Black Dialect and the School." *Elementary English* 46 (April 1969): 495–499.

Fader, Daniel N. *The Naked Children.* New York: Macmillan, 1971.

Fairbairn, Ann. *Five Smooth Stones.* New York. Crown Publishers, Inc., 1966.

Farrison, William E. *The Phonology of the Illiterate Negro Dialect of Guilford County, North Carolina.* Dissertation, Ohio State University, 1937.

Fasold, Ralph W. "Tense and the Form *Be* in Black English." *Language* 45 (April 1969): 763–776.

———. "Two Models of Socially Significant Linguistic Variation." *Language* 46 (1970): 551–563.

———. *Tense Marking in Black English: A Linguistic and Social Analysis.* Washington: Center for Applied Linguistics, 1973.

Fauset, Arthur Huff. *Black Gods of the Metropolis: Negro Religious Cults in the Urban North.* University of Pennsylvania Press edition, with Introduction by John Szwed, 1944.

———. *Folklore from Nova Scotia.* New York: American Folk-Lore Society, 1931.

———. "Negro Folk Tales from the South." *Journal of American Folklore* 40 (1927): 213–303.

Federal Writers Project. *Texas: A Guide to the Lone Star State.* New York: Hastings House, 1940.

———. *Alabama: A Guide to the Deep South.* New York: Hastings House, 1941.

———. *Florida: A Guide to the Southern-most State.* New York: Oxford University Press, 1939.

———. *Mississippi: A Guide to the Magnolia State.* New York: Hastings House, 1949.

———. *New Orleans City Guide.* Boston: Houghton Mifflin, 1938.

Ferguson, Charles. "Diglossia." *Word* 15 (1959): 325–340.

Ferris, William R., Jr. "Black Prose Narrative in the Mississippi Delta." *Journal of American Folklore* 85 (April-June 1972): 140–151.

Fickett, Joan Gleason. *Aspects of Morphemics, Syntax, and Semology of an Inner-City Dialect.* West Rush, N.Y.: Meadowood Publications, 1970.

Figurel, J. A., ed. *Reading Goals for the Disadvantaged.* Newark, Del.: International Reading Association, Inc., 1970.

Fogel, Robert William, and Engerman, Stanley L. *Time on the Cross: The Economics of American Negro Slavery.* Boston: Little, Brown, and Co., 1974.

Folb, Edith A. *A Comparative Study of Urban Black Argot.* University of California at Los Angeles Occasional Papers in Linguistics, No. 1, March 1972.

Foster, Charles William. *The Representation of Negro Dialect in Charles W. Chesnutt's The Conjure Woman.* Dissertation, University of Alabama, 1968.

Foster, Herbert Lawrence. *Dialect-Lexicon and Listening Comprehension.* Dissertation, Columbia University, 1969.

———. *A Pilot Study of the Cant of the Culturally Deprived, Emotionally Disturbed Youngster,* no date, mimeographed.

———. *Ribbin', Jivin', and Playin' the Dozens: The Unrecognized Dilemma of Inner City Schools.* Cambridge, Mass.: Ballinger Publishing Co., 1974.

Foster, Pops, as told to Stoddard, Tom. *Pops Foster: The Autobiography of a New Orleans Jazzman.* Berkeley: University of California Press, 1971.

Frazier, Edward Franklin. *The Negro Family in the United States.* Chicago: University of Chicago Press, 1939.

Funkhouser, James. "A Various Standard." *College English* 34 (1973): 806–810.

———. "Review of Dillard, *Black English,*" *College English* 35 (January 1974): 625–629.

Gaines, Ernest J. *Bloodline.* New York: The Dial Press, 1968.

Genovese, Eugene. *Roll, Jordan, Roll: The World the Slaves Made.* New York: Pantheon Books, 1974.

Gillett, Charlie. *The Sound of the City: The Rise of Rock and Roll.* New York: E. P. Dutton, 1970.

Gold, Robert J. *Jazz Talk.* Indianapolis, Ind.: The Bobbs-Merrill Co., 1975.

Gonzales, Ambrose E. *The Black Border: Gullah Stories of the Carolina Coast.* Columbia, S.C.: 1922 (includes Glossary).

———. *Laguerre: A Gascon of the Black Border.* 1924.

Goodwin, Ruby Berkeley. *It's Good to Be Black.* Garden City, N. Y.: Doubleday and Company, 1954.

Grainger, James. *The Sugar Cane: A Poem in Four Books with Notes.* London: R. P. and J. Dodsley, 1764.

Green, Paul. *The Field God, and In Abraham's Bosom.* New York: R. M. McBryde and Co., 1927.

Greenway, John. *American Folk Songs of Protest.* Philadelphia: University of Pennsylvania Press, 1953.

Hall, Robert A., Jr. *Haitian Creole: Grammar—Texts—Vocabulary,* American Anthropological Society Memoir No. 74, 1953.

———. *Pidgin and Creole Languages.* Ithaca, N. Y.: Cornell University Press, 1966.

Hall, Susan. *Gentleman of Leisure: A Year in the Life of a Pimp.* New York: New American Library, 1972.

Handy, W. C. *Father of the Blues: An Autobiography.* New York: Macmillan, 1955.

Hannerz, Ulf. *Soulside: Inquiries into Ghetto Culture and Community.* New York: Columbia University Press, 1969.

———. "The Rhetoric of Soul: Identification in a Negro Society." *Race* 9 (April 1968): 453–465.

———. "Gossip, Networks, and Culture in a Black American Ghetto." *Ethnos* 32 (1967): 35–60.

Harris, Joel Chandler. *Uncle Remus, His Songs and Sayings: The Folklore of the Plantation.* New York: D. Appleton and Co., 1881.

———. *Nights with Uncle Remus: Myths and Legends of the Old Plantation.* Boston: Houghton, Mifflin, and Co., 1883.

———. *The Tar-Baby and Other Rhymes of Uncle Remus.* New York: D. Appleton and Co., 1904.

Harrison, James A. "Negro English." *Anglia* 7 (1884): 232–279.

Haskins, Jim. *The Psychology of Black Language.* New York: Barnes and Noble, 1973.

Hawes, Bess Lomax, and Jones, Bessie. *Step It Down: Games, Plays, and Stories from the Afro-American Heritage.* New York: Harper and Row, 1972.

Hearn, Lafcadio. "The Last of the Voodoos." *Harper's Weekly,* November 7, 1885.

———. "New Orleans Superstitions." *Harper's Weekly,* December 25, 1886.

Heilbut, Tony. *The Gospel Sound: Good News and Bad Times.* New York: Simon and Schuster, 1971.

Hellman, John M., Jr. "I'm a Monkey: The Influence of the Black American Blues Argot on the Rolling Stones." *Journal of American Folklore* 86 (April-June 1973): 367–373.

Hentoff, Nat. *The Jazz Life.* New York: The Dial Press, 1961.

———, and McCarthy, Albert. *Jazz.* New York: Grove Press, 1959.

Herskovits, Melville J. *Life in a Haitian Valley.* New York: Octagon Books, 1937.

———. *Dahomeyan Narrative.* Evanston, Ill.: 1958.

———. *The Myth of the Negro Past.* Boston: Beacon Books, 1958.

———. *The New World Negro: Selected Papers in Afroamerican Studies.* Ed. Frances S. Herskovits. Bloomington: Indiana University Press, 1966.

———. and Herskovits, Frances S. *Suriname Folk-Lore.* New York: Columbia University Press, 1936.

———. *Rebel Destiny.* New York: 1934.

Hinton, Norman D. "The Language of Jazz Musicians." *Publications of the American Dialect Society,* No. 30, 1958.

Hooper, Johnson J. *The Adventures of Captain Simon Suggs.* New York: 1845.

Horsmanden, Daniel P. *A Journal of the Proceedings in the Detection of the Conspiracy Formed by Some White People, in Conjunction with Negro and Other Slaves, for Burning the City of New York . . .* New York, James Parker 1744.

Horton, Donald. "The Dialogue of Courtship in Popular Songs." *American Journal of Sociology* 62 (1956–57):569–575.

Huggins, Nathan Irwin, ed. *Voices from the Harlem Renaissance.* New York: Oxford University Press, 1976.

Hughes, Langston, and Bontemps, Arna, eds. *The Book of Negro Folklore.* New York: Dodd, Mead, and Co., 1958.

Hurston, Zora Neale. *Jonah's Gourd Vine.* Philadelphia: J. B. Lippincott Co., 1934.

———. *Mules and Men.* Philadelphia: J. B. Lippincott Co., 1935.

———. *Dust Tracks on a Road: An Autobiography.* Philadelphia: J. B. Lippincott Co., 1942.

Hyatt, Harry Middleton. *Hoodoo—Conjuration—Witchcraft—Rootwork: Beliefs Accepted by Many Negroes and White Persons, These Being Orally Recorded among Blacks and Whites.* Washington, D.C.: Memoirs of the Alma Egin Hyatt Foundation, 1970.

———. *Folklore from Adams County, Illinois.* 2nd ed. Washington, D.C.: Memoirs of the Alma Egan Hyatt Foundation, 1965.

Ingraham, Joseph Holt. *The Southwest by a Yankee.* New York: Harper and Brothers, 1835.

Jablow, Alta. *The Intimate Folklore of Africa.* New York: Horizon Press, 1961.

Jackson, Blyden. *The Waiting Years: Essays on American Negro Literature.* Baton Rouge: Louisiana State University Press, 1976.

Jackson, Bruce, ed. *The Negro and His Folklore in Nineteenth Century Periodicals.* Austin: American Folklore Society, 1967.

———. "Circus and Street: Psychosocial Aspects of the Black Toast." *Journal of American Folklore* 85 (1972): 123–139.

———. *Wake Up Dead Man.* Cambridge: Harvard University Press, 1972.

Jahn, Mike. *Rock: From Presley to the Rolling Stones.* New York: New York Times Book Co., 1973.

Jarreau, Lafayette. *Creole Folklore of Pointe Coupée Parish.* Thesis, Louisiana State University, 1931.

Jaskosi, Helen. "Power Unequal to Man: The Significance of Conjure in Works by Five

Afro-American Authors." *Southern Folklore Quarterly* 38 (1974): 91–108.

Jensen, Arthur R. "How Much Can We Boost IQ and Scholastic Achievement." *Harvard Educational Review* 39 (1969):1–123.

Johnson, Charles Spurgeon. *Growing Up in the Black Belt: Negro Youth in the Rural South.* New York: Shocken Books, 1941.

—————. *Shadow of the Plantation.* Chicago: University of Chicago Press, 1934.

Johnson, Guy B. "Double Meaning in the Popular Negro Blues." *Journal of Abnormal and Social Psychology* 30 (1927):12–20.

Johnson, Kenneth R. "Language Problems of Culturally Disadvantaged Negro Students." *California English Journal* 2 (1966):28–33.

—————. "Black Kinesics." In *Perspectives on Black English.* Ed. J.L. Dillard.

Jones, A.M. *Studies in African Music.* London: 1959.

Jones, Charles Colcock, Sr. *The Religious Instruction of the Negro.* Savannah, Ga.: Presbyterian Board of Publications, 1832.

Jones, James A. *Haverhill: Or, Memoirs of an Officer in the Army of Wolfe.* New York: J. and J. Harper, 1831.

Jones, LeRoi. *Home: Social Essays.* New York: William Morrow and Company, 1966.

—————. *Blues People: Negro Music in White America.* New York: William Morrow and Company, 1963.

Jones, Max, and Chilton, John. *Louis: The Louis Armstrong Story.* Boston: Little, Brown, and Co., 1971.

Justice, J. *The Black Apostle.* Glenmora. La.: Bartlett and Co., 1946.

Kaplan, Arthur M. "A Master of Negro Dialect." *The Jewish Tribune,* September 23, 1927, pp. 38, 61.

Katz, Bernard. *The Social Implications of Early Negro Music in the United States.* New York: Arno Press, 1969.

Kennedy, Robert Emmet. *Black Cameos.* New York: Albert and Charles Boni, 1924.

Kilham, Elizabeth. "Sketches in Color." *Putnam's* Magazine 4 (January 1870):31–38.

Kiner, Henry A. "Old Corn Meal: A Forgotten Urban Negro Folk Singer." *Journal of American Folklore* 75 (1962):29–34.

Kochman, Thomas. "Rapping in the Black Ghetto." *Trans-Action* 6 (February 1969):26–34.

—————, ed. *Rappin' and Stylin' Out: Communication in Urban Black America.* Urbana: University of Illinois Press, 1972.

Krapp, George P. "The English of the Negro." *American Mercury* 2 (1924):190–195.

—————. *The English Language in America.* New York: The Century Company, 1925.

Kurzgefasste Neger-Englische Grammatik. Bautzen, 1854.

Labov, William. "The Logic of Nonstandard English." *Florida FL Reporter* (1969).

—————. *Language in the Inner City.* Philadelphia: University of Pennsylvania Press, 1972.

—————. *Sociolinguistic Patterns.* Philadelphia: University of Pennsylvania Press, 1972.

—————. "Academic Ignorance and Black Intelligence," *Atlantic Monthly,* June 1972.

—————, and Robins, Clarence. "A Note on the Relation of Reading Failure to Peer-group Status in Urban Ghettoes." *Teachers College Record* 70 (February 1969):54–57.

—————, and Waletzky, Joshua. "Narrative Analysis." In *Essays on the Verbal and Visual Arts.* Ed. Helm. Seattle: University of Washington Press, 1967.

—————; Cohen, Paul; Robins, Clarence; and Lewis, John. *A Study of the Non-Standard English of Negro and Puerto Rican Speakers in New York City.* U. S. Office of Education, Cooperative Research Project No. 3288, 2 vols., 1968.

Lane, Harlan; Lawrence, Caroline, and Charles Curran. "The Perception of General American English by Speakers of Southern Dialects." *Studies in Language and Language Behavior* (1967).

Leaverton, Lloyd; Davis, Olga J.; Gladney, Mildred R.; Hoffman, Melvin; and Patterson, Zoerda R. *Psycholinguistics Oral Language Program: A Bidialectal Approach.* Chicago: Board of Education, 1968.

Lee, George W. *Beale Street: Where the Blues Began.* New York: Robert O. Ballou, 1934.

Leonard, Neil. *Jazz and the White American.* Chicago: University of Chicago Press, 1962.

Levinson, Boris. "A Comparative Study of the WAIS Performance of Native-Born White and Negro Homeless." *Journal of Genetic Psychology* 105, December (1964):211–218.

Liebow, Elliott. *Talley's Corner: A Study of Negro Streetcorner Men.* Boston: Little, Brown, and Co., 1966.

Lloyd, John U. "The Language of the Kentucky Negro." *Dialect Notes* 2 (1901):179–184.

Loflin, Marvin D. "A Note on the Deep Structure of Nonstandard English in Washington, D.C." *Glossa* 1 (1967):26–32.

—————. "Negro Nonstandard and Standard English: Same or Different Deep Structure." *Orbis* 18 (1969): 74–91.

————; Sobin, Nicholas; and Dillard, J. L. "Auxiliary Structures and Time Adverbs in Black American English." *American Speech* 48 (1973).

————; Guyette, Thomas; and Marlin, Marjorie. *Context: A Necessity for Semantic Interpretations.* Institute for the Study of Urban Linguistics, University of Wisconsin, Technical Report No. 1.

Loman, Bengt. *Conversations in a Negro American Dialect.* Washington, D.C.: Center for Applied Linguistics, 1967 (an earlier transcript, minus some editing that took place before this publication, was actually used).

Lomax, Alan. *The Rainbow Sign: A Southern Documentary.* New York: Duell, Sloan, and Pearce, 1959.

————. *Mister Jelly Roll.* New York: Grove Press, 1950.

Lomax, John A. *Adventures of a Ballad Hunter.* New York: The Macmillan Co., 1947.

Lomax, Ruby T. "Negro Nicknames." *Texas Folklore Society Bulletin* 18 (1943):163–171.

Long, John D. *Pictures of Slavery in Church and State.* Philadelphia: 1857.

Long, Richard A. " 'Man' and 'Evil' in American Negro Speech." *American Speech* 34 (December 1959):305–306.

Luelsdorff, Philip A. *A Segmental Phonology of Black English.* Dissertation, Georgetown University, 1970 (published by Mouton, The Hague, 1975).

Lyell, Sir Charles. *Travels in North America.* London: J. Murray, 1848.

McCormick, Virginia T. *Charcoal and Chalk.* Norfolk, Va.: Atlantic Coast Printing Co., 1931.

McCullers, Carson. *The Heart Is a Lonely Hunter.* Boston: Houghton, Mifflin and Co., 1940.

McDavid, Raven I., Jr. "The Position of the Charleston Dialect." *Publications of the American Dialect Society* 23 (April 1955):35–49.

————. "The Grunt of Negation," *American Speech* XXX (February, 1965), p. 56.

————, and McDavid, Virginia Glenn. "The Relationship of the Speech of American Negroes to the Speech of Whites." *American Speech* 26 (February 1951):3–17.

McDowell, Tremaine. "The Negro in the Southern Novel Prior to 1850." *Journal of English and Germanic Philology* 25 (October 1926): 455–473.

————. "The Use of Negro Dialect by Harriet Beecher Stowe." *American Speech* 6 (June 1931): 322–326.

McIntosh, Maria J. *The Lofty and the Lowly: Or, Good in All and None All-Good.* New York: D. Appleton and Co., 1854.

McKay, Claude. *Home to Harlem.* New York: Harper and Brothers, 1928.

Macon, John A. *Uncle Gabe Tucker: Or, Reflection, Song, and Sentiment in the Quarters.* Philadelphia: J. B. Lippincott, 1883.

Major, Clarence. *Dictionary of Afro-American Slang.* New York: International Publishers, 1970.

Mathews, Mitford M. *Some Sources of Southernisms.* Drawer: University of Alabama Press, 1948.

———— (ed). *A Dictionary of Americanisms on Historical Principles* Chicago, Illinois, U. of Chicago Press, 1951.

Maximilien, Louis. *Le Vodou Haitien, Rite Radas, Congo.* Port-au-Prince, n. d.

Mays, Benjamin Elijah, and Nicholson, Joseph William. *The Negro's Church.* New York: Arno Press, 1969. Reprinted from 1933 edition.

Meier, August, and Rudwick, Elliott. *From Plantation to Ghetto.* New York: Hill and Wang, 1966.

Mencken, Henry L. *The American Language.* Four Editions 1919, 1921, 1923, 1926 and Two Supplements, 1945, 1948.

Meredith, Mamie. "Negro Patois and Its Humor." *American Speech* 6 (June 1931): 317–321.

Merk, Frederick. *Slavery and the Annexation of Texas.* New York: Alfred A. Knopf, 1972.

Merrick, George Byron. *Old Times on the Upper Mississippi.* Cleveland, Ohio. 1909.

Mezzrow, Milton, with Wolfe, Bernard. *Really the Blues.* New York: Random House, 1946.

Miller, Warren. *The Cool World.* Boston: Little, Brown, and Co., 1959.

————. *The Siege of Harlem.* New York: McGraw-Hill, 1964.

Milner, Christina, and Milner, Richard. *Black Players: The Secret World of Black Pimps.* Boston: Little, Brown, and Co., 1972.

Minor, Mary Willis. "How to Keep Off Witches." *Journal of American Folklore* II (January-March 1898): 76.

Mitchell, Henry H. *Black Preaching.* Philadelphia: Lippincott, 1970.

Mitchell-Kernan, Claudia I. *Language Behavior in a Black Urban Community.* Monographs of the Language-Behavior Research Laboratory No. 2, University of California, Berkeley, 1969.

Moody, Minnie Hite. *Death Is a Little Man.* New York: J. Messner, Inc., 1936.

Moore, John T. *Songs and Stories from Tennessee.* Chicago: J. C. Bauer, 1897.

Morrison, Toni. *Sula.* New York: Alfred A. Knopf, 1974.

Mott, Edward H. *The Black Homer of Jimtown.* New York: Grosset and Dunlap, 1900.

Mullin, Gerald W. *Flight and Rebellion: Slave Resistance in Eighteenth Century Virginia.* New York: Oxford University Press, 1972.

Musgrave, Marianne E. "Teaching English as a Foreign Language to Students with Substandard Dialects." *CLA Journal* 7 (February 1963): 84–91.

Myrdal, Gunnar; Sterner, Richard; and Rose, Arnold. *An American Dilemma: The Negro Problem and Modern Democracy.* New York: Harper and Brothers, 1944.

Nathan, Hans. "Charles Mathews, Comedian, and the American Negro." *Southern Folklore Quarterly* 10 (1946): 191–197.

———. *Dan Emmett and the Rise of Early Negro Minstrelsy.* Norman: University of Oklahoma Press, 1962.

Newman, Edwin. *Strictly Speaking: Will America Be the Death of English?* Indianapolis, Bobbs-Merrill Co., 1974.

Odum, Howard Washington. "Folk-song and Folk-poetry as Found in the Secular Songs of the Southern Negro." *Journal of American Folklore* 24 (April-June 1911): 255–294.

———. *Rainbow Round My Shoulder: The Blue Trail of Black Ulysses.* Indianapolis, Ind.: The Bobbs-Merrill Co., 1928.

———. *Cold Blue Moon: Black Ulysses Afar Off.* Indianapolis, Ind.: The Bobbs-Merrill Co., 1931.

———, and Johnson, Guy B. *The Negro and His Songs: A Study of Typical Negro Songs in the South.* Chapel Hill: University of North Carolina Press, 1925.

———. *Negro Workaday Songs.* Chapel Hill: University of North Carolina Press, 1926.

Oliver, Paul. *Conversation with the Blues.* New York: Horizon Press, 1961.

———. *The Story of the Blues.* London: 1969.

———. *The Blues Fell This Morning.* London: Cassell 1960.

Onstott, Kyle. *Mandingo.* Greenwich, Conn.: Fawcett Publications, 1965.

———. *Drum.* Greenwich, Conn.: Fawcett Publications, 1967.

Osser, Harry. "Biological and Social Factors in Language Development." In *Language and Poverty: Perspectives on a Theme.* Frederick Williams. Chicago: Markham 1970.

Oster, Harry. *Living Country Blues.* Detroit: Folklore Associates, 1969.

Ottley, C. R. *How to Talk Old Talk in Trinidad.* Port of Spain: Diego Martin, 1965.

Ottley, Roi, and Weatherby, William J. *The Negro in New York: An Informal Social History.* New York: New York Public Library, 1967.

Otto, John Solomon, and Burns, August M. "The Use of Race and Hillbilly Recordings as Sources for Historical Research." *Journal of American Folklore* 85 (April-June 1972): 344–355.

Owen, Mary Alicia. *Old Rabbit, the Voodoo, and Other Sorcerers.* London: T. Fisher Unwin, 1893.

Page, Thomas Nelson. *In Ole Virginia: Or, Marse Chan and Other Stories.* New York: Charles Scribner's Sons, 1887.

———. *Pastime Stories.* New York: Harper and Brothers, 1894.

Palmer, Richard J., and Masling, Joseph. "Vocabulary for Skin Color in Negro and White Children." *Developmental Psychology* 1 (July 1969): 396–401.

Pardoe, T. Earl. *An Historical and Phonetic Study of the Negro Dialect.* Dissertation, Louisiana State University 1937.

Parsons, Elsie Clews. "Folk-tales Collected at Miami, Florida." *Journal of American Folklore* 30 (1917): 222–227.

———. "Folklore from Aiken, South Carolina." *Journal of American Folklore* 34 (April-June 1921): 1–139.

———. *Folk Lore of the Antilles, French and English.* 3 vols. New York: G. L. Stechert Co., 1936.

Payne, L. W., Jr. "A Word-List from East Alabama." *Dialect Notes* 3 (1908): 279–328.

Peisach, Estelle Cherry. "Children's Comprehension of Teacher and Peer Speech." *Child Development* 36 (1965): 467–480.

Peterkin, Julia. *Black April.* Indianapolis, Ind.: Bobbs-Merrill, 1927.

Peterson, Arona. *Herbs and Proverbs of the Virgin Islands.* St. Thomas, Virgin Islands: St. Thomas Graphics, 1974.

Pharr, Robert Deane. *The Book of Numbers.* Garden City, N. Y.: Doubleday and Co., 1969.

Piestrup, Ann McCormick. *Black Dialect Interference and Accommodation of Reading Instruction in the First Grade.* Berkeley Monographs of the Language-Behavior Laboratory, No. 4, 1975.

Pipes, William H. *Say Amen, Brother! Old-Time Negro Preaching.* Westport, Conn.: Negro Universities Press, 1970.

Politzer, Robert L. "Developmental Aspects of the Awareness of the Standard/Non-standard Dialect Contrast." Stanford Center for Research and Development in Teaching, Memo. No. 72, 1970.

Preston, Dennis R. "Social Dialects and College English." *Speech Teacher* 20 (November 1971): 237–246.

Preston, Laura Fitzhugh. *Uncle Bob: His Reflections.* New York: The Grafton Press, 1904.

Price, Richard. *Maroon Societies: Rebel Slave Communities in the Americas.* Garden City, N.Y.: Doubleday, 1973.

Puckett, Niles Newbell. *Folk Beliefs of the Southern Negro.* Chapel Hill: University of North Carolina Press, 1926.

Putnam, George N., and O'Hern, Edna M. *The Status Significance of an Isolated Urban Dialect.* Baltimore: Waverley Press, 1956.

Quay, Lorene C. "Language Dialect Reinforcement, and the Intelligence Test Performance of Negro Children." *Child Development* 42 (March 1971): 5–15.

Radin, Paul. *African Folktales and Sculptures.* New York: Pantheon Books, 1952.

Ramsay, Frederick, Jr., and Smith, Charles Edward. *Jazzmen.* New York: Harcourt, Brace and Co. 1939.

Rawick, George P., ed. *The American Slave: A Composite Autobiography.* Westport, Conn.: Greenwood Publishing Co. 1972. 19 volumes (Volume 1, *From Sundown to Sunup* is subtitled *The Making of the Black Community;* the other volumes are narratives by former slaves, mainly from the southern states).

Rawlings, Marjorie Kinnan. *Cross Creek.* New York: Grossett and Dunlap, 1942.

Reed, Ishmael. *Yellow Back Radio Broke-Down.* Garden City, N.Y.: Doubleday, 1969.

———. *The Last Days of Louisiana Red.* New York: Random House, 1974.

Render, Sylvia Lyons. "North Carolina Dialect, Chesnutt Style." *North Carolina Folklore* 15 (1967): 67–70.

Roberts, Elsa. "An Evaluation of Standardized Tests as Tools for the Measurement of Language Development." Language Research Foundation, 1969.

Roberts, Hermese E. "Glossary." *Living Webster Encyclopedia of the English Language* (1971).

Rohrer, John, and Edmondson, Monroe. *The Eighth Generation: Cultures and Personalities of New Orleans Negroes.* New York: Harper and Row, 1960.

Rollins, Hyder E. "The Negro in the Southern Short Story." *Sewannee Review* 24 (1916): 42–60.

Rosengarten, Theodore. *All God's Dangers: The Life of Nate Shaw.* New York: Alfred A. Knopf, 1974.

Ross, Stephen B. "On the Syntax of Written Black English." *TESOL Quarterly* 5 (1971): 115–122.

Russell, Irwin. *Christmas Night in the Quarters and Other Poems.* New York: The Century Co., 1917.

Russell, Tony. *Blacks, Whites, and Blues.* New York: Stein and Day, 1970.

Sackheim, Eric, comp. *The Blues Line: A Collection of Blues Lyrics.* New York: Grossman Publishers, 1969.

Sampson, Emma Speed. *Mammy's White Folks.* Chicago: The Reilly and Lee Co., 1919.

Saxon, Lyle; Tallant, Robert; and Dreyer, Edward. *Gumbo Ya-Ya.* Boston: Houghton Mifflin, 1945.

Scarborough, W. S. "Negro Folk-lore and Dialect." *Arena* 17 (1897): 186–92.

Schafer, William J., and Riedel, Johannes. *The Art of Ragtime: Form and Meaning of an Original Black American Art.* Baton Rouge: Louisiana State University Press, 1973.

Schneider, Gilbert. *Cameroons Creole Dictionary: First Draft.* Southern Cameroons: 1960.

———. *First Steps in Wes-Kos.* Hartford, Conn. Hartford Seminary Foundation, 1963.

———. *Pidgin English Proverbs.* East Lansing, Mich.: African Studies Center, 1965.

———. *Wes-Kos (Pidgin English) Proverbs, Idioms, Names.* Columbus Ohio University Center for International Studies, 1965.

———. *West African Pidgin English: An Historical Over-view.* Athens, Ohio: Center for International Studies, 1967.

Schotta, Sarita G. "Toward Standard English through Writing: An Experiment in Prince Edward County, Virginia." *TESOL Quarterly* 4 (1970): 261–276.

Schuller, Gunther. *Early Jazz: Its Roots and Musical Development.* New York: Oxford University Press, 1968.

Shapiro, Nat, and Hentoff, Nat. *Jazz Makers.* New York: Grove Press, 1957.

Simms, William Gilmore. *Woodcraft: Or Hawks about the Dovecote: A Story of the South at the Close of the Revolution.* New York: W. J. Widdleton, 1972.

Simpson, George Eaton. *The Shango Cult in Trinidad.* Institute of Caribbean Studies, University of Puerto Rico, Monograph No. 2, 1965.

———. *Religious Cults of the Caribbean, Trinidad, Jamaica, and Haiti,* rev. and enlarged ed.

Institute of Caribbean Studies, University of Puerto Rico, 1970.

Sledd, James. "Bi-dialectalism: The Linguistics of White Supremacy." *English Journal* 58 (December 1969): 1307–1329.

Smith, Charles S., ed. *The History of the African Methodist Episcopal Church by Daniel A. Payne.* New York: Johnson Reprint Corp., 2 vols, 1968.

Smith, Reed. *Gullah.* Bulletin of the University of South Carolina No. 190, 1926.

Smith, Riley B. "Interrelatedness of Certain Grammatical Structures in Negro Nonstandard Dialects." *Journal of English Linguistics* 3 (March 1969): 82–88.

Smitherman, Geneva. "God Don't Never Change: Black English from a Black Perspective." *College English* 34 (March 1973): 828–833.

Smyth, J. F. D. *A Tour in the United States of America.* London: 1784.

Southern, Eileen. *The Music of Black Americans: A History.* New York: W. W. Norton, 1971.

———, ed. *Readings in Black American Music.* New York: W. W. Norton and Co., 1971.

Stearns, Marshall. *The Story of Jazz.* New York: Oxford University Press, 1956.

———, and Stearns, Jean. *Jazz Dance: The Story of American Vernacular Dance.* New York: Macmillan, 1968.

Stewart, William A. "Foreign Language Teaching Methods in Quasi-Foreign Language Situations." In *Nonstandard Speech and the Teaching of English.* Ed. William A Stewart. Washington, D.C.: Center for Applied Linguistics, 1964.

———. "Nonstandard Speech Patterns." *Baltimore Bulletin of Education* 43 (1966): 52–65.

———. "Social Dialect." In *Research Planning Conference on Language Development in Disadvantaged Children.* New York: Yeshiva University, 1966.

———. "Sociolinguistic Factors in the History of American Negro Dialects." *Florida FL Reporter* 5 (1967): 11.

———. "Continuity and Change in American Negro Dialects." *Florida FL Reporter* (1968).

———. "On the Use of Negro Dialect in the Teaching of Reading." In *Teaching Black Children to Read.* Ed. Joan Baratz and Roger W. Shuy. Washington, D.C.: Center for Applied Linguistics, 1969.

———. "Negro and White Speech: Continuities and Discontinuities." *Acta Symbolica* 2 (Spring 1971): 42–43.

———. "Acculturative Processes and the Language of the American Negro." in *Language in Its Social Setting.* Ed. William Gage. Anthropological Society of Washington Association, Washington, D.C.: 1975.

Stoney, Samuel Gaillard, and Shelby, Gertrude Mathews. *Black Genesis: A Chronicle.* New York: Macmillan, 1930.

Story, Sidney A. J. *Caste: A Story of Republican Equality.* Boston: Phillips, Sampson, and Co., 1856.

Stowe, Harriet Beecher. *Uncle Tom's Cabin: Or, Life Among the Lowly.* Cleveland: Proctor and Worthington, 1852.

———. *The Key to Uncle Tom's Cabin.* London: Clarke, Beeton, and Co. 1853.

Strickland, Dorothy S. "Black Is Beautiful vs. White Is Right." *Elementary English* 49 (February 1972): 220–223.

Stuart, Ruth. *Solomon Crow's Christmas Pockets, and Other Tales.* New York: Harper and Brothers, 1897.

———. *Napoleon Jackson: The Gentleman of the Plush Rocker.* New York: The Century Company, 1902.

Szwed, John, ed. *Black America.* New York: Basic Books, 1970.

Tallant, Robert. *Voodoo in New Orleans.* New York: Macmillan, 1946.

Talley, Thomas W. *Negro Folk Rhymes.* New York: Macmillan, 1972.

Tarone, Elaine E. *Aspects of Intonation in Vernacular Black and White Speech.* Dissertation, University of Washington, 1972.

Tarpley, Fred. "Language Development Programs for Southern Negroes." In *Applications of Linguistics.* Ed. G. E. Perren and J. L. M. Trim. Cambridge at the University Press, 1969.

Taylor, Orlando L. "Some Sociolinguistic Concepts of Black Language." *Today's Speech* 19 (Spring 1971): 19–26.

Thomas, Dominic Richard. *Oral Language Sentence Structure and Vocabulary in Kindergarten Children Living in Low Socio-Economic Urban Areas.* Dissertation, Wayne State University, 1962.

Thomas, William J. *Black Language in America.* Wichita University Studies No. 94, 1973.

Tidwell, James Nathan. "Mark Twain's Representation of Negro Speech." *American Speech* 17 (October 1942): 174–176.

———. *The Literary Representation of the Phonology of the Southern Dialect.* Dissertation, Ohio State University, 1947.

Todd, Hollis Bailey. *An Analysis of the Literary*

Dialect of Irwin Russell. Dissertation, Louisiana State University, 1965.

Torrey, Jane W. "Illiteracy in the Ghetto." *Harvard Educational Review* 40 (May 1970): 253–259.

Trollope, Mrs. Frances. *Domestic Manners of the Americans.* reprinted by Russell and Russell, New York, 1953, 1832.

Tucker, G. Richard, and Lambert, Wallace E. "White and Negro Listeners' Reactions to Various American-English Dialects." *Social Forces* 47 (June 1969): 463–468.

Tucker, Nathaniel Beverly. *The Partisan Leader: A Tale of the Future.* Washington, D.C.: D. Green, 1836.

Turner, Lorenzo Dow. *Africanisms in the Gullah Dialect.* Chicago: University of Chicago Press, 1949.

Tutuola, Amos. *The Palm Wine Drinkard.* Westport, Conn.: Greenwood Press, 1953.

———. *My Life in the Bush of Ghosts.* New York: Grove Press, 1970.

Twiggs, Robert D. *Pan-African Language in the Western Hemisphere.* North Quincy, Mass.: The Christopher Publishing Co., 1973.

Udall, Elizabeth T. "[m?m], ETC." *American Speech* 29 (October 1964): 232.

Udell, Gerald. "Concerning Black McGuffey Readers." *Acta Symbolica* (Spring 1972): 63–64.

Van Patten, Nathan. "The Vocabulary of the American Negro as Set Forth in Contemporary Literature." *American Speech* 7 (October 1931): 24–31.

Van Sertima, Ivan. *They Came Before Columbus.* New York: Random House, 1976.

Venezky, Richard L. "Nonstandard Language and Reading." *Elementary English* 47 (October 1970): 334–345.

"Visit to a Negro Cabin in Virginia." *Family Magazine* 1 (October 1836): 41–45.

Voorhoeve, Jan, and Lichtveld, Ursy M., eds. *Creole Drum: An Anthology of Creole Literature in Surinam.* New Haven: Yale University Press, 1975.

Walker, Karen Van Beyer. *Black Language: A Study of the Linguistic Environments of Black Preschool Children in New Orleans.* Dissertation, Tulane University, 1972.

Walker, Saunders E. *A Dictionary of the Folk Speech of the Eastern Alabama Negro.* Dissertation, Western Reserve University, 1956.

Walker, Ursula Genung. *Structural Features of Negro English in Natchitoches Parish.* Thesis, Northwestern State University, 1968.

Walser, Richard. "Negro Dialect in Eighteenth Century Drama." *American Speech* 30 (December 1955): 269–276.

Washington, Joseph R. *Black Sects and Cults.* Garden City, N.Y.: Doubleday, 1972.

Wasson, Ben. *The Devil Beats His Wife.* New York: Harcourt and Brace, 1929.

Waterbury, Maria. *Seven Years Among the Freedmen.* Chicago: T. B. Arnold, 1891.

Weaver, Constance W. *Analyzing Literary Representations of Recent Northern Urban Negro Speech.* Dissertation, Michigan State University, 1970.

Wells, Dicky, as told to Stanley Dance. *The Night People: Reminiscences of a Jazzman.* Boston: Crescendo Publishing Co., 1971.

Whitney, Annie Weston. "Negro American Dialects." *Independent* 53 (August 1901): 1979–1981.

Whitten, Norman. *Black Frontiersmen: A South American Case.* Cambridge, Mass.: Schenkman, 1974.

———. "Patterns of Malign Occultism Among Negroes in North Carolina." In *Mother Wit from the Laughing Barrel.* Ed. Alan Dundes, pp. 402–418.

———, and Szwed, John, eds. *Afro-American Anthropology: Contemporary Perspectives.* New York: The Free Press, 1970.

Wilkinson, Andrews. *Plantation Stories of Old Louisiana.* Boston: The Page Co., 1914.

Williams, Frederick, and Rundell, Edward E. "Teaching Teachers to Comprehend Negro Nonstandard English." *Speech Teacher* 20 (September 1971): 174–177.

———, and Wood, Barbara Sundene. "Negro Children's Speech: Some Social Class Differences in Word Predictability." *Language and Speech* 13 (July–September 1970): 141–150.

Williams, George Walton. "Slave Names in Ante-Bellum South Carolina." *American Speech* 33 (1958): 294–295.

Williams, Martin, ed. *Jazz Panorama.* New York: Collier Books, 1958.

Williams, Martin J. *The Art of Jazz.* New York: Grove Press, 1959.

Williamson, Juanita V. *The Speech of Negro High School Students in Memphis, Tennessee: Final Report.* U.S. Office of Education Contract No. OEC-6-10-207, 1968.

———, and Burke, Virginia M., eds. *A Various Language: Perspectives on a Theme.* New York: Holt, Rinehart, and Winston, 1971.

Winks, Robin W. *The Blacks in Canada: A His-*

tory. Montreal: McGill-Queens University Press, 1971.

Wise, Claude M. "Negro Dialect." *Quarterly Journal of Speech* 19 (November 1933): 523–528.

———. *Applied Phonetics.* Englewood Cliffs, N.J.: Prentice-Hall, 1957.

Wolfram, Walter. *A Sociolinguistic Description of Detroit Negro Speech.* Washington, D.C.: Center for Applied Linguistics 1969.

———, and Clarke, Nona H., eds. *Black-White Speech Relationships.* Washington, D.C.: Center for Applied Linguistics 1971.

———, and Fasold, Ralph. "Some Linguistic Features of Negro Dialect." *Language, Speech, and Hearing Services in Schools* 3 (1972): 16–49, 72.

Wood, Gordon R. *Vocabulary Change: A Study of Variation in Regional Words in Eight of the Southern States.* Carbondale: Southern Illinois University Press, 1971.

Wood, Peter A. *Black Majority.* New York: Alfred A. Knopf, 1974.

Woodson, Carter G. *The History of the Negro Church.* Washington, D.C.: The Associated Publishers, 1921.

Work, John Wesley, ed. *Folk Song of the American Negro.* Nashville, Tenn. Fisk University Press, 1915.

———. *American Negro Songs and Spirituals.* New York: Bonanza Books, 1940.

Wright, Joseph. *English Dialect Dictionary.* New York: Hacker Art Books, 1962.

Wright, Richard. *Uncle Tom's Children: Four Novellas.* New York: Harper and Brothers, 1938.

———. *Native Son.* New York: Harper and Brothers, 1940.

———. *Lawd Today.* New York: Walker and Company, 1963.

———. *The Long Dream.* Garden City, N.Y.: Doubleday, 1958.

Yerby, Frank. "My Brother Went to College." In *Best Short Stories by Negro Writers.* Ed. Langston Hughes, 1967.

Yetman, Norman R. *Voices from Slavery.* New York: Holt, Rinehart, and Winston, 1970.

Young, Martha. *Plantation Bird Legends.* New York: Appleton and Co., 1916.

Young, Stark. *Feliciana.* New York: Charles Scribner's Sons, 1935.

Young, Virginia Heyer. "Family and Childhood in a Southern Negro Community." *American Anthropologist* 72 (1970): 269–288.

Yule, Sir Henry, and Burnell, Arthur Coke. *Hobson-Jobson: Being a Glossary of Anglo-Indian Colloquial Words and Phrases, and of Kindred Terms.* London: J. Murrary, 1886.

Yurick, Sol. *The Warriors.* New York: Pyramid Books, 1966.

———. *The Bag.* New York: Trident Press, 1968.

Zach, Lilian. "The IQ Test: Does It Make Black Children Unequal?" *School Review* 78 (February 1970): 249–258.

Zarco, Marcano de. *Dialecto Inglés-Africano; O, Broken-English de la Colonia Española del Golfo de Guinea.* Turnhout, Belgium: H. Proost, 1918.

Zelnick, M., and Kantner, J. F. *Sexuality, Contraception, and Pregnancy Among Young Unwed Females in the United States.* Washington, D.C. National Institute of Child Mental Health and Human Development, 1970.

Zuck, Louis V., and Goodman, Yetta M. "On Dialects and Reading." *Journal of Reading* 15 (April 1972): 500–503.

Index